Integrated Bank Analysis and Valuation

Global Financial Markets series

Global Financial Markets is a series of practical guides to the latest financial market tools, techniques and strategies. Written for practitioners across a range of disciplines it provides comprehensive but practical coverage of key topics in finance covering strategy, markets, financial products, tools and techniques and their implementation. This series will appeal to a broad readership, from new entrants to experienced practitioners across the financial services industry, including areas such as institutional investment; financial derivatives; investment strategy; private banking; risk management; corporate finance and M&A, financial accounting and governance, and many more.

Titles include:

Global Financial Markets series
Series Standing Order ISBN: 978-1-137-32734-5

You can receive future titles in this series as they are published by placing a standing order. Please contact your bookseller or, in case of difficulty, write to us at the address below with your name and address, the title of the series and the ISBN quoted above.

Customer Services Department, Macmillan Distribution Ltd, Houndmills, Basingstoke, Hampshire RG21 6XS, England

---

Integrated Bank Analysis and Valuation

A Practical Guide to the ROIC Methodology

Sandy Chen
Cenkos Securities plc, UK

First published 2014 by
PALGRAVE MACMILLAN

Palgrave Macmillan in the UK is an imprint of Macmillan Publishers Limited, registered in England, company number 785998, of Houndmills, Basingstoke, Hampshire RG21 6XS.

Palgrave Macmillan in the US is a division of St Martin's Press LLC, 175 Fifth Avenue, New York, NY 10010.

Palgrave Macmillan is the global academic imprint of the above companies and has companies and representatives throughout the world.

Palgrave® and Macmillan® are registered trademarks in the United States, the United Kingdom, Europe and other countries

ISBN: 978–1–137–30745–3

This book is printed on paper suitable for recycling and made from fully managed and sustained forest sources. Logging, pulping and manufacturing processes are expected to conform to the environmental regulations of the country of origin.

A catalogue record for this book is available from the British Library.

A catalog record for this book is available from the Library of Congress.

Contents

List of Figures

List of Tables

Preface

This book grew out of conversations with leading fund managers who use ROIC (Return on Invested Capital) models to help them with their investment decisions about banks. The gist of these conversations was that the ROIC methodology could translate the bewildering complexity of bank jargon into a simpler, clearer language while also showing how changes in a bank's key value levers can affect its valuation.

This book was written for analysts in general: non-bank analysts in both buy-side and sell-side institutions who would like to learn how to analyse banks, bank analysts who would like to link their analyses to fundamental valuations, and analysts for regulators and governments who would like to model the potential impact of new policies.

It is easy to go astray when analysing banks – with the Basel III regulations, for example. In this book, I focus on describing the ROIC for Banks Methodology, how at the company I currently work for we construct our models for ROIC analysis, and then how this links to a fundamental valuation for the bank.

A bit of background: Back in the 1990s, while working at a large investment bank, my colleagues and I spent several years developing a detailed, cash flow–based approach to analysing and valuing banks, which was then abandoned as being too complicated to use in the real 'I need the answer now, not next week!' world.

The ROIC-based approach to banks described in this book reflects the practicalities of trying to analyse and value banks in a timely manner. In practice, as a sell-side analyst, when a bank reports its results, we spend the first hour or two spotting the key points for the 'initial morning comment'. By the end of the afternoon, we should have been able to both update our ROIC model and take a revised view on the valuation for that bank for a 'further comment' to be published. The ROIC methodology is a way of doing 'battlefield triage' on a bank's results, enabling the analyst to process a lot of complex information quickly and efficiently in order to spot the key points in a bank's performance and then link that to valuation.

For putting new banks under coverage, my experience has been that roughly a week is required to go through a bank's historical financial statements and put them into the ROIC for Banks template. This compares to roughly a month when doing it without a standardised, integrated model for both bank analysis and valuation.

On the ROIC for Banks website, you will find this template as well as detailed spreadsheets for each of the banks covered in this book. I have included them to show readers how the models actually work. The links between a bank's financial statements as reported and the ROIC for Banks model are shown clearly, and key assumptions can be altered to see the potential impacts on valuation.

To be clear, using the ROIC for Banks approach does not mean giving up all the other tools for bank analysis and valuation. What, I would suggest, makes the methodology relatively unique is that it can translate this complexity into clarity – and then link it directly to valuation.

Acknowledgements

I'd like to thank my former boss, Patrick Barton, who developed key parts of this framework, and James Alexander at Prudential/M&G, who has been a stalwart supporter of ROIC for Banks for over a decade. I also thank my employer, Cenkos Securities, for allowing me to indulge my tendency to lecture.

Most of all, I'd like to thank my gorgeous wife, Carol Jarvest, for always being loving, through thick and thin.

Glossary of Terms

Book value per share   This is calculated by dividing shareholders' equity by the number of common shares at the end of a period.

Common Equity Tier 1 ratio   This measures a bank's core capital strength; it is calculated by dividing Common Equity Tier 1 capital by risk-weighted assets.

Compensation ratio   This ratio measures a bank's personnel expenses as a percentage of net operating income; it is calculated by dividing personnel expenses by net operating income.

Contractual maturity mismatch   This compares a bank's assets and liabilities by maturity buckets, e.g. within one week, one week to one month. Also called gap analysis.

Cost–income ratio   This ratio measures a bank's operating efficiency; it is calculated by dividing a bank's operating expenses by its net operating income.

Derivatives   These are a wide range of financial products that are calculated by (or derived from, thus derivatives) referring to another financial data item. For example, a call option is a derivative that refers to the price of a stock or index.

Dividend yield   This is calculated by dividing the expected dividend in a year by the current share price.

Earnings per Share (EPS)   A commonly-used valuation measure; this is calculated by dividing the net profit attributable to equity shareholders by the weighted average number of common shares in a period.

Gap analysis   See contractual maturity mismatch.

Hedges (and Hedging)   A hedge is a financial product that is intended to move in the opposite direction as the item to which it refers, thereby helping to mitigate the risk of that item.

High Quality Liquid Assets (HQLA)   These are assets that can be converted into cash quickly.

Impaired loan   A loan is classified as impaired when it fails to meet a pre-specified set of criteria; often these criteria include whether a loan has fallen behind in repayments.

Impairment allowance Formerly a loan-loss provision, an impairment allowance is the amount set aside to cover potential losses against a bad (impaired) loan.

Impairment charge This is the item on the income statement reflecting the net changes in the impairment allowances in the period.

Leverage ratio This is a ratio of a bank's core equity capital versus its assets; it is calculated by dividing Tier 1 capital by Total Assets.

Liquidity ratios These ratios measure how long a bank's liquid (cash, or near-cash) assets would withstand a period of outflows, or they measure how much cash (or near-cash) assets there is in relation to various potential demands for that cash.

Liquidity Coverage Ratio (LCR) This ratios is calculated by dividing the stock of High Quality Liquid Assets by the Total net cash outflows that would be expected over the next 30 days in a stressed environment.

Net interest margin This ratio measures how much net interest income a bank gets from its interest-earning assets; it is calculated by dividing net interest income by the average interest-earning assets in the period.

Net interest spread Net interest spread is like net interest margin in that it is a measure of a bank's income from interest, but it is calculated differently; it is calculated by subtracting the ratio of interest expense divided by average interest-bearing liabilities from the ratio of gross interest income divided by average interest-earning assets.

Net operating income This is the total net interest income plus non-interest income for a bank in a period, less insurance claims but before impairment charges.

Net Stable Funding Ratio (NSFR) This ratio looks at a bank's funding risk profile over a one-year timeframe; it is calculated by dividing the available amount of stable funding by the required amount of stable funding.

Non-performing loan Generally, a loan on which the interest or principal repayments have not been met according to their schedule; many loans are classified as non-performing when loan repayments are more than 30–90 days overdue.

Provisioning coverage ratio This is a measure of provisioning adequacy; it is calculated by dividing the impairment allowances by the impaired loans.

Return on Equity (ROE) This is calculated by dividing net profit by the average shareholders' equity in a period.

Return on Invested Capital (ROIC)   This is calculated by dividing the net risk-adjusted returns by the average invested capital in a period.

Return on Risk-Weighted Assets (RORWA)   This is calculated by dividing net risk-adjusted returns by the average risk-weighted assets in a period.

Tangible book value per share   This is calculated by subtracting goodwill and other intangible items from shareholders' equity and then dividing it by the number of common shares at the end of a period.

Value creation   This is calculated by subtracting the weighted average cost of capital from the return on invested capital (ROIC) in a period; if this is a positive number (i.e. the ROIC is higher than the WACC), then this is defined as value creation.

Introduction: Fundamentals of Bank Analysis and Valuation

Over the past several years, banks have attracted a lot of (largely unwelcome) attention, not only from their customers, but from investors, regulators, and politicians. The high costs and uncertain benefits of government support for banks have been hotly debated, and the share prices of many banks have seesawed.

Many people have also tried to learn the complicated vocabulary of interest rate derivatives, credit default swaps and hedging strategies, all in order to try to understand what's going on in the banks, and maybe even buy or sell their shares (or fund their bailouts).

However, one of the big problems has been that there hasn't been a 'grand unified theory' that can explain what makes banks do better or worse (or that can tell you whether or not to buy or sell their shares). It's all gotten far too complicated.

This is where I and my colleagues at Cenkos Securities think an ROIC (Return on Invested Capital) approach could prove helpful, not only to investors, regulators and politicians, but also to the banks' customers. The ROIC methodology is an integrated framework for both analysis and valuation of banks. It translates the complexity of banks' financials into a simpler, clearer language of risk-adjusted operating performance and capital leverage.

To be clear, we're not suggesting that the ROIC method is the grand unified theory that explains everything about banking; we do think, however, that having an integrated approach to analysis and valuation for banks is helpful, not only for investors, but for regulators, politicians, the banks themselves and, not least, their customers. And if wider use of the ROIC method were to lead to stronger banks, we think the wider economy would benefit significantly.

What makes ROIC for banks different?

The vast bulk of bank analysis and valuation has been done separately. Bank analysts churn out detailed analyses of capital structures under different regulatory regimes, do cost–income ratio and compensation ratio

1

comparisons, and look at the different liquidity profiles and collateral requirements of various trading businesses, for example, but there is a seldom a direct link between these myriad analyses and a fundamentally-derived valuation for a bank.

For each bank, although detailed analyses of operating performance and capital/liquidity risks are conducted, these tend to boil down to a forecast of EPS (earnings per share) and ROE (return on equity). These EPS and ROE forecasts are then compared with those of other banks, either on an across-the-board basis or using a regression (for example, price-to-book multiple versus ROE), in order to assess whether or not that bank's share price is high, low, or 'just right' relative to its peers. By nature, these comparisons tend to be just that, for example, comparing one bank's price-to-tangible-book multiple to another bank's multiple and deeming it higher and/or lower than the peer group average. There are more sophisticated versions of this, for example, using returns on tangible equity (ROTE) and/or tangible book value per share, but in general there isn't much of a fundamental link between analysis and valuation.

In contrast to EPS- or ROE-based analyses, our ROIC-based approach looks at underlying returns on total invested capital (i.e. both equity and debt capital). It then compares the return on invested capital with the cost of capital, in order to assess whether or not the bank is creating or destroying value. This assessment of value creation/destruction is then integrated with valuation by discounting the bank's future expected value creation to give a fundamentally-derived current valuation.

Distinguishing between operating performance and capital leverage

In understanding what makes a bank tick, we have found it useful to break down ROIC (return on invested capital) analysis into two main parts: (1) the bank's operating performance on a risk-adjusted basis, and (2) its capital leverage. In the ROIC method, these are (1) underlying returns on risk-weighted assets (RORWAs), and (2) RWA/Invested Capital. Multiplying these two factors together gives us Return on Invested Capital (ROIC).

Looking at it in this way, analysing bank performance is either a discussion of (1) what's driving changes in operating performance, or (2) a look at rising/falling leverage and different capital structures. This enables us to distinguish between higher profitability that has been achieved by improving operating performance, and increasing capital leverage; we regard higher risk-adjusted operating profitability as being a more sustainable competitive advantage than simply choosing to run with lower (read: weaker) capital ratios.

Clients have said that this ROIC methodology translates the often mind-boggling complexity of banks into a simpler, clearer language of risk-adjusted operating returns and capital leverage – and it then enables readers to derive a bank valuation that is based on fundamentals, not just on comparative valuations.

Also, despite its clarity and simplicity, the ROIC approach can still capture much of the complexity of modern banking – via the assumptions that feed into the analysis and valuation. All of the other bank ratio analysis can feed into the ROIC methodology via these key value lever assumptions. Or in other words, analysts can still use all of the other tools, but what the ROIC methodology offers in addition to those tools is a clear, integrated framework for both analysis and valuation.

Analysis integrated with valuation

Although much has changed over the past few decades – IFRS, Basel I/II/III, balance sheet structures during the recent crises – we think many of the underlying ways of evaluating bank performance have endured. For us, this boils down to comparing the returns on invested capital versus the cost of that capital – and assessing whether or not those risk-adjusted returns are sustainable.

Integrated ROIC analysis and valuation boils down to answering one basic question: whether a bank is creating or destroying value. If a bank is expected to create sustainable value, it should generally be valued at a premium to its current invested capital; if it is expected to destroy sustainable value, then it should generally be valued at a discount to its invested capital.

We thus take the ROIC analysis of historical performance and apply it our forecasts of future performance. These forecasts are then integrated with a ROIC-based valuation methodology that compares the forecasted returns on invested capital with the cost of that capital and gives a fundamentally-based, period-by-period target valuation.

But does it work?

Whilst ROIC has limited value as a short-term trading tool, we do think it does lead to good longer-term investment calls. Over the years, ROIC analysis has led us to favour those banks that have consistently generated risk-adjusted returns on capital above their cost of capital – those banks have tended to deliver the best shareholder value as well.

In our view, relative valuations will tend to flow from relative comparisons of each bank's ability to generate sustainable risk-adjusted ROICs.

We also look out for trend changes in key ROIC drivers. In other words, we hope that, by applying ROIC methodologies to banks, they be analysed and valued like other sectors.

How this book is organised

After this introduction, the book has three chapters. Chapter 1 looks at other approaches to analysing and valuing banks, Chapter 2 goes into the ROIC for Banks methodology in detail, and Chapter 3 applies it to several leading banks worldwide. There is also an appendix with references.

1
Other Approaches to Bank Analysis and Valuation

In this chapter, we will look at several other tools for bank analysis and valuation that are used in practice. These include operating performance ratios like the cost-income ratio, regulatory ratios like the Core Equity Tier 1 ratio and leverage ratio, and valuation ratios like P/E and Price-to-Tangible Book multiples.

At the end of the chapter, we'll give an example (using HSBC's 2012 annual results) of how bank analysts knit these ratios together for a bank's investment 'story' – as if we were analysing the results on the morning that they were published.

Firstly, we'll run through several key ratios that most bank analysts use when evaluating a bank's results:

Operating performance ratios

These ratios are used to compare a bank's operating performance versus its peers and/or track the changes in a bank's operating performance over time.

Cost-income ratio

This is calculated by dividing a bank's operating expenses by its net operating income over a period. The formula is as follows:

Cost-income ratio = Operating expenses/Net operating income

Note that the operating expenses do not include impairment charges; the cost-income ratio is mainly used to track whether or not a bank's operating efficiency is improving or deteriorating over time, and/or to compare a bank's operating efficiency versus its peers.

The cost-income ratio is often mentioned in a bank's management comments at the beginning of its results announcement; it also often appears in the summary table in a results announcement. Historically, retail and commercial banks have tended to have cost-income ratios in the 30–50% range, whereas investment banks have tended to have cost-income ratios in the 60–80% range. We think this is largely because of the higher compensation packages that investment bankers, as compared to retail/commercial bankers, have tended to get.

Compensation ratio

The compensation ratio (or 'comp ratio') is a sub-category of the cost-income ratio; it is calculated by dividing the personnel expenses – wages, salaries, and other employee compensation including bonuses – by net operating income. The formula is as follows:

Comp ratio = Personnel expenses (including wages, bonuses and related personnel expenses)/Net operating income

The comp ratio is often used when analysing investment banks. For many investment bankers, bonuses have often been linked to the revenue that they have generated in the period (for example, bonuses could be defined as 20% of an investment banker's revenues), so the comp ratio is basically used as a management tool. During the recent financial crisis, some investment banks used this performance-linked compensation structure to ratchet bonuses down as well as up.

Note that some EU countries have been tinkering with compensation structures for senior bankers and investment bankers; for example, in the UK, there are proposals to defer bonuses for up to ten years and to claw back compensation if there has been financial misconduct. This could add to volatility and uncertainty in comp ratios.

Net interest margin

Net interest margin is calculated by taking net interest income (from the income statement) and dividing it by average interest-earning assets (from the balance sheet). The formula is as follows:

Net interest margin = Net interest income/Average interest-earning assets

We generally take net interest income directly from the income statement; for interest-earning assets, we include cash, customer loans, debt assets, and anything else that could be a source of interest income.

For the past several years, quantitative easing and other unconventional monetary policies have caused net interest margins to decline at many banks; indeed, one of the stated aims of quantitative easing was to bring down interest rates in general (and borrowing rates in particular) – this has put downward pressure on net interest margins. If these unconventional monetary policies begin to be unwound, it could be expected that net interest margins would increase again as interest rates increased.

Net interest spread analysis

Net interest spread is another way of looking at how banks generate net interest income; it compares the average rates on lending and other interest-earning assets with the average rate on deposits and other interest-bearing liabilities. The formula is as follows:

$$\text{Net interest spread} = (\text{Gross interest income/Average interest-earning assets}) - (\text{Interest expense/Average interest-bearing liabilities})$$

Or in other words, the net interest spread is calculated by subtracting the liability spread from the asset spread in a period. The asset spread is calculated by taking gross interest income and dividing by average interest-earning assets; the liability spread is calculated by taking interest expense and dividing it by average interest-bearing liabilities. As with interest-earning assets, we include customer deposits, deposits held with other banks (including central banks), debt liabilities and any other liability where interest expense is recognised.

Net interest spread analysis is often used to distinguish between the competitive environments on each side of balance sheet. For example, if the liability spread for a bank has remained relatively stable whilst its asset spreads have fallen, we can guess that competition on the asset side (e.g. in lending) is tougher than on the deposit or wholesale markets funding side of the balance sheet.

Derivatives hedging structures

Some banks disclose how their derivatives positions affect their net interest margins and/or spreads. For example, a structural hedge, whereby a bank holds a position in interest-rate swaps that are designed to offset swings in the interest rate environment, could be used to smooth out some of the volatility in net interest margins.

However, we have found the disclosure on derivatives to be relatively minimal for most banks, thus it is often difficult to analyse or predict the performance of derivatives hedging structures as an external analyst.

Credit quality: non-performing/impaired loans ratios

On a bank's income statement, the impairment charge (and before that the loan-loss provisioning charge) tended to be one of the most volatile line items. This is partly because of the way it is calculated: a bank will add up its bad loans, estimate the provisions that are required to cover those bad loans (taking into account the likely realisable value of the collateral backing those loans and the cost of foreclosure etc.), and then adjust those numbers by the amount of actual loan write-offs and recoveries in that period, with the net change in these factors being the impairment charge. All of these factors can be relatively big, moving parts – especially if the credit environment has suddenly changed – and thus the impairment charge number can swing around quite widely and unpredictably.

It is important to note that the terminology of bad debts has not been unified yet. Definitions of what constitutes a non-performing loan, or an impaired loan have yet to be agreed globally, and for banks reporting under IFRS there was a big transition from, say, UK GAAP to IFRS that led to the non-performing loans item being replaced by an impaired loans line item that was calculated in a different manner. We expect that over the next few years, these definitions will be standardised – making cross-bank comparisons much easier.

One key indicator of the impairment charge is the level of non-performing (or, in the IFRS parlance, impaired) loans. The formula for the NPL ratio is as follows:

Non-performing loans (NPL) ratio = Non-performing (or impaired) loans/Gross customer loans

An increase in the NPL ratio is often a sign that impairment charges will rise (and a fall in the NPL ratio often presages falling impairment charges). It is also a useful measure of the extent to which a bank's bad debts have been addressed.

Note that the standards for what constitutes a non-performing loan, or an impaired loan, can vary from country to country, and even from bank to bank within a country, so although we do compare NPL ratios across banks, these comparisons should not be regarded as entirely apples-to-apples.

Provisioning adequacy: provisioning coverage ratio

One related measure is provisioning adequacy, which measures the extent to which a bank's loan-loss provisions (or, under IFRS, impairment allowances) cover that bank's non-performing (or impaired) loans. The formula is as follows:

Provisioning coverage = Loan-loss provisions (or impairment allowances)/Non-performing (or impaired) loans

As with the NPL ratio above, it should be noted that apples-to-apples comparisons across banks may not be wholly accurate because of different recognition policies being used. We tend to look for changes in provisioning coverage over time in a single bank.

Regulatory ratios

The recent financial crisis triggered a wave of new regulations on capital and liquidity, commonly referred to as Basel III. These new regulations aim to both improve the transparency and consistency of bank regulatory disclosures as well as strengthen capital and liquidity requirements. Although the Basel III requirements are being phased in over several years (mostly to 2019), many of the Basel III disclosures are already becoming available.

For analysts, these Basel III disclosures are extremely helpful in giving a clearer picture of a bank's robustness and enabling it to be compared with other banks. In this book we will focus on how the published regulatory ratios can be used in bank analysis; trying to build up those ratios according to the regulatory formulas would require data that are not available to external analysts.

Capital adequacy ratios

Under Basel III, a bank's capital is divided into two buckets: Tier 1 capital, which is described as 'going-concern' capital (i.e. capital that can be used when a bank is operating), and Tier 2 capital, which is described as 'gone-concern' capital (i.e. capital that can be drawn upon if the bank is no longer operating).

Tier 1 capital is further divided into two components, Common Equity Tier 1, which is regarded as the highest quality capital in a bank, and Additional Tier 1 capital, which is other capital that is available to a bank to cover losses.

For all banks under Basel III, the Common Equity Tier 1 ratio will be required to be at least 4.5% of risk-weighted assets, the Tier 1 capital ratio will be required to be at least 6.0% of RWAs, and the Total Capital (Tier 1 capital plus Tier 2 capital) ratio will be required to be at least 8.0% of RWAs. Larger banks that are deemed to be systemically important will be subject to higher capital requirements.

Common Equity Tier 1 ratio

Over the next few years, the Basel III Common Equity Tier 1 ratio will replace the Basel II Core Equity Tier 1 ratio in bank reporting. Somewhat confusingly, both are abbreviated as the 'CET1 ratio' (although they are calculated quite differently). Because it is the measure of a bank's highest quality capital (or in other words, this layer will be the first to absorb any losses), we focus on a bank's Common Equity Tier 1 ratio as the core measure of its capital strength.

The ratio is calculated as follows:

Common Equity Tier 1 ratio = Common Equity Tier 1 capital/Risk-weighted assets

Common Equity Tier 1 capital consists of:
a bank's common shares
plus additional paid-in capital (share premium)
plus retained earnings
plus minority interests
minus goodwill and other intangible assets
minus deferred tax assets
minus cash-flow hedging reserves
minus expected losses over existing provisions
minus gains (plus losses) on sale related to securitisation transactions
minus gains (plus losses) on changes in the fair value of own debt
minus defined benefit pension assets net liabilities
minus treasury shares
minus reciprocal cross-shareholdings in financial institutions
minus financial investments outside the scope of regulatory consolidation accounting for more than 10% of a bank's common equity in aggregate.

The Basel III regulations go into far greater detail on the recognition policies for all of the above items, but as we mentioned earlier, we regard the calculation of these components as mainly the concern of the bank's internal personnel and its auditors; as external analysts, our main focus is knowing that the Common Equity Tier 1 capital number represents a bank's core capital, and that core capital will be fully available to cover any losses that might occur.

The 2019 timetable for the full implementation of the Basel III requirements has been raised as an issue, but in our opinion what matters is the timing of the Basel III disclosures; once the Basel III ratios become available, we expect that they will be used as the de facto standard for analyzing capital adequacy.

Leverage ratio

In addition to the Tier 1 capital ratios, which are calculated using risk-weighted assets, Basel III also uses a Leverage Ratio based on a bank's assets as reported; this is intended to provide a simpler measure of a bank's capital strength. This Leverage Ratio is calculated as follows:

Leverage Ratio = Tier 1 capital/Assets (with some adjustments)

In effect, the Leverage Ratio takes the Tier 1 capital as calculated for the risk-based Basel III ratios, and divides it by an asset number that is not adjusted for risk weights. The total assets number reported on a bank's balance sheet is generally adjusted downwards in the leverage ratio calculation; one of the main adjustments involves netting out derivatives assets and liabilities.

A minimum leverage ratio of 3% has been set by the Basel committee on bank supervision; this 3% requirement will be assessed over the next several years. Some countries, such as the US, already have a higher leverage ratio requirement (in the case of the US, it is 4% for the largest US banks and is now scheduled to be 5% for most large US banks and 6% for the largest US banks by 2018).

As with the Common Equity Tier 1 ratio, although there are some adjustments to the assets that are prescribed by Basel III, we regard these as mainly the concern of a bank's internal staff and its auditors. We tend to focus on the Leverage Ratio number as reported, checking it against the 3% minimum as a measure of a bank's capital strength.

Liquidity ratios

Basel III uses two main ratios to assess the robustness of a bank's liquidity position – the Liquidity Coverage Ratio, or LCR, and the Net Stable Funding Ratio, or NSFR. The LCR focuses on short-term liquidity (i.e. a bank's ability to meet funding demands in a one-month crisis scenario), whereas the NSFR looks at the robustness of a bank's funding structures with a one-year timeframe in mind.

Liquidity Coverage Ratio (LCR)

The Liquidity Coverage Ratio, or LCR, is calculated as follows:

Liquidity Coverage Ratio = Stock of High Quality Liquid Assets/ Total net cash outflows over the next 30 calendar days in a stressed environment

High Quality Liquid Assets, or HQLAs, are defined as the assets that can be converted into cash quickly and easily, with little or no loss of value. These are generally assets that are considered low risk (e.g. because of their high credit ratings, short duration, low inflation/currency risk), with easy and reliable valuations (because they are actively traded on public markets). As a rule of thumb, the assets that investors tend to buy when there is bad economic news (e.g. US treasuries, UK gilts) would probably be regarded as High Quality Liquid Assets.

The 'total net cash outflows over 30 calendar days in a stressed environment' number is an internal bank calculation; it requires access to non-public data. For example, the likely cash outflows if a bank were to be downgraded by three notches needs to be calculated, along with the likely impacts on customer deposit withdrawals by specific categories and maturities and repo/reverse repo cash flows. Accordingly, as with the regulatory capital ratios, we tend to use a bank's published LCR numbers instead of trying to derive it by ourselves. The timetable for the implementation of the LCR changed in January 2013; the bibliography at the end of this book has the URLs for an update of this and other regulatory implementations.

As with the capital requirements, the LCR requirement is being phased in over the next several years, starting with a 60% LCR requirement on 1 January 2015 (e.g. HQLAs/30-day net cash outflows =/> 60%) and going up to 10% notches each year until a 100% LCR requirement is reached for 1 January 2019.

That said, we do think that a bank's LCR gives a good snapshot of its liquidity profile. In particular, a low LCR can indicate a higher exposure to short-term funding risks, so if the macroeconomic environment were beginning to show indications of another liquidity crisis, we would use the LCR ratios to identify those banks that could be at greater risk of funding problems.

Net Stable Funding Ratio (NSFR)

The Net Stable Funding Ratio, or NSFR, looks at a bank's funding risk profile in a one-year timeframe, rather than the 30-day stressed environment used in the LCR calculation. The NSFR compares balance sheet assets and off-balance sheet commitments with the amount of stable funding on the balance sheet, using 'haircuts' (or discounts) to adjust the value of some items. The stated intent of the NSFR is 'to limit over-reliance on short-term wholesale funding during times of buoyant market liquidity and encourage better assessment of liquidity risk across all on- and off-balance sheet items' (footnote BCBS165 section 42).

The Net Stable Funding Ratio is calculated as follows:

Net Stable Funding Ratio = Available amount of stable funding/
Required amount of stable funding

The target minimum NSFR is 100% – although please note that this is under review by the Basel committee.

Available stable funding is defined as a bank's capital and preferred stock (with maturities of one year or greater), plus liabilities with maturities of one year or greater, plus an estimated portion of term deposits with less than one year maturities that would remain with a bank even in a bank-specific stress event, plus an estimated portion of deposits without maturities (e.g. current accounts) that would remain in a stressed environment.

The required stable funding is calculated by multiplying certain on- and off-balance sheet items by a Required Stable Funding (RSF) factor in order to adjust for liquidity risk, and then adding up the RSF-adjusted numbers.

As with the other regulatory ratios, we tend to use the NSFR as reported by the banks. External analysts simply do not have access to the data required to calculate the NSFR. In addition, with the NSFR currently under review by the Basel committee and other supervisors/regulators, we tend to focus more on the LCR.

Other regulatory monitoring tools

The Basel Committee has been working on implementing other risk monitoring tools that can be used to both analyse a bank's historical performance as well as compare it with other banks. Some of these are outlined below:

Contractual maturity mismatch

This is also called 'gap analysis', and a table on this can often be found in a bank's annual report and accounts. Contractual maturity mismatch looks at contractual maturities for a bank's assets and liabilities by time bucket, e.g. assets and liabilities with residual maturities of less than one week, one week to one month, one to three months etc. By subtracting liabilities from assets for each time bucket, gaps are identified. This is useful in getting a sense for whether or not a bank is overly reliant on short-term funding.

Funding concentration

This table is sometimes disclosed in a bank's annual report and accounts; it tends to show the top five or ten counterparties in wholesale funding. If a relatively high proportion of a bank's wholesale funding comes from only a few counterparties, we would regard this as an indicator of concentration risk. It could then lead us to cross-check the funding concentration with the shareholder register, to see if there might be a relatively concentrated shareholder base as well.

Lending concentration

Similar to funding concentration, this table is generally disclosed in a bank's annual report and accounts, and it tends to show the top five or ten loan customers. This is often expressed as a percentage of a bank's shareholders' equity, because many country regulators require this disclosure. Lending concentration can help to identify whether a bank has large exposures to an investor or customer group.

Available unencumbered assets

Some banks have begun to disclose this number; it shows the amount of unencumbered assets, which could potentially be used as collateral for secured funding, either in the market (e.g. for repo funding) or with central banks.

Available unencumbered assets is a key measure in the repurchase (or repo) or reverse repurchase (reverse repo) markets – a bank's ability to access short-term wholesale, interbank or central bank funding via the repo markets is often determined by the availability of collateral to pledge against the repo.

Bank valuation measures

Although most of the ratios described above would be found in most equity analyst reports, most bank valuations tend to boil down to two sets of valuation ratios – EPS for P/E ratios, and ROE (and its variant, ROTE or return on tangible equity) for price-to-book multiples. Dividend yield is also used in relative valuation comparisons, but because many banks had stopped paying or cut dividends during the financial crisis, this valuation ratio had become less relevant for across-the-board valuation comparisons.

Other performance measures that are commonly used in the stock markets – free cash flow and EBITDA-based measures, for example – haven't been used on the banks because of the difficulties in determining what debt capital is. (More on this when we cover the ROIC for Banks Methodology in Chapter 2.)

EPS

EPS, or earnings per share, is the standard performance measure for almost all listed equities. This is because it can be calculated for nearly every company, and for valuation, a 'forward P/E', or the price-earnings ratio forecast for the next future period, is the most commonly used way of describing a stock's valuation in the markets.

Basic EPS is the net profit attributable to equity shareholders divided by the weighted average number of common equity shares in the period; diluted EPS includes valid share options in the number of shares and thus diluted EPS tends to be lower than basic EPS.

Alongside their statutory EPS, banks have tended to report an adjusted, or management basis, EPS, that adjusts for various items on the income statement related to either accounting standards or management items.

A common adjustment is taking out the effects of changes in the fair value of own debt; this began to show up in the 2008 results for banks reporting under IFRS, and in the 2009 results for banks reporting under US GAAP. Many US banks called this a 'debt valuation adjustment', or DVA. The changes in fair value of own debt was generally calculated in reference to the credit default swaps (CDSs) against the bank's own subordinated and long-term debt; the bigger the swings in CDS spreads, the bigger the swing in the fair value of own debt item in the income statement. In many cases from 2008 through 2011, the fair value of own debt adjustment comprised a significant proportion of overall reported earnings, but because it was not a 'real' change (only an accounting change because the reference CDS spread had moved), we think it was justified to exclude this item from the Group income statement. Note also that accounting standards are being revised to reduce or eliminate the distortion from the fair value of own debt item, so from a longer-term perspective, earnings that have adjusted to exclude changes in the fair value of own debt should show a better pattern of underlying earnings both before and after the time that the IFRS/US GAAP treatment had been in place.

Also, a credit valuation adjustment, or CVA, has been made to some bank earnings under IFRS/US GAAP since 2008 and 2009. The credit valuation adjustment is generally driven by changes in either the credit rating or the CDS spread of a financial counterparty; for example, if the credit ratings of a financial counterparty were downgraded, the value of that counterparty's financial contract would be judged to be weaker, and a negative credit valuation adjustment would be made. This adjustment essentially reflects the changes in the market value of a financial asset that result from changes in the credit risk of the financial counterparty. CVAs tend to be disclosed less often than DVAs – we tend to keep them in our EPS calculations.

Several banks also exclude expense items like restructuring costs, charges that management deem as one-off in nature, and gains/losses associated with disposals. For these management/restructuring items, we tend to side with a bank's auditors, recognising only those items that the auditors classify as being extraordinary items as extraordinary items. This often results in our adding back items into our EPS calculation that have been excluded by a bank's management.

EPS and P/E ratios

In the equity markets, the forward P/E ratio is the most commonly used way to describe a company's valuation, i.e., 'Company A is trading at a forward P/E of 10x', meaning that the company's share price is currently

10x the forecast earnings for the next year. P/E ratios have been used for banks as well, but with the losses reported by some banks in recent years (negative P/E ratios aren't used with negative EPS, instead 'n/a' or 'not applicable' is printed), and volatile reported EPS numbers as well, P/E ratios have been less useful.

ROE

ROE, or return on equity, is calculated by dividing a bank's net profit attributable to common equity shareholders by the weighted-average common shareholders' equity in the period. ROTE, or return on tangible equity, is calculated by dividing a bank's net profit attributable to common equity shareholders by the period average tangible shareholders' equity, i.e. common shareholders' equity minus intangible assets.

Some analysts prefer ROTE to ROE, on the basis that the capital tied up in goodwill shouldn't be used when calculating profitability. We prefer using ROE, on the basis that common shareholders' equity reflects the capital invested by the common shareholders, via both organic growth and acquisitions. With ROTE, we would also see an incentive to pay more for acquisitions, in order to use the goodwill to reduce tangible shareholders' equity and thus boost ROTE. This doesn't make sense, in our opinion.

ROE and price-to-book multiples

Over the past several years, there has been a relatively reliable correlation between the profitability of a bank, measured by its ROE (or ROTE), and its valuation, expressed as price-to-book multiple (or price-to-tangible book multiple). When we have run regressions on ROE vs price-to-book or price-to-tangible book multiples, we have tended to get correlations (i.e., r-squared) of 0.5 or higher – which generally indicates a decent level of correlation. In plain English, if a bank is producing higher ROEs, it does tend to trade at a higher price-to-book multiple.

In practice, we prefer using a bank's forecast ROE versus its forward price-to-tangible book multiple as a traditional valuation comparison. Our rationale for using the price-to-tangible book multiple over the price-to-book multiple is similar to our preference for ROE over ROTE – using the price-to-tangible book multiple provides an incentive to minimise the goodwill associated with acquisitions (i.e. pay a lower price for those acquisitions), because the higher the goodwill, the lower the tangible shareholders' equity, and thus the higher the price-to-tangible book value multiple. Or, in plain English again, if a bank paid a higher price for an acquisition, its price-to-tangible book multiple would be higher, and thus it would appear more expensively priced than if it had paid less for that acquisition.

Dividend yield

Another relative valuation tool that is commonly used is the dividend ratio. This is often used as a rule of thumb: for example, UK banks tended to have dividend yields of 4–6% in the 1980s and early 1990s, and 2–4% through the bulk of the past decade (if the bank was paying dividends at all). If a bank had a higher dividend yield, the relative attractiveness of the yield would be weighted against questions about sustainability and capital adequacy.

Note: Pillar 3 disclosures and the enhanced risk disclosure task force

In addition to their annual report and accounts, banks are now required to publish a Pillar 3 disclosure; this report shows in detail how a bank manages its risks, from the organisational structures and processes to the underlying assumptions about credit risks.

We have found the Pillar 3 disclosures extremely valuable in helping to assess a bank's capital strength, because of the depth of detail that is generally required by regulators. For example, there are generally details about the probability of default (PD), Loss Given Default (LGD) and Exposure At Default (EAD) assumptions, that are not generally found in a bank's annual report.

From our point of view, one of the sections in most Pillar 3 reports is a comparison between the expected probability of default that was used to make provisioning assumptions at the beginning of a period versus the actual default rates. We look for major discrepancies, for example, if the actual period default rates in a particular area were significantly higher than the probability of default expectation at the beginning of a period, this could indicate that a bank may have been under-provisioning.

The Enhanced Risk Disclosure Task Force (a working group of institutional investors, investment banks and other financial professionals, under the aegis of the Global Financial Stability Board) has supported the strengthening of the Pillar 3 disclosure requirements, calling for more timely publication of the Pillar 3 disclosure (e.g. on results days, rather than one or two months afterwards) as well as quarterly reporting of the Pillar 3 disclosure. The prospect of more timely Pillar 3 disclosure and more depth of disclosure has been welcomed by many analysts, including ourselves.

Note: using regulatory publications

There are several regular publications by various central banks and other organisations that we have found useful in reviewing current macro trends and identifying key potential risks. Here are some examples:

IMF Global Financial Stability Report (http://www.imf.org/external/pubs/ft/GFSR/)

This is produced twice yearly by the IMF, generally in April and October; the IMF's GFSR looks at key risks facing the global financial system, and it discusses policy actions that may address these risks.

IMF World Economic Outlook
(http://www.imf.org/external/ns/cs.aspx?id=29)

Generally produced on a quarterly basis, the IMF WEO analyses key macro trends. The IMF also publishes its forecasts of GDP growth and other macro forecasts by country in the WEO.

IMF Staff Discussion Notes and Working Papers
(http://www.imf.org/external/research/index.aspx)

These are ad hoc papers produced by IMF staff analysing various aspects of macroeconomic and banking affairs. For example, several notes in the past few years have looked at collateral rehypothecation chains and their effect on the repo markets, and there have been recent reviews of the quantitative easing and other unconventional monetary policies.

BIS Consultation Documents and Working Papers (http://www.bis.org)

Published by the Bank for International Settlements in Basel, Switzerland, BIS consultation documents set out the framework for future central bank regulation. An example is the revised Basel III leverage ratio framework consultative document published in June 2013, which set out the recommended principles for calculating leverage ratios as well as giving a timetable for implementation (in this case, a phased schedule leading to full implementation starting 1 January 2015). These consultative documents effectively set out the recommended path of bank regulation that individual country/regional regulators are likely to follow. The BIS working papers tend to focus on specific points that can feed into consultative documents and future recommended regulations.

The individual country central banks (e.g. US Federal Reserve, Bank of England) tend to have similar publications, i.e. financial stability reports, as well as working papers and quarterly forecasts/reviews. We have found these extremely helpful in identifying key macroeconomic trends as well as specific concerns for banks and other financial institutions.

Example of analysis and valuation in practice: HSBC

One caveat: One obvious but major problem with a reference book is that its references are, by nature, out of date by the time it is published. However, since this is intended as a practical guide to bank analysis and valuation, we thought it would be valuable to show which ratios were used (and how they were used) in analysing an actual set of results as they were reported – and then how that analysis was turned into an investment 'story'.

We have used HSBC's 2012 annual results as our example; it is one of the banks that we actually cover. HSBC published its 2012 results on 4 March 2013; the annual report, analyst's presentation and transcript can be accessed here: (http://www.hsbc.com/investor-relations/events-and-presentations).

From the 546-page 2012 Annual Report, we extracted data and put them into the tables on the following pages. Given the time constraints (typically, there is one hour between the time results are published and the time that an initial analyst comment is expected), analysis tends to jump around. Flowing through these tables, here is an example of a chain of analysis:

Table 1.1 HSBC: standardised income statement and balance sheet items

Performance summary	2010	2011	2012
Net interest income	39,441	40,662	37,672
Net fee & commission income	17,355	17,160	16,430
Net trading income	7,210	6,506	7,091
Other banking income	1,080	1,056	1,410
Net insurance income	(621)	1,691	(1,171)
Other operating income	2,562	1,766	2,100
Subtotal non-interest income	27,586	28,179	25,860
Net operating income	67,027	68,841	63,532
Administrative expenses	(34,992)	(38,625)	(40,474)
Depreciation and amortisation	(2,696)	(2,920)	(2,453)
Other operating expenses	–	–	–
Operating expenses	(37,688)	(41,545)	(42,927)
Trading surplus	29,339	27,296	20,605
Impairment charges	(14,039)	(12,127)	(8,311)
Operating profit (pre-goodwill)	15,300	15,169	12,294
Goodwill impairment	–	–	–
Operating profit	15,300	15,169	12,294
Fair value gains/(losses) on own debt	(258)	4,161	(4,327)
Changes in fair value of financial assets	1,478	(722)	2,101
Income from associates and JVs	2,517	3,264	3,557
Exceptional items	–	–	7,024
Profit before tax	19,037	21,872	20,649
Income tax	(4,846)	(3,928)	(5,315)
Net profit	14,191	17,944	15,334
Minority interests (non-equity)	–	–	–
Minority interests (equity)	(1,032)	(1,147)	(1,307)
Preference dividends	–	0	0
Net profit attributable to equity shareholders	13,159	16,797	14,027
Dividends	(5,937)	(7,726)	(8,314)
Retained earnings	7,222	9,071	5,713
Risk-weighted assets (RWA), end of period	1,103,113	1,209,514	1,123,943
RWA growth in period	–2.7%	9.6%	–7.1%
Period average RWAs	1,096,725	1,162,421	1,163,312

Source: HSBC annual reports, author's analysis.

At first glance of the income statement, the fall in net operating income (from \$68.8bn to \$63.5bn) jumps out; looking at the bottom of the table, this correlates with a 7% year-on-year fall in RWAs in 2012, following a 10% increase in 2011. We know that HSBC has disposed of several (circa 50) businesses since a global streamlining/restructuring programme was announced in 2011, so this fall in RWAs and net operating income could just be a result of those disposals. However, we will keep an eye on profitability as we go through our analysis.

Working down the income statement, the increase in administrative expenses (from \$38.6bn to \$40.5bn) jumps out – especially since net operating income has come down. HSBC had circa \$1bn in fines related a US anti-money laundering investigation in late 2012, and there were charges in the UK from payment protection insurance (PPI) mis-selling and other items; although these probably accounted for the bulk of the increase in operating expenses, we would look further into the notes to the financial statements to explain why operating expenses did not fall as much as net operating income. In many restructuring programmes, income falls more quickly than operating expenses; after all, if an employee is made redundant, they tend to stop generating income immediately, but they tend to remain on the payroll for several more months.

The combination of fall in net operating income and increased operating expenses has led to a big fall in HSBC's trading surplus (from \$27.3bn in 2011 to \$20.6bn in 2012); this is only partly mitigated by a fall in impairment charges (from \$12.1bn to \$8.3bn). Operating profit (excluding movements in the fair value of own debt) has fallen from \$15.2bn in 2011 to \$12.3bn in 2012.

To dig a bit deeper into what has been driving this drop in operating profit (and in order to take a view if this trend will continue), we go to our value levers table, which looks at various income statement line items on a per RWA basis as well as tracking cost-income ratios. We will go into more detail about the Value Levers table when we get into the ROIC methodology in Chapter 2, but here I would note that there has been a fall in both net interest income per RWA and non-interest income per RWA in HSBC's 2012 results, whilst administrative expenses have increased from 3.3% to 3.5% on a per RWA basis. Impairment charges per RWA have improved, at 71bp in 2012 down from 104bp in 2011, but as we saw above, the improvement has not been enough to mitigate the broad-based fall in income.

We would then look at credit quality metrics for HSBC. Because of the cyclical nature of bad debts and provisioning, we tend to look at longer-term streams of data when assessing credit quality trends. Non-performing (or impaired) loans have fallen significantly, from 4.3% at end-2011 to 3.7% at end-2012; provisioning coverage has stayed quite stable at 42%

Table 1.2 HSBC: value levers

Value levers	2011	2012
RWA growth	**9.6%**	**–7.1%**
Net interest income/Average RWA	3.50%	3.24%
Non-interest income/Average RWA	2.42%	2.22%
Net fee & commission income/Average RWA	1.48%	1.41%
Net trading income/Average RWA	0.56%	0.61%
Other banking income/Average RWA	0.09%	0.12%
Net insurance income growth in period	–372.3%	–169.2%
Other operating income growth in period	–31.1%	18.9%
Administrative expenses/Average RWA	–3.32%	–3.48%
Depreciation expenses/Average RWA	–0.25%	–0.21%
Other operating expenses/Average RWA	0.00%	0.00%
Operating expenses/Average RWA	–3.57%	–3.69%
Cost-income ratio	**60.3%**	**67.6%**
Impairment charges/Average RWA	–1.04%	–0.71%

Source: HSBC annual reports, author's analysis.

Table 1.3 HSBC: credit quality

Asset quality	2009	2010	2011	2012
Impaired (non-performing) loans	30,606	28,091	41,584	38,001
Gross customer loans	921,773	978,449	957,940	1,031,373
Impairment provisions	23,909	20,083	17,511	16,112
Non-performing loans as % Gross customer loans	3.32%	2.87%	4.34%	3.68%
NPLs as % of RWAs	2.70%	2.55%	3.44%	3.38%
Provisioning coverage				
Impairment provisions/NPLs	78.1%	71.5%	42.1%	42.4%
Impairment provisions/RWA	2.12%	1.83%	1.46%	1.43%
Impairment charges/Average RWA	–2.30%	–1.28%	–1.04%	–0.71%

Source: HSBC annual reports, author's analysis.

(impairment provisions/NPLs), and stock of impaired loans has fallen from \$41.6bn at end-2011 to \$38.0bn at end-2012. We would find this trend encouraging, and in keeping with the overall global streamlining strategy.

A quick look at capital ratios – with Core Equity Tier 1 strengthening from 10.1% at end-2011 to 12.3% at end-2012, shows that HSBC remains strongly capitalised.

Moving onto valuation, HSBC's P/E ratio is much higher than those of the UK domestically-orientated banks (RBS, Lloyds, Barclays) but lower than those of its emerging markets rival, Standard Chartered. A similar pattern occurs with the price/tangible book value multiples.

In a real analyst report, at this point there would be a reference to forecasts and valuation comparisons; to illustrate how the analysis of

Table 1.4   HSBC: capital ratios

	2011	2012
Core Equity Tier 1 ratio	10.1%	12.3%
Debt Capital/Invested Capital	13%	12%

Source: HSBC annual reports, author's analysis.

Table 1.5   HSBC: standard valuation ratios

Traditional valuation ratios		2011	2012
	GBP 736		
	1,119		
	1.5200		
Profit before tax pre-exceptionals & FV		18,433	15,851
% growth year-on-year		3.5%	–14.0%
Net profit pre-exceptionals & FV		13,167	11,465
% growth year-on-year		6.6%	–12.9%
Adjusted EPS, fully-diluted		73.5	62.7
% growth year-on-year		4.9%	–14.6%
Adjusted P/E		**15.2**	**17.8**
Dividends per share		41.0	45.0
% growth year-on-year		20.6%	**9.8%**
Dividend yield		3.7%	4.0%
Dividend payout ratio		46.0%	59.3%
ROE		11.0%	8.4%
P/BVPS multiple		**1.25**	**1.16**
Book value per share		897	967
% growth in period		5.7%	7.8%
Balance sheet goodwill		29,034	**29,853**
Tangible shareholders' equity		129,691	145,389
Tangible book value per share (US cents)		726	787
Price/Tangible BVPS multiple (x)		**1.54**	**1.42**

Source: HSBC annual reports, author's analysis.

HSBC's 2012 annual results were woven into a investment story, we have reprinted here the two analyst comments published by Cenkos on the day of the results. The first was produced within an hour of the results being published, and the second was produced after an analyst conference call.

---

* 1. HSBC (HSBA LN, £135bn mkt cap, 728p, Hold) – The pbt headline missed consensus, but it's worth noting that shareholders' equity still did grow by 10% yoy, to $175bn, in contrast with the UK-focussed banks where shareholders' equity keeps on falling.

One of the reasons for the miss is higher-than-expected operating expenses, but whereas other banks try to exclude regulatory fines, HSBC has always included them in their calculations. So although HSBC's cost – income ratio did worsen, from 57.5% in 2011 to 62.8% in 2012 (66.0% underlying), these ratios included the US anti-money laundering fines as well as additional UK PPI and SME swap provisions.

On the face of it, these numbers don't look good, but they're actually no worse than the others in terms of fines and charges, and we credit HSBC with not trying to hide them from view. And despite this HSBC still generated $20.6bn of pbt in 2012 ($16.4bn underlying, i.e. excluding FV of own debt and several disposal gains).

Fundamentally, the global streamlining programme is showing results. Underlying pbt in Hong Kong (the biggest geographical contributor) was up 24% yoy to $7.2bn and Rest of Asia-Pac was up 2% to $6.4bn; these two regions produced a combined 83% ($13.6bn of the $16.4bn) in underlying pbt. The loss in North America was down 51% yoy to $1.5bn, and LatAm pbt up 19% to $2.2bn. The key region of concern was Europe, where underlying pbt dropped 57% to $0.7bn.

Risk-adjusted revenue growth dipped 0.2% in 2012 after growing 11% in 2011, but underlying revenue growth was 13% in 2012, HSBC's balance sheet grew by 5.4% (to $2.7tn), and customer loans grew by 6.1% (to $998bn), which is decent growth for such a big bank. So, although the headline numbers did miss, we think the fundamentals are still pointing in the right direction. Maintain Hold.

* 2. HSBC (HSBA LN, £131bn mkt cap, 708p, Hold) – Does today's miss represent a downward shift in HSBC's earnings trendline? We don't think so, although from the headline numbers (e.g. net interest income –7% yoy, net fee income –4%, operating expenses +3%) we can understand the concerns. Which begs the question, why would HSBC's famously Scottish Presbyterian board have the confidence to approve a 10% increase in 2012's dividends to $0.45 (increasing the payout ratio from 42% to 55%) and indicate an 11% rise in the first three quarterly dividends for 2013?

We think that their thinking would be (1) the $1.9bn US anti-money laundering fine was a true one-off, (2) the $1.4bn UK PPI and SME interest-rate swap charges would continue into 2013, but HSBC's exposures are actually rather limited compared to both UK peers and HSBC's overall earnings, and (3) underlying Group revenue growth was 7%, balance sheet growth was 5% and customer loan growth was 6%, i.e. roughly corresponding to the overall GDP growth in the Asian and other emerging markets regions where HSBC is re-allocating its resources. And a fully-loaded Basel 3 Common Equity Tier 1 of 9.0% as at end-2012 (10.3% post-2013 management actions) points to ample capital adequacy.

To be clear, we are concerned about the dip in underlying RORWAs (from 2.1% in 2011 to 1.9% in 2012) as well as the shrinking net interest margins (from 2.51% in 2011 to 2.32% in 2012, with the 39bp fall in gross interest yields outpacing the 20bp fall in cost of funds), but when we look at the regional split of RORWAs (Hong Kong 6.6% in 2012 vs 5.3% in 2011, Rest of Asia-Pac 2.3% vs 2.7% compared with Europe 0.2% in 2012 vs 0.5% in 2011) and the comparison of RORWAs by business (Commercial Banking 2.1%, Global Markets 2.0%, Retail Banking 1.4%, Private Banking 4.3%), management's strategy of emphasising growth in Asian emerging markets and global trade should support a firming of overall Group returns, not a weakening.

---

* Any extracts from previously published research by Cenkos Securities plc included within this publication are for illustrative purposes only and should not be relied upon for any investment purpose. Such extracts have been reproduced with the kind permission of Cenkos Securities plc.

2
ROIC for Banks Methodology

This section shows how we do integrated analysis and valuation using the ROIC methodology. We will use a bank's financial statements to calculate Invested Capital and ROIC, analysing those results along the way. We will then link that analysis to valuation, showing how the ROIC valuation model can be used to discover what the market expectations of a bank's future sustainable profitability are. All this can then inform our own views on a bank's valuation.

It is important to emphasise that the ROIC methodology is not a replacement for the tools that we looked at in Chapter 1. Rather, we think it complements those tools by highlighting key value levers that affect a bank's performance, and showing how operating performance can link directly with a bottom-up, fundamental valuation.

Distinguishing between operating performance and capital leverage

In understanding what makes a bank tick, we have found it useful to break down the return on invested capital analysis into two main parts: (1) the bank's operating performance on a risk-adjusted basis (measured as underlying returns on risk-weighted assets, RORWAs), and (2) its capital leverage (measured as RWA/Invested Capital). Multiplying these two factors together gives us Return on Invested Capital (ROIC).

In many ways, this echoes a DuPont-style ROE analysis. The DuPont approach breaks down ROE (return on equity) into its main components with the following formula:

DuPont ROE decomposition:

$$\text{ROE} = (\text{Net Income/Sales}) \times (\text{Sales/Total Assets}) \times (\text{Total Assets/Shareholders' Equity})$$

Where Net Income/Sales is the net profit margin, Sales/Total Assets is the asset turnover, and Total Assets/Shareholders' Equity is the leverage component.

Similarly, the ROIC approach breaks down ROIC (return on invested capital) into its main components with the following formula:

ROIC decomposition:

$$\text{ROIC} = (\text{Net Returns/Risk-Weighted Assets}) \times (\text{Risk-Weighted Assets/Invested Capital})$$

Where Net Returns/Risk-Weighted Assets is the net risk-adjusted profit margin, and Risk-Weighted Assets/Invested Capital is the capital leverage component.

Looking at it in this way, analysing bank performance tends to be a discussion of either (1) what's driving changes in operating performance (RORWA components), or (2) whether capital leverage (RWA/Invested Capital ratios, and within Invested Capital the debt capital/equity capital funding mix) is rising or falling. We have found this a simpler, clearer way of analysing a bank's performance.

The fundamental link between analysis and valuation: value creation

The key link between analysis and valuation in the ROIC methodology is value creation (or destruction). If a bank's return on invested capital (ROIC) is higher than the cost of that capital (WACC), then it is deemed to be creating value in that period; if its ROIC is below its WACC, it is deemed to be destroying value.

The ROIC methodology adds up a bank's future value creation/destruction period-by-period, discounting it back to net present value. This net present value of future value creation/destruction is then added to (or subtracted from) current invested capital to derive a fundamental valuation for the bank.

By understanding how changes in some of the key levers (e.g. operating return on risk-weighted assets, capital leverage) influence the bank's fundamental ability to create value, we think there can be a clearer assessment of the robustness of a bank's business model, as well as a half-decent pointer towards likely movements in its share price.

Of course, as we saw in Section I, there is plenty of room for complexity in analysing a bank's operating performance and capital structure. In practice, we tend to do all of the analysis outlined in Section I when analysing and valuing banks – but we also use the ROIC methodology to gain additional insights into risk-adjusted operating performance, capital leverage, and key value drivers.

The ROIC methodology also puts an emphasis on understanding how a bank is creating (or destroying) value – and it links those trends in value creation (or destruction) directly with that bank's valuation.

Some guiding principles

In calculating ROIC, we want to get a sense of the 'true' returns on total invested capital. These 'true' earnings often differ from either the statutory earnings number or the 'underlying/core' earnings that banks often present. And total invested capital includes other balance sheet items besides shareholders' equity that, in effect, represent appropriations of shareholders' funds. So, the ROICs that are calculated often differ markedly from the ROEs that the banks report.

We tend to look at 'underlying' or 'core' earnings numbers with a great deal of scepticism; after all, for the listed banks, it is impossible to buy a share in just these 'underlying' or 'core' banks – the only share available is that for the bank as a whole. These 'underlying' or 'core' numbers also beg the question of what happens to those balance sheet and income statement items that aren't deemed underlying or core. How is a particular customer treated if their banking relationship includes both core and non-core exposures?

In our ROIC analysis, we have tended to rely mainly on the statutory, audited financial statements for our numbers – thus avoiding the core/non-core distinction in the management accounts that many banks also show.

We should also note that the ROIC methodology parallels the Basel capital adequacy methodologies in many ways – for example, the Invested Capital calculations are very similar to the calculations for Common Tier 1 capital, Tier 1 capital and Total Capital according to BIS. However, whilst the BIS has moved from Basel I to III (and many banks have moved from their country's GAAP to IFRS), we have tried to keep the Invested Capital calculation relatively constant throughout.

A note: using risk-weighted assets

We have used risk-weighted assets (RWAs) as our main basis for performance analysis; returns are expressed on a per-RWA basis, as are income statement line items. This enables line-by-line analysis of returns on a risk-adjusted basis. However, although our ROIC analyses are based on RWAs, note that there are several different ways that can be used to calculate RWAs, with very different results.

For example, most of the larger banks and nearly all of the listed banks use internal ratings-based (IRB) methodologies to calculate their RWAs; these are based on internal models and datasets, and thus it is impossible for an external analyst to determine whether the RWAs as calculated by one bank for its assets would be the same if those RWAs were calculated using another bank's IRB models. Recent studies by the Basel Committee on Bank Supervision (BCBS) have shown that for a model portfolio of assets, the RWAs calculated using IRB models tend to be much lower than if the standardised models were used. Or in other words, banks that use IRB models in their RWA calculations (which are nearly all of the large global banks) may be reporting RWAs that are significantly lower than what they would be reporting under the standardised Basel rules.

All of this makes a true apples-to-apples comparison across banks extremely difficult; even comparing one bank's RWAs over time is not entirely consistent, because some risk weights are likely to have changed over time.

That said, despite these flaws, RWAs are the only practical foundation for broad risk-based analysis that we have found. Also, several regulatory bodies, including the BCBS, Bank of England, and the Global Financial Stability Board, have been working on ways to address the inconsistencies in RWA calculations. In particular, the Enhanced Disclosure Task Force (EDTF) have developed a series of templates for risk disclosures that aim to improve transparency and disclosure; although these templates have been initially developed for the large, global, systemically-important banks (the 'G-SIBs'), there is support for much broader application of these disclosure templates amongst smaller banks. This could help make comparisons more apples-to-apples.

ROIC analysis: a step-by-step guide

The following pages describe how we calculate a bank's ROIC, step-by-step, from building up Invested Capital to determining the through-the-cycle Returns on that Invested Capital. Please note that the following ROIC methodology that we describe is only the particular one that we have used; others may choose to implement their ROIC methodology differently – with equal validity. The key point is that by using a standardised ROIC methodology, peer comparisons are both more valid and more useful.

First step: standardised ROIC model templates

One of the first things that we did when building our ROIC models was to standardise a template that would be used across all the banks that we

Table 2.1 Standard financials template

Performance summary	2010	2011	2012
Net interest income	39,441	40,662	37,672
Net fee & commission income	17,355	17,160	16,430
Net trading income	7,210	6,506	7,091
Other banking income	1,080	1,056	1,410
Net insurance income	(621)	1,691	(1,171)
Other operating income	2,562	1,766	2,100
Subtotal non-interest income	27,586	28,179	25,860
Net operating income	67,027	68,841	63,532
Administrative expenses	(34,992)	(38,625)	(40,474)
Depreciation and amortisation	(2,696)	(2,920)	(2,453)
Other operating expenses	–	–	–
Operating expenses	(37,688)	(41,545)	(42,927)
Trading surplus	29,339	27,296	20,605
Impairment charges	(14,039)	(12,127)	(8,311)
Operating profit (pre-goodwill)	15,300	15,169	12,294
Goodwill impairment	–	–	–
Operating profit	15,300	15,169	12,294
Fair value gains/(losses) on own debt	(258)	4,161	(4,327)
Changes in fair value of financial assets	1,478	(722)	2,101
Income from associates and JVs	2,517	3,264	3,557
Exceptional items	–	–	7,024
Profit before tax	19,037	21,872	20,649
Income tax	(4,846)	(3,928)	(5,315)
Net profit	14,191	17,944	15,334
Minority interests (non-equity)	–	–	–
Minority interests (equity)	(1,032)	(1,147)	(1,307)
Preference dividends	–	0	–
Net profit attributable to equity shareholders	13,159	16,797	14,027
Dividends	(5,937)	(7,726)	(8,314)
Retained earnings	7,222	9,071	5,713
Risk-weighted assets (RWA), end of period	1,103,113	1,209,514	1,123,943
RWA growth in period	–2.7%	9.6%	–7.1%
Period average RWAs	1,096,725	1,162,421	1,163,312
Total assets	2,454,689	2,555,579	2,692,538
RWA/Assets	45%	47%	42%

covered. This made data entry and cross-comparisons much easier, and it also helped to highlight any banks whose accounting disclosures differed radically from those of its peers.

These standard ROIC templates are extracted from a bank's financial statements as reported. In practice, we generally type in a bank's financial statements on a separate worksheet tab, adding detailed notes as appropriate, and then we link the cells in the ROIC model worksheet with the relevant cells in the financials worksheet. If a bank changes its reporting format (which seems to happen every three to five years for most banks), then the cell links simply change; the structure of the ROIC model stays the same.

A standard ROIC template makes it easier not only to see longer-term trends in a bank's performance and valuation, but also to compare that bank with others. Also, when evaluating mergers, acquisitions or disposals, we have also found that having a standard ROIC template makes it far easier to model potential scenarios.

We have put HSBC financials into our standard template as an example (see below). Note that although we have only shown 2010 through 2012, in practice we usually collect as much historical financial data as possible – in HSBC's case our model has data going back to 1989 (when Basel I data on RWAs etc first became available).

On the ROIC for Banks website, you can find both our standard ROIC model template as well as the ROIC models with linked financials for the banks in Chapter 3.

Calculating Invested Capital

We start our ROIC analysis by getting a clear idea of the total capital that has been invested in a bank. This starts with shareholders' equity and then adds items that are also regarded as capital.

A bank's balance sheet (along with supporting notes) is the main data source for calculating Invested Capital. Unless there has been a change in the bank's auditors, there tends to be more continuity in the presentation of the balance sheet than in the income statement, thus making it easier to do period-on-period comparisons. In recent years, the balance sheet disclosure has been augmented by the Pillar 3 disclosures for many banks.

Note that Invested Capital is split into Adjusted Equity and Debt Capital, in order to track the debt and equity components separately. This will prove useful in the ROIC analysis later in this section. Remember that we use the same Invested Capital and ROIC templates for all the banks that we cover; this is so that we can compare banks across regions and countries in a relatively consistent manner.

Before we go into the line-by-line detail of how we calculate Invested Capital, it is worth noting the difference between Invested Capital and the Basel definitions of regulatory capital (e.g. Core Tier 1 capital). Whilst both tend to look at the same line items in a bank's financial statements, they are looking at these items for different purposes – the

Invested Capital calculation is looking for all the capital that has been invested in the bank, whereas the purpose of the regulatory capital calculations is to clarify the ability of bank to absorb potential losses. Thus, the regulatory capital ratios distinguish among layers of capital in terms of their ability to absorb losses, starting with tangible shareholders' equity as the core part of a bank's capital. In the ROIC methodology, we do pay attention to the relative distinctions among Core Tier 1 capital, other Tier 1 capital and Tier 2 capital, but we are also interested in the overall returns on the total amount of capital that has been invested in the bank.

Using HSBC as an example, we will now build up Invested Capital from the financial statements, line-by-line.

Shareholders' equity

This is taken directly from the balance sheet. Note that some banks include other shareholders besides common equity shareholders in this line item (e.g. preference shares). Taking only common shareholders' equity enables us to get a 'clean' equity leverage ratio.

Goodwill charges – track and add back

We add back the accumulated goodwill amortisation (or under IFRS, goodwill impairment charges) to Invested Capital. The reasoning behind this is that the goodwill is the excess over book value that was paid for an acquisition; at the time of the acquisition, it was a use of shareholders' funds. Although subsequent goodwill amortisation and goodwill impairment charges would reduce reported earnings and thus shareholders' equity, nothing would have changed from the point of view of tracking how much capital has been invested.

Thus, in calculating Invested Capital, we keep a running tally of cumulative goodwill charges on the P&L, adding them back to Invested Capital. Note that for HSBC and other UK banks, UK generally accepted accounting principles (GAAP) had required goodwill to be written off directly against reserves in reporting prior to 1998; in our ROIC models, we have

Table 2.2 Building Invested Capital: shareholders' equity

Invested Capital	2008	2009	2010	2011	2012
Adjusted equity Shareholders' equity	93,591	128,299	147,667	158,725	175,242

Source: HSBC annual reports, author's analysis.

Table 2.3   Building Invested Capital: goodwill and other intangibles

Invested Capital	2008	2009	2010	2011	2012
Adjusted equity					
Shareholders' equity	93,591	128,299	147,667	158,725	175,242
+ Goodwill written off directly to reserves (pre-98)	**5,138**	**5,138**	**5,138**	**5,138**	**5,138**
+ Cumulative intangibles amortised	**14,238**	**14,238**	**14,238**	**14,238**	**14,238**

Source: HSBC annual reports, author's analysis.

Table 2.4   Building Invested Capital: cumulative unrealised fair value adjustments

Invested Capital	2008	2009	2010	2011	2012
Adjusted equity					
Shareholders' equity	93,591	128,299	147,667	158,725	175,242
+ Goodwill written off directly to reserves (pre-98)	5,138	5,138	5,138	5,138	5,138
+ Cumulative intangibles amortised	14,238	14,238	14,238	14,238	14,238
– Cumulative unrealised FV adjustments	**(9,626)**	**(6,095)**	**(7,315)**	**(10,754)**	**(8,528)**

Source: HSBC annual reports, author's analysis.

included a line item to account for this, but this line item will be blank for banks that did not report in UK GAAP.

Changes in fair value items – track

We have excluded changes in fair value P&L items from our RORWA calculation but included them as a running tally in our Invested Capital calculation. This is particularly relevant for the 'changes in fair value of own debt' items that have appeared in banks' financial statements, as well as for changes in the value of various derivatives.

Most of these changes in fair value for own debt and derivatives tend to net themselves out over the life of the underlying asset or liability, thus using a running tally as part of Invested Capital makes sense in our opinion.

Table 2.5 Building Invested Capital: loan–loss provisions

Invested Capital	2008	2009	2010	2011	2012
Adjusted equity					
Shareholders' equity	93,591	128,299	147,667	158,725	175,242
+ Goodwill written off directly to reserves (pre-98)	5,138	5,138	5,138	5,138	5,138
+ Cumulative intangibles amortised	14,238	14,238	14,238	14,238	14,238
– Cumulative unrealised FV adjustments	(9,626)	(6,095)	(7,315)	(10,754)	(8,528)
+ Loss provisions (Balance Sheet)	**23,972**	**23,972**	**20,241**	**17,636**	**16,112**

Source: HSBC annual reports, author's analysis.

Impairment allowances – add

Like the regulators, we also treat impairment allowances (or loan–loss provisions in pre-IFRS accounts) as Invested Capital. In effect, they represent appropriations of shareholders' funds – in other words, the bank needs to keep this money back from shareholders in order to cover potential bad debts.

Of course, there is a range of other allowances (or provisions), including those for lawsuits. Although we have chosen not to include those provisions in our calculation of Invested Capital, we can understand the arguments for including them. Instead, we tend to capture the additional provisioning charges by including them in our calculation of ROIC (rather than excluding them from 'underlying earnings' calculations as many banks have done).

Pension liabilities – add

As with impairment allowances, we also treat pension liabilities as appropriations of shareholders' funds; thus, we regard it as Invested Capital in our calculations. The caveat with pension liabilities is that if long-term interest rate or inflation assumptions become volatile, then the estimated pension liabilities could become quite volatile as well. Note that the calculation methodologies for pension assets and liabilities changed when IFRS/IAS was introduced in the mid-2000s; we have taken only pension liabilities under IFRS accounting.

Table 2.6   Building Invested Capital: pensions

Invested Capital	2008	2009	2010	2011	2012
Adjusted equity					
Shareholders' equity	93,591	128,299	147,667	158,725	175,242
+ Goodwill written off directly to reserves (pre-98)	5,138	5,138	5,138	5,138	5,138
+ Cumulative intangibles amortised	14,238	14,238	14,238	14,238	14,238
– Cumulative unrealised FV adjustments	(9,626)	(6,095)	(7,315)	(10,754)	(8,528)
+ Loss provisions (Balance Sheet)	23,972	23,972	20,241	17,636	16,112
+ Pension liabilities (post IFRS only)	**3,888**	**6,967**	**3,856**	**3,666**	**3,905**

Source: HSBC annual reports, author's analysis.

Table 2.7   Building Invested Capital: minority interests (equity)

Invested Capital	2008	2009	2010	2011	2012
Adjusted equity					
Shareholders' equity	93,591	128,299	147,667	158,725	175,242
+ Goodwill written off directly to reserves (pre-98)	5,138	5,138	5,138	5,138	5,138
+ Cumulative intangibles amortised	14,238	14,238	14,238	14,238	14,238
– Cumulative unrealised FV adjustments	(9,626)	(6,095)	(7,315)	(10,754)	(8,528)
+ Loss provisions (Balance Sheet)	23,972	23,972	20,241	17,636	16,112
+ Pension liabilities (post IFRS only)	3,888	6,967	3,856	3,666	3,905
+ Minority interests (equity)	**6,638**	**7,362**	**7,248**	**7,368**	**7,887**

Source: HSBC annual reports, author's analysis.

Minority interests (equity) – add

We add equity minority interests because we think that if the bank has operating control over a subsidiary, then it has effectively mustered the equity minority interests to support its strategies. Thus, we include them as part of Invested Capital.

We can also understand if other analysts choose to exclude equity minority interests from a bank's invested capital; indeed, under the BIS rules, minority interests are excluded when calculating Core Tier 1 capital. We have chosen to include equity minority interests in invested capital because in many cases, these equity minority interests arise from acquisitions where the original shareholders in the acquired bank retain a minority stake, even whilst ceding management control to the acquiring bank. In these cases, we think that the acquiring bank can effectively do what it wants with the acquired bank, and thus those equity minority interests have effectively added themselves to the acquiring bank's invested capital, in our opinion.

Revaluation gains – subtract

When property prices were booming, many banks recognised revaluation gains from their own properties in shareholders' equity. The recent financial crises have reminded us that prices can go down as well as up, even with property; we thus subtract these revaluation gains from our calculation of Invested Capital.

Table 2.8 Building Invested Capital: revaluation gains

Invested Capital	2008	2009	2010	2011	2012
Adjusted equity					
Shareholders' equity	93,591	128,299	147,667	158,725	175,242
+ Goodwill written off directly to reserves (pre-98)	5,138	5,138	5,138	5,138	5,138
+ Cumulative intangibles amortised	14,238	14,238	14,238	14,238	14,238
– Cumulative unrealised FV adjustments	(9,626)	(6,095)	(7,315)	(10,754)	(8,528)
+ Loss provisions (Balance Sheet)	23,972	23,972	20,241	17,636	16,112
+ Pension liabilities (post IFRS only)	3,888	6,967	3,856	3,666	3,905
+ Minority interests (equity)	6,638	7,362	7,248	7,368	7,887
– Revaluation gains	**(1,726)**	**(2,226)**	**(3,121)**	**(2,678)**	**(3,290)**

Source: HSBC annual reports, author's analysis.

Table 2.9 Building Invested Capital: adjusted equity

Invested Capital	2008	2009	2010	2011	2012
Adjusted equity					
Shareholders' equity	93,591	128,299	147,667	158,725	175,242
+ Goodwill written off directly to reserves (pre-98)	5,138	5,138	5,138	5,138	5,138
+ Cumulative intangibles amortised	14,238	14,238	14,238	14,238	14,238
– Cumulative unrealised FV adjustments	(9,626)	(6,095)	(7,315)	(10,754)	(8,528)
+ Loss provisions (Balance Sheet)	23,972	23,972	20,241	17,636	16,112
+ Pension liabilities (post IFRS only)	3,888	6,967	3,856	3,666	3,905
+ Minority interests (equity)	6,638	7,362	7,248	7,368	7,887
– Revaluation gains	(1,726)	(2,226)	(3,121)	(2,678)	(3,290)
Adjusted equity	**136,113**	**177,655**	**187,952**	**193,339**	**210,704**
Average adjusted equity in period	**152,869**	**159,515**	**180,985**	**194,555**	**202,236**

Source: HSBC annual reports, author's analysis.

Result: Adjusted Equity in Invested Capital

The above items produce our Adjusted Equity part of Invested Capital. We've separated the equity and debt components of Invested Capital because these two parts tend to behave differently, especially in crises.

Whereas the dividends to equity shareholders can be changed relatively easily, the interest and preference dividends on debt capital instruments tend to be much harder to change. Separating equity and debt in Invested Capital also enables us to compare debt/equity capital ratios, historically for a given bank, but also in bank cross-comparisons.

Now, onto the debt capital part of Invested Capital:

Long-term subordinated debt – add

We consider long-term subordinated debt as part of invested capital, mainly because next to shareholders' equity this long-term, junior debt tends to be the next layer in a bank's capital structure that would absorb any losses. Regulators also consider these items as acceptable when calculating Tier 2 capital (and in some cases, Tier 1 capital as well). Indeed, many

Table 2.10   Building Invested Capital: subordinated debt

Invested Capital	2008	2009	2010	2011	2012
Debt capital					
Subordinated debt (incl IFRS FV accounted)	52,394	52,394	33,387	30,606	29,479

Source: HSBC annual reports, author's analysis.

Table 2.11   Building Invested Capital: minority interests (non-equity)

Invested Capital	2008	2009	2010	2011	2012
Debt capital					
Subordinated debt (incl IFRS FV accounted)	52,394	52,394	33,387	30,606	29,479
+ Minority interests (non-equity)	–	–	–	–	–

Source: HSBC annual reports, author's analysis.

subordinated debt issues are specifically designed to be acceptable to the regulators for capital adequacy calculations.

Note that there are often discrepancies between the long-term subordinated debt numbers on the balance sheet and the amounts in the regulatory capital disclosures, but compared to overall invested capital, these differences tend to be minor.

Minority Interests (debt) – add

As noted above, we treat equity minority interests as part of adjusted equity in Invested Capital; non-equity minority interests are treated as part of debt Invested Capital. This is similar to the regulatory recognition of minority interests in Core Tier 1 and other Tier 1 capital.

Preference shares – add

We add preference shares to invested capital because they effectively sit alongside common shareholders' equity in terms of loss absorption; for example, when many banks reported losses in 2008 and 2009, they often cancelled dividends on both common and preference shares. If dividends are restarted, preference shares, by definition, are preferred, or in other

Table 2.12 Building Invested Capital: preference shares

Invested Capital	2008	2009	2010	2011	2012
Debt capital					
Subordinated debt (incl IFRS FV accounted)	52,394	52,394	33,387	30,606	29,479
+ Minority interests (non-equity)	–	–	–	–	–
+ Preference shares	–	–	–	–	–

Source: HSBC annual reports, author's analysis.

words, the dividends would be restarted for preference shares before common shares.

In recent years, preference shares have dwindled as a component of the capital structures for banks; this is because many regulators have decided not to include many types of preference shares as part of their regulatory capital calculations. Without the regulatory capital benefit from preference shares anymore, most banks have chosen to issue other forms of debt capital that get better regulatory treatment. Thus, some banks still have some preference shares as part of Invested Capital, but these tend to be older sources of funding.

Taken together, these items give us Debt Capital within Invested Capital.

Invested Capital – some observations and analyses

So, going back to HSBC as our example:

As with nearly all of the banks we have analysed, HSBC's adjusted equity in Invested Capital is significantly higher than shareholders' equity. Previously written-off goodwill, loss provisions, pension liabilities, and equity minority interests add up quite quickly.

Note that including impairment provisions helps to regulate Invested Capital in a crisis. For example, if a bank took a big impairment charge (as many have in the past several years) and thus books a big loss, it may take a big chunk out of shareholders' equity. But if the actual loan write-offs haven't picked up yet, then the additional impairment allowances would be added back to Invested Capital. In our view, this gives us a fairer, less volatile Invested Capital number.

Table 2.13 Building Invested Capital: total

Invested Capital	2008	2009	2010	2011	2012
Adjusted equity					
Shareholders' equity	93,591	128,299	147,667	158,725	175,242
+ Goodwill written off directly to reserves (pre-98)	5,138	5,138	5,138	5,138	5,138
+ Cumulative intangibles amortised	14,238	14,238	14,238	14,238	14,238
– Cumulative unrealised FV adjustments	(9,626)	(6,095)	(7,315)	(10,754)	(8,528)
+ Loss provisions (Balance Sheet)	23,972	23,972	20,241	17,636	16,112
+ Pension liabilities (post IFRS only)	3,888	6,967	3,856	3,666	3,905
+ Minority interests (equity)	6,638	7,362	7,248	7,368	7,887
– Revaluation gains	(1,726)	(2,226)	(3,121)	(2,678)	(3,290)
Adjusted equity	136,113	177,655	187,952	193,339	210,704
Average adjusted equity in period	152,869	159,515	180,985	194,555	202,236
Debt capital					
Subordinated debt (incl IFRS FV accounted)	52,394	52,394	33,387	30,606	29,479
+ Minority interests (non-equity)	–	–	–	–	–
+ Preference shares	–	–	–	–	–
Debt capital	**52,394**	**52,394**	**33,387**	**30,606**	**29,479**
Average debt capital in period	**51,243**	**50,552**	**35,569**	**32,375**	**29,869**
Invested capital	188,507	230,049	221,339	223,945	240,183
Invested capital growth in period	–10%	22%	–4%	1%	7%
Average invested capital in period	204,112	210,067	216,554	226,930	232,106

Source: HSBC annual reports, author's analysis.

Table 2.14   Invested Capital: analysis

Invested Capital	2008	2009	2010	2011	2012
Adjusted equity					
Shareholders' equity	93,591	128,299	147,667	158,725	175,242
+ Goodwill written off directly to reserves (pre-98)	5,138	5,138	5,138	5,138	5,138
+ Cumulative intangibles amortised	14,238	14,238	14,238	14,238	14,238
− Cumulative unrealised FV adjustments	(9,626)	(6,095)	(7,315)	(10,754)	(8,528)
+ Loss provisions (Balance Sheet)	23,972	23,972	20,241	17,636	16,112
+ Pension liabilities (post IFRS only)	3,888	6,967	3,856	3,666	3,905
+ Minority interests (equity)	6,638	7,362	7,248	7,368	7,887
- Revaluation gains	(1,726)	(2,226)	(3,121)	(2,678)	(3,290)
Adjusted equity	136,113	177,655	187,952	193,339	210,704
Average adjusted equity in period	152,869	159,515	180,985	194,555	202,236
Debt capital					
Subordinated debt (incl IFRS FV accounted)	52,394	52,394	33,387	30,606	29,479
+ Minority interests (non-equity)	–	–	–	–	–
+ Preference shares	–	–	–	–	–
Debt capital	52,394	52,394	33,387	30,606	29,479
Average debt capital in period	51,243	50,552	35,569	32,375	29,869
Invested capital	188,507	230,049	221,339	223,945	240,183
Invested capital growth in period	–10%	22%	–4%	1%	7%
Average invested capital in period	204,112	210,067	216,554	226,930	232,106

Source: HSBC annual reports, author's analysis.

Calculating Return on Invested Capital (ROIC)

Reflecting the principles used in calculating invested capital, we have made corresponding adjustments to net profit in calculating the return on invested capital (see below).

Guiding principles for calculating ROIC

In calculating ROIC for banks, we are trying to get something like 'free cash flow' as is used in analysing most other companies – whilst acknowledging how difficult it is to determine and/or agree what 'free cash flow' actually is for a bank. What we're trying to get a sense of is the 'real' profitability of the bank – particularly after adjusting for the debt capital portion of the bank's invested capital base.

We wanted the ROIC for Banks approach to be both useful and practical – so that it can actually be used to analyse and value banks, instead of sitting unused on a bookshelf. In practice, that has meant being able to take a fresh set of bank financial statements in the morning and having a decent view on what makes the bank tick and how much it should be worth by the end of the day. We can indulge our habit to veer into complexity later, but the needs for analysis and valuation are often immediate.

Avoiding core/non-core distinctions

In this quest for clarity, we tend to ignore the core/non-core distinctions that have been created by many banks. In our opinion, these always beg the question of exactly how it was decided that something was 'core' or 'non-core' – for example, can a customer have some of their loans labelled as 'core' and others labelled as 'non-core'? Or could a customer loan be labelled as 'core', but the interest-rate swap that was sold alongside it be labelled as 'non-core'? And have any rules for recognition been applied consistently throughout?

As we have noted earlier, if shareholders can't buy a share of only the 'core' bank, then we don't think it's really that worthwhile to make the distinction.

Leaving in 'one-off' restructuring charges

Similarly, we don't take out 'one-off' charges associated with restructuring programmes. We have seen a bank announce a big restructuring programme even though their previously announced restructuring programme was still running, and another bank excluded 5–10% of its operating costs as restructuring expenses in its presentation of management profits for nearly a decade. We note that in almost all of these cases, these 'one-off' expenses are included as part operating expenses in the statutory accounts, even though in the 'management' or 'adjusted' presentation they have been stripped out. In our opinion, if the bank's auditor thought that it should be included in operating expenses in the audited financial statements, we tend to agree with them.

Tracking fair value movements in a rolling account

Under IFRS and US GAAP, accountants have agreed that the changes in the 'fair value' of some balance sheet items (e.g. some derivatives, debt securities and other marketable securities) can be recognised separately.

One of the most prominent examples of this is changes in fair value of own debt. We don't tend to regard these movements as 'real', however – for example, if the own debt liability is paid back at maturity (and most of these own debts are held to maturity), any changes in fair value along the way will have netted themselves out. We thus would not regard these fair value changes as affecting Invested Capital.

In order to counterbalance the effect of these fair value items on Invested Capital, we keep track of them in a rolling tally in Invested Capital as outlined above.

Show unlevered returns

In order to show the unlevered returns (i.e., before debt servicing costs), we add back the interest paid on subordinated debt. We can usually find this disclosed in either the bank's cash flow statement or in the detailed interest expense breakdown in the notes to the financial statements.

We also add back minority interests. Often these haven't been broken out into debt or equity minority interests at the bottom of the income statement, but in the notes to the financial statements you can generally get the debt/equity minority interests broken out separately in the details on shareholders' equity.

As an example, here are our ROIC calculations for HSBC in 2011 and 2012:

Table 2.15 ROIC: HSBC examples 2011 & 2012

Return on Invested Capital (ROIC)	2011	2012
Net profit attributable to equity shareholders	16,797	14,027
+ Goodwill/intangibles amortisation	–	–
+ Exceptional items	–	(7,024)
– Unrealised fair value (gains)/losses	(3,439)	2,226
+ Preference share dividends	–	–
+ Interest paid on subordinated debt	1,619	1,493
+ Minority Interests charge (non-equity)	–	–
+ Minority Interests charge (equity)	–	–
+ Provisioning charge (P&L as reported)	12,127	8,311
+ Tax charge (P&L as reported)	3,928	5,315
Pre-provisioning Operating Profit	31,032	24,348
– Provisioning charge (P&L as reported)	(12,127)	(8,311)
Adjusted Operating Profit	18,905	16,037
Operating ROIC (12-month)	8.31%	6.85%
– Tax charge (P&L as reported)	(3,928)	(5,315)
– Implied tax charge on debt capital interest	(486)	(448)
Adjusted Net Profit	14,491	10,274
RORWA (12-month)	1.25%	0.88%
Net ROIC (12-month)	6.37%	4.39%

As we mentioned earlier, we use the same ROIC template across all of the banks that we analyse. Having a standard template not only encourages peer-to-peer and cross-border comparisons, it makes them easier to do.

We have also found that when accounting rules and/or capital/liquidity regulations do change, it's easier to make any changes across a standardised template instead of trying to recall all the idiosyncratic tweaks that have been made along the way.

So, again, taking it line-by-line:

Start with net profit attributable to equity shareholders

This is the statutory net profit attributable to common equity shareholders. Some banks tend to show net profit including equity minority interests and preference share dividends. We usually double-check this; if a bank is showing minority interests and preference shares on its balance sheet, we then start looking for the corresponding charge in the income statement, either in the interest expense details or at the bottom of income statement. We'll get to add back these items later in the ROIC analysis.

Add back goodwill charges

Since IFRS accounting rules came into effect (around 2004), goodwill amortisation charges have been replaced by goodwill impairment charges that are recognised when the value of the acquisition is judged to have deteriorated. These goodwill impairments tend to be lumpier, with several years having no goodwill charges, followed by a year where a significant impairment of goodwill is recognised.

In calculating ROIC, we have added back both of these types of goodwill charges. After all, these aren't cash items, they're accepted accounting conventions for recognising the cost of acquisitions over time (long after shareholders' funds have already been spent on the acquisition).

Table 2.16   Building ROIC: net profit

Return on Invested Capital (ROIC)	2008	2009	2010	2011	2012
Net profit attributable to equity shareholders	5,728	5,834	13,159	16,797	14,027

Source: HSBC annual reports, author's analysis.

Table 2.17   Building ROIC: goodwill/intangibles

Return on Invested Capital (ROIC)	2008	2009	2010	2011	2012
Net profit attributable to equity shareholders	5,728	5,834	13,159	16,797	14,027
+ Goodwill/intangibles amortisation	**10,564**	–	–	–	–

Source: HSBC annual reports, author's analysis.

Table 2.18   Building ROIC: exceptional items

Return on Invested Capital (ROIC)	2008	2009	2010	2011	2012
Net profit attributable to equity shareholders	5,728	5,834	13,159	16,797	14,027
+ Goodwill/intangibles amortisation	10,564	–	–	–	–
+ Exceptional items	**(2,445)**	–	–	–	**(7,024)**

Source: HSBC annual reports, author's analysis.

Note that we treat the amortisation of other intangibles differently from goodwill charges. These 'other intangibles' items tend to be software-related, e.g. where the cost of an IT project is capitalised and recognised as an intangible asset, and the cost of that project is spread out over a set number of years. We regard these as operating expenses.

Add back restructuring/exceptional items

We add the restructuring/exceptional items back to our ROIC calculation, keeping in mind that we are quite strict in terms of what qualifies as an extraordinary item (that we would exclude from our ROIC calculation). In general, if the bank's accountants have classified it as an extraordinary (or exceptional) item in the audited income statement, we'd also accept it as such.

In practice, these items are often linked with acquisitions or disposals, so there are often corresponding goodwill items in both the income statement (e.g. goodwill impairments) and balance sheet (e.g. changes in goodwill). There can often be changes in the deferred tax asset/liability on the balance sheet as well.

Table 2.19 Building ROIC: unrealised fair value gains

Return on Invested Capital (ROIC)	2008	2009	2010	2011	2012
Net profit attributable to equity shareholders	5,728	5,834	13,159	16,797	14,027
+ Goodwill/intangibles amortisation	10,564	–	–	–	–
+ Exceptional items	(2,445)	–	–	–	(7,024)
– **Unrealised fair value (gains)/losses**	**(3,852)**	**3,531**	**(1,220)**	**(3,439)**	**2,226**

Source: HSBC annual reports, author's analysis.

Subtract unrealised fair value gains

Unrealised fair value gains come in two main categories: changes in the fair value of own debts, and changes in the fair value of assets. Note that most banks now tend to take the fair value of own debt items out of their adjusted earnings; these changes also tend to be excluded from the regulatory calculation of Tier 1 capital.

Unrealised fair value gains (or losses) are often associated with changes in the market value of a bank's own debt (e.g. subordinated liabilities); in recent years, this line item has been extremely volatile, swinging from positive to negative as the credit markets swing around.

This is often disclosed in the management accounts, in either or both the investment banking/trading income details, or as part of head office/HQ performance. It is also tends to be disclosed in the Tier 1 capital details.

Debt capital interest expense – add

In addition to the adjustments identified above, we also add back interest expense associated with the bank's debt capital funding. This is in order to show the returns on total invested capital, in other words including the interest expense from subordinated debt and other forms of debt capital that are accepted by the regulators.

The next three items add back the interest expense on debt capital:

Preference share dividends – add

This can usually be found either in the interest expense details in the notes to the financial statements, or at the bottom of the income statement.

Table 2.20 Building ROIC: preference share dividends

Return on Invested Capital (ROIC)	2008	2009	2010	2011	2012
Net profit attributable to equity shareholders	5,728	5,834	13,159	16,797	14,027
+ Goodwill/intangibles amortisation	10,564	–	–	–	–
+ Exceptional items	(2,445)	–	–	–	(7,024)
– Unrealised fair value (gains)/losses	(3,852)	3,531	(1,220)	(3,439)	2,226
+ Preference share dividends	–	–	–	–	–

Source: HSBC annual reports, author's analysis.

Table 2.21 Building ROIC: interest paid on subordinated debt

Return on Invested Capital (ROIC)	2008	2009	2010	2011	2012
Net profit attributable to equity shareholders	5,728	5,834	13,159	16,797	14,027
+ Goodwill/intangibles amortisation	10,564	–	–	–	–
+ Exceptional items	(2,445)	–	–	–	(7,024)
– Unrealised fair value (gains)/losses	(3,852)	3,531	(1,220)	(3,439)	2,226
+ Preference share dividends	–	–	–	–	–
+ Interest paid on subordinated debt	2,178	2,528	1,778	1,619	1,493

Source: HSBC annual reports, author's analysis.

Add back interest paid on subordinated debt

This can usually be found in the cash flow statement (we've seen it in the cash flow from operations or cash flow from financing sections) or in the interest expense details in the notes to the financial statements. Sometimes this item isn't broken out separately; in those cases, we usually look for a recent subordinated debt issue (via a web search or financial information source) and check what the coupon is, or ideally we could search for news items describing the results (i.e. yield, proceeds) of that bank's subordinated debt auction.

Table 2.22   Building ROIC: minority interests

Return on Invested Capital (ROIC)	2008	2009	2010	2011	2012
Net profit attributable to equity shareholders	5,728	5,834	13,159	16,797	14,027
+ Goodwill/intangibles amortisation	10,564	–	–	–	–
+ Exceptional items	(2,445)	–	–	–	(7,024)
– Unrealised fair value (gains)/losses	(3,852)	3,531	(1,220)	(3,439)	2,226
+ Preference share dividends	–	–	–	–	–
+ Interest paid on subordinated debt	2,178	2,528	1,778	1,619	1,493
+ Minority interests charge (non-equity)	–	–	–	–	–
+ Minority interests charge (equity)	–	–	–	–	–

Source: HSBC annual reports, author's analysis.

Add back (debt) minority interest charges

These are usually broken out separately at the bottom of the income statement; if the equity and debt portions of minority interest charges aren't broken out separately, we usually cross-reference back to the balance sheet data to see the relative weightings in equity versus debt minority interests. If the debt minority interests are broken out separately, we also adjust for the debt tax shield.

Look at pre-provisioning operating profit

Once we have adjusted for the debt capital items, we can get to an estimate of pre-provisioning operating profit by adding back (1) impairment charges, and (2) income tax charged in the period. This gives a view of operating cash flows before the accounting-driven charge for bad debts as well as taxes due – note that in a later section, we will adjust for long-term average impairment charges to get a view of through-the-cycle operating profitability.

Adjusted Operating Profit and Operating ROIC

Taking impairment charges back into account gives us Adjusted Operating Profit. Dividing Adjusted Operating Profit by average Invested Capital gives us Operating ROIC in the period.

Table 2.23   Building ROIC: provisioning/impairment charge

Return on Invested Capital (ROIC)	2008	2009	2010	2011	2012
Net profit attributable to equity shareholders	5,728	5,834	13,159	16,797	14,027
+ Goodwill/intangibles amortisation	10,564	–	–	–	–
+ Exceptional items	(2,445)	–	–	–	(7,024)
– Unrealised fair value (gains)/losses	(3,852)	3,531	(1,220)	(3,439)	2,226
+ Preference share dividends	–	–	–	–	–
+ Interest paid on subordinated debt	2,178	2,528	1,778	1,619	1,493
+ Minority interests charge (non-equity)	–	–	–	–	–
+ Minority interests charge (equity)	–	–	–	–	–
+ Provisioning charge (P&L as reported)	**24,937**	**26,488**	**14,039**	**12,127**	**8,311**

Source: HSBC annual reports, author's analysis.

Adjusted Net Profit and Net ROIC

Taking income taxes back into account gives us Adjusted Net Profit. Dividing Adjusted Net Profit by average Invested Capital gives us Net ROIC in the period. We also calculated Return on Average Risk-Weighted Assets (RORWA) in the period by dividing Adjusted Net Profit by average RWAs.

Note that in the online Appendix, you can download the ROIC models and then trace back to the reported financials. We've found that's the best way to learn how to use ROIC analysis in practice.

Through-the-cycle (TTC) ROIC

Net ROIC in banks is often quite volatile, with impairment charges being a key factor in that volatility. We find it quite valuable to have an estimate of long-term profitability, adjusting for the volatility of impairment charges by using a long-term average impairment charge.

There is much debate about how long a period should be used for this average. We prefer taking as long-term a view on this as possible, trying to include as many cycles as we can; for some banks (e.g. Barclays), this

Table 2.24 Building ROIC: Adjusted Operating Profit and Operating ROIC

Return on Invested Capital (ROIC)	2008	2009	2010	2011	2012
Net profit attributable to equity shareholders	5,728	5,834	13,159	16,797	14,027
+ Goodwill/intangibles amortisation	10,564	–	–	–	–
+ Exceptional items	(2,445)	–	–	–	(7,024)
– Unrealised fair value (gains)/losses	(3,852)	3,531	(1,220)	(3,439)	2,226
+ Preference share dividends	–	–	–	–	–
+ Interest paid on subordinated debt	2,178	2,528	1,778	1,619	1,493
+ Minority interests charge (non-equity)	–	–	–	–	–
+ Minority interests charge (equity)	–	–	–	–	–
+ Provisioning charge (P&L as reported)	24,937	26,488	14,039	12,127	8,311
+ Tax charge (P&L as reported)	2,809	385	4,846	3,928	5,315
Pre-provisioning Operating Profit	39,919	38,766	32,602	31,032	24,348
– Provisioning charge (P&L as reported)	(24,937)	(26,488)	(14,039)	(12,127)	(8,311)
Adjusted Operating Profit	**14,982**	**12,278**	**18,563**	**18,905**	**16,037**
Operating ROIC (12-month)	**7.34%**	**5.84%**	**8.57%**	**8.33%**	**6.91%**

Source: HSBC annual reports, author's analysis.

can mean having data as far back as 1989 (when the first Basel regime was adopted).

For most of the banks that we have analysed, the long-term average impairment charge has tended to be higher than what we had expected. We think this could mean that the probability of disappointing earnings (from higher-than-expected impairments) is higher than what we (or the markets) might expect.

Here are our overall ROIC calculations for HSBC from 2008 through 2012. Note that in the supporting website, you can access our ROIC model on HSBC, which goes back to 1989.

Table 2.25 Building ROIC: Adjusted Net Profit and Net ROIC

Return on Invested Capital (ROIC)	2008	2009	2010	2011	2012
Net profit attributable to equity shareholders	5,728	5,834	13,159	16,797	14,027
+ Goodwill/intangibles amortisation	10,564	–	–	–	–
+ Exceptional items	(2,445)	–	–	–	(7,024)
– Unrealised fair value (gains)/losses	(3,852)	3,531	(1,220)	(3,439)	2,226
+ Preference share dividends	–	–	–	–	–
+ Interest paid on subordinated debt	2,178	2,528	1,778	1,619	1,493
+ Minority interests charge (non-equity)	–	–	–	–	–
+ Minority interests charge (equity)	–	–	–	–	–
+ Provisioning charge (P&L as reported)	24,937	26,488	14,039	12,127	8,311
+ Tax charge (P&L as reported)	2,809	385	4,846	3,928	5,315
Pre-provisioning Operating Profit	39,919	38,766	32,602	31,032	24,348
– Provisioning charge (P&L as reported)	(24,937)	(26,488)	(14,039)	(12,127)	(8,311)
Adjusted Operating Profit	14,982	12,278	18,563	18,905	16,037
Operating ROIC (12-month)	7.34%	5.84%	8.57%	8.33%	6.91%
– Tax charge (P&L as reported)	(2,809)	(385)	(4,846)	(3,928)	(5,315)
– Implied tax charge on debt capital interest	(653)	(758)	(534)	(486)	(448)
Adjusted Net Profit	11,519	11,134	13,184	14,491	10,274
RORWA (12-month)	**0.96%**	**0.97%**	**1.20%**	**1.25%**	**0.88%**
Net ROIC (12-month)	**5.64%**	**5.30%**	**6.09%**	**6.39%**	**4.43%**

Source: HSBC annual reports, author's analysis.

To help analyse these Invested Capital and ROIC data, we tend to start with a top-line ROIC decomposition (similar to the DuPont ROE decomposition described earlier in this section), and then we move on to a line-by-line RORWA analysis and Value Levers analysis.

Table 2.26 Building ROIC: through-the-cycle (TTC) ROIC

Return on Invested Capital (ROIC)	2008	2009	2010	2011	2012
Net profit attributable to equity shareholders	5,728	5,834	13,159	16,797	14,027
+ Goodwill/intangibles amortisation	10,564	–	–	–	–
+ Exceptional items	(2,445)	–	–	–	(7,024)
– Unrealised fair value (gains)/losses	(3,852)	3,531	(1,220)	(3,439)	2,226
+ Preference share dividends	–	–	–	–	–
+ Interest paid on subordinated debt	2,178	2,528	1,778	1,619	1,493
+ Minority interests charge (non-equity)	–	–	–	–	–
+ Minority interests charge (equity)	–	–	–	–	–
+ Provisioning charge (P&L as reported)	24,937	26,488	14,039	12,127	8,311
+ Tax charge (P&L as reported)	2,809	385	4,846	3,928	5,315
Pre-provisioning Operating Profit	39,919	38,766	32,602	31,032	24,348
– Provisioning charge (P&L as reported)	(24,937)	(26,488)	(14,039)	(12,127)	(8,311)
Adjusted Operating Profit	14,982	12,278	18,563	18,905	16,037
Operating ROIC (12-month)	7.34%	5.84%	8.57%	8.33%	6.91%
– Tax charge (P&L as reported)	(2,809)	(385)	(4,846)	(3,928)	(5,315)
– Implied tax charge on debt capital interest	(653)	(758)	(534)	(486)	(448)
Adjusted Net Profit	11,519	11,134	13,184	14,491	10,274
RORWA (12-month)	**0.96%**	**0.97%**	**1.20%**	**1.25%**	**0.88%**
Net ROIC (12-month)	**5.64%**	**5.30%**	**6.09%**	**6.39%**	**4.43%**

Source: HSBC annual reports, author's analysis.

ROIC decomposition

As described earlier, we have also found it useful to decompose ROIC (similar to how DuPont analysis uses ROE decomposition), breaking ROIC into its main components of RORWA and capital leverage (RWA/Invested Capital).

Table 2.27   ROIC analysis: ROIC decomposition, HSBC

ROIC drivers	2008	2009	2010	2011	2012
Return on risk-weighted assets (RoRWA)	0.96%	0.97%	1.20%	1.25%	0.88%
× Avg RWA/Avg Invested Capital	5.8	5.5	5.1	5.1	5.0
= Return on Invested Capital (ROIC)	5.6%	5.3%	6.1%	6.4%	4.4%
NB: Core Equity Tier 1 ratio	7.0%	9.4%	10.5%	10.1%	12.3%
NB: Debt Capital/ Invested Capital	28%	23%	15%	13%	12%

Source: HSBC annual reports, author's analysis.

DuPont ROE decomposition:

ROE = (Net Income/Sales) × (Sales/Total Assets) × (Total Assets/ Shareholders' Equity)

ROIC decomposition:

ROIC = (Net Returns/Risk-Weighted Assets) × (Risk-Weighted Assets/ Invested Capital)

ROIC decomposition enables us to distinguish between an improvement in ROIC driven by an improvement in operating performance (using the RORWA analysis described above), and one which is driven by an increase in capital leverage. Of these two main drivers for ROIC, we tend to prefer an improvement in RORWAs; increasing capital leverage (or its inverse, a decreasing Invested Capital/RWA ratio) generally indicates a higher risk profile.

Here is the ROIC decomposition for HSBC from 2008 through 2012.

At HSBC, capital leverage (RWA/Invested Capital) reached 5.8x in 2008 followed by a decrease and then levelling off at 5.1x in 2010 and 2011 with a slight dip to 5.0x in 2012; we think this decrease in capital leverage was mainly driven by the 50+ disposals since a global restructuring/streamlining programme was announced by the new CEO in 2011, plus an earlier decision to exit much of the Household U.S. consumer finance business. Many of these disposals were achieved at a premium to their net book value at the time, which both boosted capital and reduced RWAs, thus reducing capital leverage. At this data point (early 2013), it could be expected that HSBC would continue with its global streamlining programme, and that further reduction in RWAs and potential disposal gains would provide a further boost to regulatory capital ratios as well as bringing down HSBC's capital leverage.

HSBC's risk-adjusted returns (RORWA) dropped to 0.96% in 2008 and recovered to 1.25% by 2011, before dipping again in 2012 (to 0.88%). One of the key drivers behind the jump in administrative expenses in 2012 included major regulatory fines related to a U.S. anti-money laundering investigation and other expenses related to UK conduct-risk fines for payment protection insurance and other mis-selling. This showed up in the standardised income statement, RORWA table and Value Levers table as well.

As operating performance had improved from 2008 through 2011, ROIC had recovered, from 5.6% in 2008 to 6.4% in 2011 despite a decrease in capital leverage. In 2012, however, as operating performance dipped again, with RORWA falling from 1.25% in 2011 to 0.88% in 2012, this, combined with a small dip in leverage (5.1x to 5.0x) drove a significant decline in ROIC in 2012, from 6.4% in 4.4%.

Of course, we delve much deeper into the complex drivers behind the trends in HSBC's risk-adjusted operating performance and its capital leverage, but our main point about ROIC analysis is that it can boil down this complexity into a clearer, simpler set of key levers. Or in other words, we find that using the ROIC methodology enables us to do 'joined-up' analysis without getting lost in the complexity.

RORWA analysis: trends and comparisons

By using a standardised template for ROIC analysis, we have been able to look at a bank's performance over time (through, e.g., changes in accounting standards, corporate configurations) as well being able to cross-compare banks on a roughly apples-to-apples basis.

Dividing the standardised income statement line items by the average risk-weighted assets (RWAs) in the period helps with this by recasting performance on a risk-adjusted basis. As noted earlier, we acknowledge that the various methodologies for calculating RWAs are evolving constantly and that apples-to-apples comparisons may be using different apples, but despite this we think that having a risk-adjusted filter with which to evaluate operating performance still helps in giving a bit more consistency.

Using HSBC as an example again, here are our RORWA analyses for 2008 through 2012:

When we do RORWA analysis, we tend to look for shifts in the net interest income and non-interest income per RWA items. We have tended to find that looking at the P&L on a per RWA basis helps to adjust for

Table 2.28 ROIC analysis: Return on Risk-Weighted Assets (RORWA) analysis, HSBC

Performance per risk-weighted asset	2008	2009	2010	2011	2012
Net interest income	3.57%	3.54%	3.60%	3.50%	3.24%
Net fee & commission income	1.68%	1.54%	1.58%	1.48%	1.41%
Net trading income	0.55%	0.86%	0.66%	0.56%	0.61%
Other banking income	0.04%	0.06%	0.10%	0.09%	0.12%
Net insurance income	0.33%	−0.17%	−0.06%	0.15%	−0.10%
Other operating income	0.15%	0.24%	0.23%	0.15%	0.18%
Subtotal non-interest income	2.75%	2.52%	2.52%	2.42%	2.22%
Net operating income	6.31%	6.06%	6.11%	5.92%	5.46%
Administrative expenses	−3.02%	−2.77%	−3.19%	−3.32%	−3.48%
Depreciation	−0.21%	−0.22%	−0.25%	−0.25%	−0.21%
Other operating expenses	0.00%	0.00%	0.00%	0.00%	0.00%
Operating expenses	−3.23%	−2.99%	−3.44%	−3.57%	−3.69%
Trading surplus	3.09%	3.07%	2.68%	2.35%	1.77%
Impairment charges	−2.09%	−2.30%	−1.28%	−1.04%	−0.71%
Operating profit (pre-goodwill)	1.00%	0.77%	1.40%	1.30%	1.06%
Intangibles amortisation	−0.88%	0.00%	0.00%	0.00%	0.00%
Operating profit	0.11%	0.77%	1.40%	1.30%	1.06%
Fair value gains/(losses) on own debt	0.00%	0.00%	0.00%	0.00%	0.00%
Changes in fair value of financial assets	0.32%	−0.31%	0.13%	−0.06%	0.18%
Income from associates and JVs	0.14%	0.15%	0.23%	0.28%	0.31%
Exceptional items	0.20%	0.00%	0.00%	0.00%	0.60%
Profit before tax	0.78%	0.62%	1.74%	1.88%	1.78%
Income tax	−0.24%	−0.03%	−0.44%	−0.34%	−0.46%
Net profit	0.54%	0.58%	1.29%	1.54%	1.32%
Minority interests (non-equity)	0.00%	0.00%	0.00%	0.00%	0.00%
Minority interests (equity)	−0.06%	−0.07%	−0.09%	−0.10%	−0.11%
Preference dividends	0.00%	0.00%	0.00%	0.00%	0.00%
Net profit attributable to equity shareholders	0.48%	0.51%	1.20%	1.45%	1.21%

changes in the risk profile of the assets, i.e. assets offering higher returns often carry higher-risk weightings, and thus moving to a per RWA basis shows a smaller difference in risk-adjusted returns than using a per asset (or per interest-earning asset) basis.

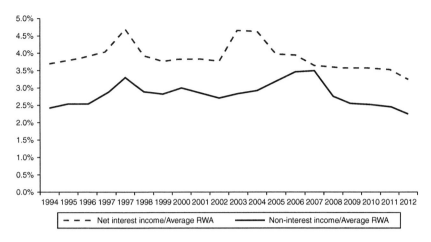

Figure 2.1 HSBC net interest income v. non-interest income per RWA

Going back to our HSBC example – and using a long dataset going back to 1994 – we can see that HSBC has consistently generated the majority of its income from net interest income (versus non-interest income). Both sources of income declined in recent years, with non-interest income declining further. Doing this high-level analysis helps to direct the focus of more detailed analysis; for HSBC, we'll want to understand what has been driving the relatively sharper decline in non-interest income per RWA in recent years, as well as understanding what has helped make net interest income per RWA relatively stable.

Value levers analysis

The RORWA analysis often boils down to a smaller number of key value levers, where we look at both trends and cross-comparisons in order to understand what makes a particular bank tick, and how it differs from its peers.

We include a Value Levers section as part of our standard ROIC model template; it simply refers to the relevant cells in the Invested Capital, ROIC and RORWA sections. We note that we tend to prefer longer time spans when analysing ROIC value levers; it helps in spotting trends.

Our Value Levers table for HSBC is shown below:

As noted earlier, the rise in administrative expenses per RWA (from 2.8% in 2009 to 3.5% in 2012) is substantial. Although much of this was related to disposals, there was also a substantial component of conduct-risk related expenses (for example, the U.S. anti-money laundering fines and the UK mis-selling customer redress charges).

Table 2.29　ROIC analysis: value levers, HSBC

Value levers	2008	2009	2010	2011	2012
RWA growth	2.2%	–1.3%	–2.7%	9.6%	–7.1%
Net interest income/ Average RWA	3.57%	3.54%	3.60%	3.50%	3.24%
Non-interest income/ Average RWA	2.75%	2.52%	2.52%	2.42%	2.22%
Net fee & commission income/Avg RWA	1.68%	1.54%	1.58%	1.48%	1.41%
Net trading income/ Average RWA	0.55%	0.86%	0.66%	0.56%	0.61%
Other banking income/Average RWA	0.04%	0.06%	0.10%	0.09%	0.12%
Net insurance income growth in period	746.4%	–150.0%	–68.6%	–372.3%	–169.2%
Other operating income growth in period	25.6%	54.2%	–8.1%	–31.1%	18.9%
Administrative expenses/Average RWA	–3.02%	–2.77%	–3.19%	–3.32%	–3.48%
Depreciation expenses/Average RWA	–0.21%	–0.22%	–0.25%	–0.25%	–0.21%
Other operating expenses/Average RWA	0.00%	0.00%	0.00%	0.00%	0.00%
Operating expenses/ Average RWA	–3.23%	–2.99%	–3.44%	–3.57%	–3.69%
Cost:income ratio	51.1%	49.3%	56.2%	60.3%	67.6%
Interest coupon on subordinated debt	4.25%	5.00%	5.77%	5.11%	5.05%
Income tax/Profit before tax	–30.2%	–5.4%	–25.5%	–18.0%	–25.7%

Source: HSBC annual and interim reports, author's analysis.

In terms of top-line operating income, both net interest income and non-interest income per RWA appear to be caught in a broadly weakening trend. The use of quantitative easing and other unconventional monetary policies in many of HSBC's key markets (U.S., UK, Eurozone and Japan) has kept net interest margins under continued pressure, and although HSBC's global streamlining programme is boosting capital ratios by reducing RWAs, the net effect of declining RWAs and lower risk-adjusted operating margins has been lower top-line income. Looking ahead, when analysing HSBC we would keep an eye on its overall prospects for top-line growth.

Credit quality analysis

As discussed above, the impairment charge line item tends to be one of the most volatile line items in a bank's income statement. Trends in credit quality and the adequacy of provisioning coverage are thus key concerns when analysing a bank, both in terms of looking at a bank's historical trends and comparing it with others. We have a specific section of the ROIC model that tracks this, in order to inform our forecasts.

HSBC's credit quality metrics are shown below:

HSBC's impaired (formerly non-performing) loans came down significantly – from impaired loans as a percentage of gross customer loans of 4.3% at the end of 2011 to 3.7% by the end of 2012. Interestingly, impaired loans as a percentage of RWAs stayed relatively flat, at 3.44% at the end of 2011 versus 3.38% at the end of 2012. This discrepancy is explained by the increase in gross customer loans (from $958bn at the end of 2011 to $1.03 trillion by the end of 2012) versus the 7% decline in RWAs. Provisioning coverage (impairment provisions/NPLs) strengthened slightly, at 42.1% at the end of 2011 versus 42.4% at the end of 2012. This was a big step down from 94% in 2008 and 71.5% in

Table 2.30 ROIC analysis: credit quality analysis, HSBC

	2008	2009	2010	2011	2012
Impaired (non-performing) loans	25,352	30,606	28,091	41,584	38,001
Gross customer loans	956,777	921,773	978,449	957,940	1,031,373
Impairment provisions	23,909	23,909	20,083	17,511	16,112
Non-performing loans as % gross customer loans	2.65%	3.32%	2.87%	4.34%	3.68%
NPLs as % of RWAs	2.21%	2.70%	2.55%	3.44%	3.38%
Provisioning coverage					
Impairment provisions/NPLs	94.3%	78.1%	71.5%	42.1%	42.4%
Impairment provisions/RWA	2.09%	2.12%	1.83%	1.46%	1.43%
Impairment charges/ Average RWA	−2.09%	−2.30%	−1.28%	−1.04%	−0.71%

Source: HSBC annual and interim reports, author's analysis.

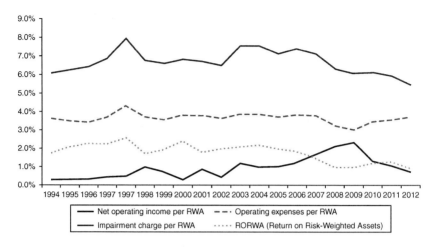

Figure 2.2   Key value levers, HSBC
Source: HSBC annual and interim reports, author's analysis.

2010, but further analysis showed that the bulk of impaired loans in from 2008 through 2010 were in the Household consumer finance area, which being mostly unsecured or with low levels of collateral required significantly higher provisioning coverage. These consumer finance books were one of the main areas that HSBC targeted for disposals, and thus the decline in provisioning coverage fits with the other trends examined above.

Having done this credit quality analysis on HSBC, we would keep an eye on the mix of impaired loans and the associated provisioning requirements, in order to inform our impairment forecasts.

To help spot longer-term trends, we think a graph of some key value levers is helpful:

For HSBC, the decrease in net operating income/RWA since 2005 and 2006 caught our eye; that could indicate potential difficulties in generating top-line growth in the sluggish U.S./UK/European macro-environments.

Comparing the absolute decline in net operating income/RWA with that in operating expenses/RWA would indicate rising cost–income pressures. In particular, administrative expenses/RWA look to be trending up after hitting a trough in 2009. For future periods, this would be a key area on which to focus.

Comparing HSBC's ROE versus its ROIC from 1995 through 2012, it is clear that ROIC is generally lower and less volatile than ROE. Thus, trend changes (for example, the downshift in ROIC in 2004 and 2005, as well as the bottoming out/flattening in 2008/9) become more meaningful, in our view.

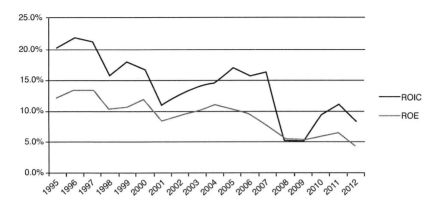

Figure 2.3   ROIC v. ROE, HSBC

Source: HSBC annual and interim reports, author's analysis.

Looking ahead, the downward tick in ROIC in 2012 – after three years of halting recovery – would make us re-examine the key value levers for HSBC. In particular, we would focus on the probability of another round of conduct-related fines (relatively low, in our view) and the challenge of bringing down operating expenses (achievable given HSBC's track record and a strong culture of Scottish Presbyterian thrift, in our view).

Translating complexity to clarity

Although this ROIC analytical methodology is quite simple, its structure can incorporate a great deal of complexity via the assumptions underlying the key ROIC drivers.

For example, the net interest per average RWA assumption can be further broken down into interest-earning asset versus interest-bearing liability margin assumptions, as well as incorporating contribution from hedging structures (balance sheet or derivatives-based); and the operating expense per RWA line item could be broken out into individual business units.

In practice, where the data are available, we have extended ROIC analysis to the individual business units – retail banking, corporate and investment banking divisions, for example. The debt capital allocation to various divisions is rarely disclosed, however, so this level of analysis is often limited to RORWA analysis – although the RWAs by division could also be used to allocate Invested Capital for ROIC analysis.

A divisional RORWA analysis can often help to explain some of the group-level changes in various ROIC components. For example, the operating expense per RWA in investment banking can be 40–80% higher than for retail banking whilst also being more volatile, and non-interest income per RWA from investment banking tends to be much higher than net interest income; a group shift to emphasise investment banking could thus result in an increase in group non-interest income per RWA as well as a higher and more volatile operating expense per RWA line item.

For an overall perspective on a bank, however, we tend to revert to group-level ROIC analysis; after all, it's more practical to keep track of 20 data trend lines than 200. From an analyst perspective, it's also normally impossible to buy the equity shares of a single division; thus, the overall Group ROIC and its associated valuation is what's important, in our view.

Rationale for taking a long-term, through-the-cycle view

Also, from our analyst perspective, we tend to find that whilst the day-to-day changes in banks' share prices tend to be driven by the news in that particular day, longer-term shifts in valuations (re-rating or de-ratings of the sector or the individual bank) tend to correspond with shifts in ROIC trends.

Two of the biggest swing factors in a specific period's ROIC tend to be trading income/RWA and impairment charges/RWA. These two factors tend to have different trend characteristics: trading income/RWA has tended to be seasonal, with lulls in Q3 (for the summer holidays in the Northern Hemisphere) and Q4 (for the winter holidays), and in recent years there has been a correlation with various central bank liquidity injections (e.g. quantitative easing by the Fed and the Bank of England, long-term repo operations by the ECB); whereas impairment charges/RWA have tracked the economic/business cycle.

For impairment charges, we think that taking a through-the-cycle view of impairment charges when calculating ROIC helps to avoid getting carried away by over-optimistic assessments of profitability when impairment charges are at the bottom of the cycle, as well as not getting too gloomy when impairment charges are peaking.

Applying the ROIC method to forecasts

We have shown how the ROIC analysis tools can be applied to analysing the historical performance of a bank; we can then take what we've learned from that analysis and use it in our forecasts for that bank. We can also incorporate all of the other analytical tools described in Section I (regulatory ratios, other performance ratios) when setting the input numbers in our forecasts.

In practice, we use the ROIC Value Levers table to drive the bulk of our forecasting on a line item basis. We do this by 'turning our formulas around' – reorienting the spreadsheet formulas from historical analysis to forecasting. For example, we would take the formula for net interest margins (net interest income divided by average interest-earning assets), and instead of the inputs being net interest income and average interest-earning assets producing the net interest margin, the inputs would be the net interest margin and average interest-earning assets producing the net interest income line item.

In our spreadsheets, we usually highlight the cells that are forecast inputs, for example, by using a different font colour or cell shading. This helps to distinguish between the numbers in the spreadsheet that are the driving assumptions, and those that are being produced by the various formulas. In our forecasting, we tend to start by inputting our assumptions for the Value Drivers items, then inputting assumptions for any of the other items in the RORWA table and the standardised income statement. By that point, we will have gotten a decent feel for the shape of the forecasts, e.g. what the key drivers for changes in earnings and ROIC are. We then tidy up any remaining assumptions in the various tables to finalise our forecast.

One key note: Although we have included forecasts for HSBC and the other banks that we analyse and value in this book, these should not be regarded as real forecasts. They have been included in order to show how to build forecasts using the ROIC method. Also, in the real world of bank results reporting and news updates, forecasts tend to change nearly every time one reviews them.

ROIC valuation: calculating value-added margin

Linking ROIC analysis to valuation

The link between ROIC analysis and valuation is value creation. In other words, we first use ROIC analysis to understand the key drivers of profitability, then we compare that profitability to the cost of the capital used to generate those profits, in order to assess how much value was created (or destroyed) in a period. Adding the estimated total value creation in the future to the current invested capital gives us the total entity value.

Table 2.31 ROIC valuation: value creation, HSBC

Value creation	2008	2009	2010	2011	2012
WACC					
Cost of debt					
Interest rate on subordinated debt	4.16%	4.82%	4.15%	5.06%	4.97%
less: tax shield at 30%	−1.25%	−1.45%	−1.24%	−1.52%	−1.49%
Subordinated debt coupon with tax shield	2.91%	3.38%	2.90%	3.54%	3.48%
Subordinated debt as % Invested Capital	27.8%	22.8%	15.1%	13.4%	12.3%
Rate on minorities and preference shares					
Minorities and prefs as % Invested Capital	0.0%	0.0%	0.0%	0.0%	0.0%
Cost of equity					
Risk-free rate (10-yr gilt yield)	4.24%	3.62%	3.41%	2.87%	1.87%
Equity risk premium	4.00%	6.00%	6.00%	6.00%	6.00%
Stock beta	1.200	0.980	0.980	0.980	0.980
Cost of equity	9.04%	9.50%	9.29%	8.75%	7.75%
Adjusted equity as % Invested Capital	72.2%	77.2%	84.9%	86.6%	87.7%
WACC	7.33%	8.10%	8.33%	8.05%	7.23%
Value Creation					
Net ROIC	5.64%	5.30%	6.07%	6.37%	4.39%
− WACC	7.33%	8.10%	8.33%	8.05%	7.23%
= Value Added Margin	−1.69%	−2.80%	−2.25%	−1.68%	−2.84%
x Average Invested Capital	204,112	210,067	217,052	227,465	234,022
= Value Created/ (Destroyed)	(3,450)	(5,886)	(4,886)	(3,819)	(6,635)
Value Creation growth in period	2669%	71%	−17%	−22%	74%
Value Creation per share (p)	(25.2)	(35.8)	(27.7)	(21.3)	(36.3)
Value Creation – Through the cycle					
Through-the-cycle Net ROIC	10.66%	9.08%	6.86%	5.75%	2.77%
- WACC	7.33%	8.10%	8.33%	8.05%	7.23%
= Value Added Margin	3.33%	0.97%	−1.46%	−2.30%	−4.45%
x Average Invested Capital	204,112	210,067	217,052	227,465	234,022
= Value Created/ (Destroyed)	6,792	2,048	(3,177)	(5,236)	(10,416)
Value Creation growth in period	115%	−70%	−255%	65%	99%
Value Creation per share (p)	49.7	12.5	(18.0)	(29.2)	(57.0)

Source: HSBC annual and interim reports, author's analysis.

As with other sectors, we measure value creation (or destruction) by subtracting a bank's WACC from its ROIC to get the value-added margin.

There is a lively debate about how to derive WACC (and whether or not any of these methodologies are 'valid'). In our models, WACC is calculated by using the ten-year benchmark sovereign debt yield as the 'risk-free rate' (irony acknowledged) adding an equity risk premium and multiplying by the stock beta to get a cost of equity, and for the cost of debt capital, taking (if possible) the actual interest expense on debt capital and adjusting for the tax shield. This has generally resulted in a WACC of 8–10%, largely depending on the stock's beta and the estimate of the equity risk premium.

If ROIC is higher than WACC, then the bank has created value in the period; if ROIC is lower than WACC, it has destroyed value. The quantum of value creation/destruction in a period is then calculated by multiplying the value-added margin times the average invested capital in that period.

Aggregating value creation/destruction

Deriving a fundamental ROIC valuation

To derive a fundamental ROIC-based valuation, we simply aggregate the forecasted value creation/destruction. In essence, this is simply an extension of the standard Gordon Growth valuation formula:

Stock Price = Dividends/(Cost of Equity – Growth Rate of
            Dividends)

In our ROIC valuation, we rebase the Gordon Growth model from dividends and the cost of equity to returns on total invested capital (ROIC), and add an explicit forecast period instead of a single-period continuing-growth assumption.

Our models use a ten-year explicit forecast period for value-added margins, starting with the current forecast year and ending with a value-added margin assumption ten years ahead. Having this relatively long forecast period means that the continuing value assumption tends to be a smaller component of the overall valuation than with a standard Gordon Growth-type formula.

The ten-year explicit forecasts and methodology for calculating net present value of future value creation (or destruction) for HSBC are shown below:

Table 2.32   ROIC valuation: value-added margin forecasted, HSBC

Value added margin in forecast year:	2007	2008	2009	2010	2011	2012
1	1.62%	2.94%	1.11%	−1.24%	−2.08%	−3.91%
2	1.59%	2.57%	1.28%	−1.01%	−1.84%	−3.34%
3	1.57%	2.20%	1.44%	−0.77%	−1.60%	−2.77%
4	1.54%	1.83%	1.60%	−0.53%	−1.35%	−2.20%
5	1.52%	1.46%	1.76%	−0.30%	−1.11%	−1.63%
6	1.50%	1.09%	1.92%	−0.06%	−0.86%	−1.06%
7	1.47%	0.72%	2.08%	0.17%	−0.62%	−0.49%
8	1.45%	0.35%	2.24%	0.41%	−0.38%	0.08%
9	1.42%	−0.02%	2.41%	0.64%	−0.13%	0.66%
10	1.40%	−0.39%	2.57%	0.88%	0.11%	1.23%

Source: HSBC annual and interim reports, author's analysis.

We take the Value-Added Margin from the most recent historical period, and then the long-term sustainable value-added margin assumption, and use a straight-line progression from the most recent actual period to the terminal value-added margin assumption in year ten of our specific forecast period.

Table 2.33   ROIC valuation: Invested Capital forecasted, HSBC

Invested Capital in forecast period	2007	2008	2009	2010	2011	2012
1	207,790	220,441	218,469	225,734	236,564	243,383
2	224,413	238,076	227,208	234,763	246,026	253,118
3	242,366	257,122	236,296	244,153	255,867	263,243
4	261,755	277,692	245,748	253,920	266,102	273,772
5	282,695	299,907	255,578	264,076	276,746	284,723
6	305,311	323,900	265,801	274,639	287,816	296,112
7	329,736	349,812	276,433	285,625	299,329	307,957
8	356,115	377,797	287,491	297,050	311,302	320,275
9	384,604	408,020	298,990	308,932	323,754	333,086
10	415,372	440,662	310,950	321,289	336,704	346,409

Source: HSBC annual and interim reports, author's analysis.

We then grow Invested Capital according to the assumed annual growth rate used in our ROIC valuation model.

Table 2.34 ROIC valuation: value creation/destruction forecasted, HSBC

Value created in forecast period	2007	2008	2009	2010	2011	2012
1	3,357	6,482	2,434	(2,801)	(4,926)	(9,524)
2	3,572	6,120	2,899	(2,360)	(4,524)	(8,460)
3	3,800	5,659	3,396	(1,880)	(4,082)	(7,295)
4	4,041	5,084	3,928	(1,357)	(3,597)	(6,023)
5	4,297	4,382	4,498	(790)	(3,068)	(4,638)
6	4,568	3,535	5,107	(175)	(2,490)	(3,132)
7	4,855	2,524	5,757	491	(1,861)	(1,499)
8	5,159	1,328	6,451	1,210	(1,177)	270
9	5,480	(74)	7,192	1,985	(436)	2,183
10	5,819	(1,710)	7,981	2,821	366	4,249

Source: HSBC annual and interim reports, author's analysis.

The quantum of Value Creation/(or Destruction) in the period is the forecasted Value-Added Margin times the forecasted Invested Capital in the specific forecast period.

Table 2.35 ROIC valuation: present value of value created forecasted, HSBC

PV of value created in forecast period	2007	2008	2009	2010	2011	2012
1	3,111	6,038	2,252	(2,585)	(4,558)	(8,880)
2	3,068	5,311	2,479	(2,011)	(3,873)	(7,353)
3	3,025	4,574	2,686	(1,478)	(3,234)	(5,912)
4	2,982	3,828	2,874	(985)	(2,637)	(4,551)
5	2,938	3,073	3,044	(529)	(2,081)	(3,267)
6	2,895	2,309	3,196	(108)	(1,563)	(2,057)
7	2,851	1,536	3,332	280	(1,080)	(918)
8	2,808	753	3,454	637	(633)	154
9	2,764	(39)	3,561	966	(217)	1,162
10	2,720	(841)	3,655	1,266	168	2,108
PV of Value Created in forecast period	29,162	26,542	30,533	(4,547)	(19,706)	(29,513)

Source: HSBC annual and interim reports, author's analysis.

We then use the WACC to discount the forecasted Value Creation (or Destruction) to get its net present value; we can then add up these net present values to get the present value of Value Creation (or Destruction) in the specific forecast period.

The Continuing Value is calculated similarly to the Gordon Growth Model, by taking the quantum of Value Creation/Destruction in year eleven, and dividing it by the WACC minus the assumed continuing growth rate. This number is then discounted back to the net present value by using WACC.

The cumulative results for HSBC's historical valuation are shown below; note that the terminal value-added margin is the 'plug' variable that makes the calculated equity valuation match the actual valuation at the end of each period. It is our estimate of what the market was expecting in terms of long-term sustainable value-added margins and ROIC, given the bank's operating performance at the time.

Table 2.36   ROIC valuation: fundamental ROIC valuation, HSBC

Fundamental valuation	2008	2009	2010	2011	2012
Value-Added Margin in period	−1.69%	−2.80%	−2.25%	−1.68%	−2.84%
Through-the-cycle Value-Added Margin	3.33%	0.97%	−1.46%	−2.30%	−4.45%
Invested Capital growth pa (next 10 years)	8.0%	4.0%	4.0%	4.0%	4.0%
Terminal Value-Added Margin assumption	−0.39%	2.55%	0.87%	0.10%	1.21%
Assumed continuing growth of Value Added	4.0%	4.0%	4.0%	4.0%	4.0%
Invested Capital (beginning of period)	208,560	188,507	230,049	221,081	227,848
PV of Value Created/ (Destroyed) in forecast period	26,716	30,569	(4,489)	(19,557)	(29,412)
PV of Continuing Value	(23,561)	81,923	26,891	3,677	60,208
Total firm value	211,715	300,999	252,451	205,201	258,644
Less: Debt Capital	(52,394)	(52,394)	(33,387)	(30,606)	(29,479)
Less: Equity Adjustments	(42,522)	(49,356)	(40,027)	(38,517)	(35,038)
Target Equity Value	116,799	199,249	179,037	136,078	194,127
Market Capitalisation (end of period)	116,799	199,249	179,037	136,078	194,127
Target Equity Value per share (US$)	8.62	12.24	10.29	7.69	10.71
Target Equity Value per share (GBP)	5.67	8.05	6.77	5.06	7.05
Exchange rate (GBP:USD)	1.46	1.61	1.55	1.55	1.62

Source: HSBC annual and interim reports, author's analysis.

ROIC valuations flex on expectations of value creation/destruction

One of the reasons why we prefer using our ROIC-based valuation methodology versus the standard Gordon Growth formula is that the way the ROIC valuation is built up makes more intuitive sense in our view. The ROIC valuation starts with the current invested capital base and then adds or subtracts the net present value of the value created or destroyed during the ten-year forecast period, as well as a smaller continuing value component.

This fits better with how we think markets work when pricing bank shares; we think it starts with the invested capital base, then decides whether the current management/strategy and other factors will create or destroy value, and adjusts the valuation accordingly.

Running ROIC valuation backwards to get a sense of what markets expect

Deriving implied market assumptions of value creation/destruction

For listed banks, we have found it useful to run the ROIC valuation formula backwards in order to get a sense of what market expectations of a bank's future sustainable profitability are. We do this by solving for the terminal value-added margin that makes the ROIC equity valuation equal to the actual equity valuation. Microsoft Excel users can use the Goal Seek function to do this. Doing this for past periods thus compares a bank's actual ROIC performance to the future expected performance that is reflected in its share price.

In other words, we have used the ROIC valuation framework on a bank's historical share price to make an educated guess at what the market was thinking about the prospects for value creation/destruction at the time. When applied over several years, this approach can give a sense for how market expectations of a bank's profitability – or more specifically, its ability to earn more than its cost of capital – have varied over time. This can then be used to inform the assumptions about a bank's future sustainable profitability.

For example, looking at HSBC in 2007 in the table above, a terminal value-added margin assumption of 1.2% gets the target equity value reasonably close to the end-2007 market capitalisation. We thus think that back in 2007, the markets thought that HSBC would be able to maintain a 1.2% value-added margin in perpetuity. That changed in 2008; a terminal value-added margin of 0.3% gets the target equity value close to the end-2008 market capitalisation. In other words, in 2008, it seems the market dropped its assumption of HSBC's ability to generate sustainable value-added margins from 1.2% to 0.3%. With the QE-driven rally in 2009, the continuing value-added margin assumption appears to have jumped back to 1.8%, only to fall again as the QE boosts faded.

Obviously, boiling the complexity of HSBC's myriad macro and micro conditions down to one set of numbers may seem far too reductionist, but – following the Buffet/Graham market dictum of 'in the short-term, it's a voting machine, in the long-term, it's a weighing machine', we assert that this dynamic – of adjusting the invested capital base for an assessment of whether a company's actions are creating or destroying value – isn't too far off from how the markets actually work.

Getting a feel for how valuations flex

When valuing listed banks, one of the practices that we have found useful is running the ROIC model backwards and solving for the implied long-term value-added margin on any given day, and comparing that with the previous value-added margin implied by the earlier valuation to get a sense of how a bank's implied expectations of long-term profitability flex with its share price.

Taking an informed view on valuation

In our fundamental ROIC valuation model, all the analysis and forecast assumptions for a bank boil down to a view on its long-term, sustainable value-added margin – all the work has been done in order to take an informed view on this.

Keep in mind that there is no intrinsically 'right' number that will give the 'correct' valuation for a bank – however, with this integrated methodology for ROIC analysis and valuation, there is at least a clear path that leads from a bank's financials to a valuation for that bank.

Forecasting with ROIC

A note on our forecasts and analyses: In the real day-to-day job, of course, a banks analyst does not have the luxury of weeks or months of hindsight before making decisions – there is often less than an hour between the time that a bank's results are published and when an initial analyst comment is expected. Markets can move very quickly.

With this time urgency, it is extremely useful to have a framework for fast, effective analysis such as the ROIC methodology, so that changes in a bank's key value levers (and thus likely changes in the market's valuation of that bank) are spotted quickly.

In the analyses, forecasts, and valuations in this book, we have tried to avoid the temptation of appearing prescient by taking advantage of the time lag between the date of the reported results (in this case, the 2012 results published in early 2013) and the publication date of this book. Instead, we try to capture the immediate analysis as at the time of the results, or in other words, how we would have analysed those results on the actual day. This approach, we think, will be more valuable to readers of this book when you find yourself analysing bank results 'on the day'.

In practice, if the core of the analysis of a bank's operating performance can be boiled down to a manageable set of key value levers, then forecasting can be done in a simpler, clearer way, by casting those value levers forward based on the insights gained ROIC analysis and other tools. This also makes it easier to explain to others how and why forecasts and valuations have changed.

Thus, in making forecasts, we tend to spend the bulk of time adjusting the variables in the Key Value Levers table, doing cross-checks along the way to make sure the overall forecasts make sense. For example, when we input the number for the forecasted administrative expenses per RWA in a period, we would cross-check that with the cost–income ratio to make sure that ratio was reasonable. We would also compare the forecasted net operating income per RWA for a bank with its peers, as well as cross-checking the RWA density (RWA/Assets ratio), looking at, for example, whether an abnormally low net interest income per RWA number could be partly explained by a higher RWA/Assets ratio. In other words, we give our Value Levers table a general check for common sense; we would prefer to be 'roughly right' than 'exactly wrong' in our forecasts.

Making forecasts in practice

As an example, our forecasted Value Levers table for HSBC is below:

Using the Value Levers table enables us to distil our forecast for HSBC into changes in relatively few key variables. In many ways, it enables us to 'tell an investment story' about HSBC – one of the largest, most complex financial institutions in the world – in clear, simple terms. Here is a potential narrative:

In building up the forecast for HSBC at the time of its 2012 results (in early 2013), one of the key management goals was cost-cutting, following two years of global streamlining where over 50 businesses had been sold off or shut down. Also, costs associated with conduct risks – e.g. redress charges for PPI mis-selling in the UK, fines for violations of U.S. anti-money laundering laws – were a significant component of the 2012 results, and the management of reputational/conduct risks was identified as a key priority.

Accordingly, when looking at making forecasts with the Value Levers table, we would focus firstly on Administrative expenses per RWA, which were 3.32% in 2011, rising to 3.48% in 2012. Looking further back at this line item, we could see that the 3.48% in 2012 was quite high in comparison to the past few years, and after reading the operational/divisional details in the annual report, we could assume that this was partly due to the costs of the global streamlining programme as well as the conduct-risk charges. Both of these costs could be regarded as likely to decline in the future. Looking ahead, it could then be expected that Administrative expenses per RWA could trend downwards as the benefits from the streamlining and cost-cutting programmes took hold. Keeping in mind the historical context of

Table 2.37   ROIC valuation: value levers table, 2011–2012 actuals and 2013–2015E forecasts, HSBC

Value Levers	2011	2012	2013E	2014E	2015E
RWA growth	**9.6%**	**–7.1%**	**6.1%**	**8.2%**	**8.2%**
Net interest income/ Average RWA	3.50%	3.24%	3.23%	3.23%	3.23%
Non-interest income/ Average RWA	2.42%	2.22%	2.55%	2.51%	2.52%
Net fee & commission income/Average RWA	1.48%	1.41%	1.45%	1.45%	1.45%
Net trading income/ Average RWA	0.56%	0.61%	0.72%	0.67%	0.67%
Other banking income/Average RWA	0.09%	0.12%	0.10%	0.10%	0.10%
Net insurance income growth in period	–372.3%	–169.2%	–138.2%	10.3%	10.3%
Other operating income growth in period	–31.1%	18.9%	33.3%	10.3%	10.3%
Administrative expenses/Average RWA	–3.32%	–3.48%	–3.27%	–3.13%	–3.03%
Depreciation expenses/ Average RWA	–0.25%	–0.21%	–0.20%	–0.20%	–0.20%
Other operating expenses/Average RWA	0.00%	0.00%	–0.05%	–0.05%	0.00%
Operating expenses/ Average RWA	–3.57%	–3.69%	–3.52%	–3.38%	–3.23%
Cost:income ratio	**60.3%**	**67.6%**	**60.9%**	**58.9%**	**56.2%**
Impairment charges/ Average RWA	–1.04%	–0.71%	–0.65%	–0.67%	–0.68%
Interest coupon on subordinated debt	5.11%	5.05%	4.93%	4.90%	4.90%
Income tax/Profit before tax	–18.0%	–25.7%	–23.3%	–21.5%	–20.3%

Source: HSBC annual and interim reports, author's analysis.

changes in this line item, a reduction of forecasted Administrative expenses per RWA from 3.48% in 2012 to 3.03% in 2015 would make sense.

We would then cross-check this estimate with the cost–income ratio forecast: with these Administrative expenses per RWA assumptions, HSBC's cost–income ratio would fall from 67.6% in 2012 to 56.2% in 2015. Looking back at HSBC's cost–income ratios, this would not seem out of line.

Compared to the management guidance on cost-cutting, the expectations on balance sheet growth prospects and net interest margin growth were rather muted, thus in the forecasts, an assumption of roughly flat Net interest income per RWA (3.23% in 2015 versus 3.24% in 2012) would seem reasonable, on the assumption that the U.S., UK, Europe and Japan maintain low base rates and other unconventional monetary policies for several more years. Regarding Non-interest income, management discussion of a greater focus on higher RORWA businesses (especially the Commercial Banking and trade-linked businesses) would encourage the view that trade-related fee income and related client-driven trading income (from forex hedging, for example) could rise. Non-interest income per RWA could accordingly be expected to strengthen from 2.2% in 2012 to 2.5% for 2013 through 2015.

Regarding credit quality, at the time of the 2012 results (in March 2013) there was still significant uncertainty as to whether key markets including China would experience another round of bad debt crises; thus, although impairment charges could be expected to fall as a result of the disposals of poorly-performing businesses (for example, most of the U.S. consumer finance businesses), these could be counterbalanced by rising bad debts if China were to suffer a major correction. Accordingly, only a slight forecasted improvement in Impairment charges per RWA (from 0.71% in 2012 to 0.68% in 2015) would seem reasonable.

The RWA growth assumption (and the nature of that RWA growth) also plays a key role in the value levers dynamics. Management discussion of balance sheet growth prospects were rather muted, but there was also the broader context of higher risk weights being imposed by regulators (for example, the Basel Committee's review of risk weights in proprietary trading, and another review of credit risk weights). Thus, the banking sector as a whole, and investment banks in particular, faced the prospect of higher RWAs as a result of increased risk weights – over and above any balance sheet growth. In HSBC's case, however, recalling that HSBC's RWA density (RWA/Assets ratio) was already relatively high compared to its peers, the view could be taken that HSBC would be relatively less affected by these regulatory changes. Taking this into account, forecasting 6.1% RWA growth in 2013, 8.2% in 2014 and 8.2% in 2015 would seem reasonable.

The other items on the Value Levers can be forecasted using the same approach, cross-checking for reasonableness along the way. In this way, HSBC's complicated investment story can be boiled down to the expected movements in relatively few, key value levers.

In addition, by changing the key value levers, various forecast scenarios can be modelled quickly using the ROIC methodology – for example, higher/lower RWA growth, higher/lower impairments – and the potential effect on operating performance could be gauged.

Integrating forecasts with valuation

Continuing with the HSBC example, the forecast assumptions in the Value Levers table would result in the following forecasts for HSBC:

These valuation ratios could then be compared to those of HSBC's peers in order to take a view on HSBC's relative valuation. Note that in the ROIC models that are on this book's website, you can trace the cell references to see the connections between the assumptions made and the resulting forecast numbers.

Table 2.38   ROIC valuation: standard valuation ratios, HSBC

Traditional Valuation Ratios	2011	2012	2013E	2014E	2015E
GBP 736 1,119 1.5200					
Profit before tax pre-exceptionals & FV	18,433	15,851	21,636	24,133	27,990
% growth year-on-year	3.5%	–14.0%	36.5%	11.5%	16.0%
Net profit pre-exceptionals & FV	13,167	11,465	15,246	17,476	20,737
% growth year-on-year	6.6%	–12.9%	33.0%	14.6%	18.7%
Adjusted EPS, fully-diluted	73.5	62.7	81.4	91.4	106.2
% growth year-on-year	4.9%	–14.6%	29.7%	12.2%	16.2%
Adjusted P/E	**15.2**	**17.8**	**13.7**	**12.2**	**10.5**
Dividends per share	41.0	45.0	51.8	58.0	64.9
% growth year-on-year	20.6%	9.8%	15.0%	12.0%	12.0%
Dividend yield	3.7%	4.0%	4.6%	5.2%	5.8%
Dividend payout ratio	46.0%	59.3%	56.9%	63.9%	61.6%
ROE	11.0%	8.4%	9.6%	9.3%	10.6%
P/BVPS multiple	**1.25**	**1.16**	**1.14**	**1.12**	**1.09**
Book value per share	897	967	983	1,000	1,026
% growth in period	5.7%	7.8%	1.7%	1.7%	2.5%
Balance sheet goodwill	29,034	29,853	29,853	29,853	29,853
Tangible shareholders' equity	129,691	145,389	153,784	160,954	169,906
Tangible book value per share (US cents)	726	787	815	835	864
Price/Tangible BVPS multiple (×)	**1.54**	**1.42**	**1.37**	**1.34**	**1.30**

Source: HSBC annual and interim reports, author's analysis.

Table 2.39 ROIC valuation: fundamental ROIC valuation, HSBC

Fundamental valuation	2011	2012	2013E	2014E	2015E
Value-Added Margin in period	−1.70%	−2.87%	−1.50%	−0.59%	0.39%
Through-the-cycle Value-Added Margin	−2.33%	−4.48%	−3.11%	−2.26%	−1.43%
Invested Capital growth pa (next 10 years)	4.0%	4.0%	4.0%	4.0%	4.0%
Terminal Value-Added Margin assumption	0.11%	1.23%	1.50%	1.50%	1.50%
Assumed continuing growth of Value Added	4.0%	4.0%	4.0%	4.0%	4.0%
Invested Capital (beginning of period)	221,081	227,848	239,759	249,891	259,785
PV of Value Created/ (Destroyed) in forecast period	(19,706)	(29,513)	(14,389)	(6,413)	2,001
PV of Continuing Value	3,826	60,309	59,848	62,446	65,384
Total firm value	205,201	258,644	285,217	305,924	327,169
Less: Debt Capital	(30,606)	(29,479)	(31,271)	(33,823)	(36,583)
Less: Equity Adjustments	(38,517)	(35,038)	(34,983)	(35,155)	(35,229)
Target Equity Value	**136,078**	**194,127**	**218,963**	**236,946**	**255,357**
Market Capitalisation (end of period)	136,078	194,127	208,932	208,932	208,932
Target Equity Value per share (US$)	7.69	10.71	11.72	12.42	13.11
Target Equity Value per share (GBp)	5.06	7.05	7.71	8.17	8.63
Exchange rate (GBP:USD)	1.55	1.62	1.52	1.52	1.52

Source: HSBC annual and interim reports, author's analysis.

For a view on fundamental valuation, we would apply the ROIC valuation model as follows:

The key variable in the fundamental ROIC valuation model is the Terminal Value-Added Margin assumption; most of the other items – Value-Added Margin in the period and Through-the-Cycle Value-Added Margin, for example – come from the forecasts in the Value Levers table.

Running the ROIC valuation model backwards to derive the implied market expectation of terminal value-added margin, we can see that the market's implied expectation had improved, from 0.11% at the end of 2011 to 1.23% by the end of 2012. With the expectations of improved operating performance in the Value Levers table, it could be expected that the market would increase further its expectation of HSBC's terminal value-added margin – an estimate of 1.50% would seem reasonable. This assumption, along with relatively conservative expectations of 4% growth per annum in both Invested Capital and Value-Added, would then drive the fundamental valuation forecast of $327bn of firm value by the end of 2015. Subtracting the forecasted debt capital and equity adjustments from the forecasted firm value would give a forecasted equity value of $255bn at the end of 2015. At the prevailing GBP:USD exchange rate at the time, this would translate into a fundamental share price target of 863p.

The example of HSBC shows how the ROIC methodology is applied to analyse a bank's results, make forecasts and derive a fundamental target equity valuation. As described earlier, analysts can use this methodology to quickly model various forecast scenarios. It can be used by a bank's management team and board to evaluate the potential impact that various strategic options (e.g. acquisitions or disposals, new business development) would have on operating performance and the bank's share price. Similarly, regulators could use this to model the potential effect of regulatory changes (e.g. higher risk weights on specific areas like investment banking operations).

A few methodological notes on ROIC valuation

1. Terminal value-added margin as the 'plug'. Instead of using the terminal value-added margin as the 'plug', we could vary any or all of the other variables in the ROIC valuation formula (e.g. growth rate), but in our experience it makes more sense to hold these steady on the view that a bank's share price tends to move because market expectations of future profitability have changed, not because expectations of longer-term growth rates have shifted. That said, when it appears that market expectations of growth rates have shifted (e.g. during the recent financial crises), we have changed those variables as well.
2. Applying ROIC valuation to unlisted banks. Obviously, this methodology only works for listed banks. For banks that are privately held, we would look for look for listed banks with similar ROIC valuation profiles (historical value-added margins, growth rates, terminal value-added margin assumption) to get a sense of their likely market valuation.
3. Volatility and valuation. The volatility of the historical chain of market-implied terminal value-added margins can inform how volatile

the forecast terminal value-added margin (and thus the target valuation) is likely to be. This could then feed into the assumption of the stock's future beta in the WACC calculation. In other words, the ROIC valuation methodology tends to reward banks that produce consistent returns.

4. Number of years in the specific forecast period. In our ROIC valuation models, we have used a ten-year specific forecast period, with value-added margins moving in a straight line from the most recent actual period to the estimated value-added margin ten years ahead. In the past, we have used five-year forecast periods (which were deemed too short to capture some macro cycles) and twenty-year forecast periods (which were deemed too long a view to have relevance for a current valuation). Ten years seems about right to us, but feel free to use a different timeframe.

Section summary – integrated ROIC analysis and valuation

This section has shown how Invested Capital and ROIC can be calculated, and how RORWA, Value Levers and ROIC decomposition tools can be used to analyse a bank's operating performance and capital leverage. We have also seen how ROIC analysis feeds into fundamental ROIC-based valuation via a long-term value-added margin assumption, and how we can run the ROIC valuation model backwards to get a sense of the market's expectations of future profitability.

In the next section, we'll apply this integrated ROIC analysis and valuation methodology to several banks – as well as covering some current topics affecting banks.

3
Case Studies

In this next section, we have analyses, indicative forecasts and valuations for the following banks:

1. Bank of China
2. Barclays
3. Citigroup
4. Credit Suisse
5. Deutsche Bank
6. HSBC
7. JP Morgan Chase
8. Lloyds Banking Group
9. RBS
10. Standard Chartered

Some overall observations

Before delving into each of these banks, we thought it would be useful to discuss some broader themes and make some overall observations.

Basel III could become a significant issue for some management and regulators

Although many of the UK and European banks that we analysed already include Basel III reporting in their results announcements, many of the US and Chinese banks have provided less disclosure on a Basel III basis.

A reluctance to move from Basel I or II is understandable, especially if risk-weighted assets (and thus capital requirements) are likely to increase for several banks on the move to Basel III. However, we think that analysts would be likely to interpret a relative lack of disclosure negatively. In other words, clear disclosure about higher RWAs under Basel III is preferable to the uncertainty from a lack of disclosure.

How to encourage greater transparency and completeness of disclosure

We think that a move towards greater transparency and disclosure is generally received well by the market – even if the news is not good. One case in point would be the analyst response to the increased disclosure by RBS following its change of management in late 2008 and early 2009.

Market expectations of future profitability have deteriorated markedly

For nearly all of the banks that we have analysed in this book, market expectations of future sustainable profitability have deteriorated markedly. The terminal value-added margin in our fundamental ROIC valuation models is a good indicator of market expectations of long-term sustainable profitability, with ROIC (returns on invested capital) compared to the cost of that capital (WACC).

For all of the banks that we analysed, when we derived the implied market assumption of terminal value-added margins based on past valuations, the terminal value-added margins for 2011–12 are significantly lower than those for 2005–07.

Given the recent financial and sovereign crises, combined with rising RWAs and other regulatory pressures on capital, it is understandable that market expectations of long-term profitability have diminished for banks generally.

Some methodological comments

Now for some comments about how we have applied the ROIC methodology to making forecasts and deriving valuations.

Forecasts and valuations are only indicative

Firstly, we must note that the forecasts and valuations in this book should only be taken as indicative. Our forecasts change practically every time we re-open our spreadsheets, because something has inevitably changed since the last time that we looked at any particular bank.

The main reason why we have included forecasts and valuations for the banks that we analyse is that want to show how the analysis of historical financials is used to inform the assumptions that are being made in our forecasts, and we also want to show how those forecasts are then linked to our target valuations.

The main link between our analyses and our forecasts is via our Value Levers tables; these have distilled the operating performance of each bank into a few key variables. It is important both how each of those value levers has evolved, and how they interact with each other.

For example, one key dynamic that we examine is whether or not operating expenses per RWA can adjust to changes in net operating income per RWA. Another key dynamic is the interaction between RWA growth and capital adequacy (with the RWA/Invested Capital ratio and RORWA as key indicators) – if a bank's ROIC is below its WACC, then adding more RWAs might destroy, not create, value.

Fair value accounting has not helped managers or regulators

One aspect of IFRS accounting – fair value changes – has made analysis and valuation harder, not easier, in our view. Although we can appreciate why fair value accounting is used for trading portfolios, we do not think it should be applied to long-term debt funding. Several commentators have noted that recording the decline in the market price of a bank's long-term debt as a gain seems counterintuitive, and, indeed, if the decline in market price was followed by a default on that long-term debt, the accounting might have to switch suddenly from accounting for that deterioration as a gain to recognising a major loss.

Quarterly reporting may discourage longer-term

In our modelling, we have chosen to use semi-annual (half-yearly) and annual accounts, and although we review quarterly earnings reports, we have not put them into our model. This is a philosophical bias; in our experience, the volatility of quarterly earnings reports is significantly higher than for semi-annual reports.

We also agree with those who think that quarterly reporting may discourage longer-term planning by senior management; instead, especially with listed banks, the temptation is to meet or exceed the analysts' quarterly forecasts.

1. Bank of China

Background

Bank of China, founded in 1912, provides financial services to customers in Greater China and 36 other countries. Bank of China's core businesses are commercial banking, corporate banking, personal banking and financial markets services.

Analysis

Looking at the standardised income statement for Bank of China, it is clear that the vast bulk of net operating income comes from net interest income. Net interest income accounted for CNY257bn of the CNY348bn in net operating income in 2012, and CNY153bn of the CNY188bn total in 2007. This, we think, reflects the bank's focus on commercial banking.

In contrast to many of the other banks that we have analysed, net trading income is a relatively small component of income – excluding changes in fair value items, it was CNY7bn of the CNY348bn net operating income in 2012, for example. Interestingly, Bank of China's losses in net trading and other banking income came in 2007 (when it booked CNY6bn in trading losses (ex-fair value items) and –CNY3bn in other banking income) – a year earlier than with the other, mainly Western, banks that we have profiled. We think this is an indicator that the financial markets in Greater China have different trading dynamics than the more tightly-correlated Western financial markets.

Impairment charges have been lower at Bank of China than with developed-country banks; with the exception of a spike at CNY45bn in 2008, impairment charges have ranged between CNY13bn and CNY20bn from 2007 through 2012. It is also worth noting that Bank of China's RWA intensity (RWA/Total Assets) is relatively high at 57% – this is probably a reflection of the emphasis on commercial banking, which tends to carry higher risk weights than, say, mortgage lending or lending to large corporates.

Looking at the ROIC decomposition table, we can see how the strong RORWAs have combined with relatively high capital leverage (RWA/ Invested Capital) to produce consistently strong ROICs, of 13.7% in 2012 and 10–14% throughout the past six years.

Note, however, that our calculated Core Equity Tier 1 ratio for Bank of China is relatively weaker than for many Western banks; this corresponds with the higher capital leverage ratios. With the move towards Basel 3, these capital leverage ratios may increase further, particularly if RWAs increase under the Basel 3 methodologies. This would put pressure

Table 3.1   Bank of China: standardised financials

(US$ millions)	2007	2008	2009	2010	2011	2012
Net interest income	152,745	162,936	158,881	193,962	228,064	256,964
Net fee & commission income	35,535	39,947	46,013	54,483	64,662	69,923
Net trading income	(5,909)	3,903	6,255	2,588	7,770	7,332
Other banking income	(3,263)	2,009	1,664	3,749	4,087	3,049
Net insurance income	(666)	(1,225)	1,161	(411)	100	405
Other operating income	9,496	11,941	8,240	8,643	9,639	10,048
Subtotal non-interest income	35,193	56,575	63,333	69,052	86,258	90,757
Net operating income	187,938	219,511	222,214	263,014	314,322	347,721
Administrative expenses	(66,723)	(74,664)	(84,030)	(98,650)	(114,835)	(127,072)
Depreciation & amortisation	(7,094)	(7,816)	(8,691)	(10,319)	(10,651)	(12,289)
Other operating expenses	(1,624)	(6,689)	(3,824)	(839)	(1,441)	(3,325)
Operating expenses	(75,441)	(89,169)	(96,545)	(109,808)	(126,927)	(142,686)
Trading surplus	112,497	130,342	125,669	153,206	187,395	205,035
Impairment charges	(20,263)	(45,031)	(14,987)	(12,993)	(19,355)	(19,387)
Operating profit (pre-goodwill)	92,234	85,311	110,682	140,213	168,040	185,648
Goodwill impairment	–	–	–	–	–	–
Operating profit	92,234	85,311	110,682	140,213	168,040	185,648
Fair value changes on own debt	–	–	–	–	–	–
Changes in fair value of financial assets	(2,800)	1,142	(406)	903	88	1,119
Income from associates and JVs	1,263	726	821	1,029	516	613
Exceptional items	–	–	–	–	–	–
Profit before tax	90,697	87,179	111,097	142,145	168,644	187,380
Income tax	(28,661)	(21,285)	(25,748)	(32,454)	(38,142)	(41,858)
Net profit	62,036	65,894	85,349	109,691	130,502	145,522
Minority interests (non-equity)	–	–	–	–	–	–
Minority interests (equity)	(5,788)	(1,534)	(4,530)	(5,273)	(6,226)	(6,090)
Preference dividends	0	0	0	0	0	0

Continued

Table 3.1 Continued

(US$ millions)	2007	2008	2009	2010	2011	2012
Net profit attributable to equity shareholders	56,248	64,360	80,819	104,418	124,276	139,432
Dividends	(10,154)	(25,384)	(32,999)	(35,537)	(40,756)	(43,268)
Retained earnings	46,094	38,976	47,820	68,881	83,520	96,164
Risk-weighted assets (RWA), end of period	3,754,108	3,966,943	5,163,848	5,887,170	6,656,034	7,253,230
RWA growth in period	8.2%	5.7%	30.2%	14.0%	13.1%	9.0%
Period average RWAs	3,677,100	3,899,634	4,768,311	5,566,048	6,410,765	7,019,839
Total assets	5,991,217	6,951,680	8,751,943	10,459,865	11,829,789	12,680,615
RWA/Assets	62.7%	57.1%	59.0%	56.3%	56.3%	57.2%

Source: Bank of China interim and annual reports, author's analysis.

Table 3.2 Bank of China: ROIC decomposition

ROIC drivers	2007	2008	2009	2010	2011	2012
Return on risk-weighted assets (RORWA)	1.82%	1.71%	1.85%	2.01%	2.10%	2.12%
× Avg RWA/Avg Invested Capital	6.2	6.2	6.9	6.9	6.6	6.5
= Return on Invested Capital (ROIC)	11.3%	10.5%	12.8%	13.9%	13.9%	13.7%
NB: Core Equity Tier 1 ratio		9.8%	7.8%	8.8%	9.0%	9.5%
NB: Debt Capital/ Invested Capital	10%	9%	10%	10%	12%	13%
− WACC	7.7%	7.2%	8.4%	8.7%	9.3%	9.2%
= Value-Added Margin	3.6%	3.3%	4.3%	5.2%	4.6%	4.5%
Through-the-cycle ROIC	11.2%	13.6%	11.7%	12.3%	12.6%	12.3%
− WACC	7.7%	7.2%	8.4%	8.7%	9.3%	9.2%
= Through-the-cycle Value-Added Margin	3.5%	6.4%	3.2%	3.6%	3.3%	3.1%
ROIC/WACC	1.5	1.5	1.5	1.6	1.5	1.5
Enterprise Value/ Invested Capital	2.4	1.1	1.5	1.1	0.9	0.8

Source: Bank of China interim and annual reports, author's analysis.

on Bank of China to raise more equity capital. However, given Bank of China's relatively high RWA intensity (because of its asset allocation towards commercial banking that already has high risk weights), there may be less of an increase in RWAs under Basel 3 for Bank of China than for other banks.

From a valuation perspective, looking at the ROIC/WACC versus Enterprise Value/Invested Capital ratios, it would appear that the market has tended to undervalue Bank of China's profitability by a significant degree. For example, at the end of 2012, the ROIC/WACC multiple of 1.5x would 'normally' imply a similar valuation multiple of EV/IC, but instead it was just 0.8x.

Looking at it from an RORWA perspective helps to highlight the relative differences in asset allocation. The first thing to note is the bottom-line performance; net profit per RWA at 2.0% in 2012 and 1.9% in 2011 is roughly double that of many Western banks.

Interestingly, net operating income per RWA, at 5.0% in 2012 and 4.9% in 2011, is roughly comparable with Western banks, but the operating expenses per RWA, at 2.0% in 2012 and 2011, are much lower. Administrative expenses per RWA, at 1.8–1.9% from 2007 through 2012, are the key drivers behind this better cost performance.

Impairment charges per RWA, at 0.3% in 2012, are less than half of what many of the Western banks reported, and this pattern of relatively lower impairments appears to have held throughout the period, even including 2008. We think that Bank of China's emphasis on commercial banking, and in particular trade finance, helps to explain why this is the case; despite the higher risk weights that tend to be attached to commercial banking, impairments tends to be lower because of the short-term, secured nature of most of this type of lending.

The Value Levers table gives a more concise view; we can also see that RWA growth has remained quite strong, at 9% in 2012 and 13% in 2011. Bank of China's cost-income ratio, at 40–43% throughout the period, is much lower than the ratios at the other banks we have analysed.

An analysis of Bank of China's asset quality gives more detail about the relatively lower impairment charges; we can see that the level of non-performing (or impaired) loans as a percentage of gross loans has been much lower than those reported by the Western banks. And provisioning coverage (impairment allowances/NPLs) levels, at 236% in 2012, are much higher. This provides decent support for the low impairment charges.

Looking on a slightly longer timeframe (from 2005 through 2012), we can see that the emphasis on net interest income as the Bank of China's main source of income has been consistent throughout the period.

Table 3.3 Bank of China: RORWA analysis

Performance per risk-weighted asset	2007	2008	2009	2010	2011	2012
Net interest income	4.15%	4.18%	3.33%	3.48%	3.56%	3.66%
Net fee & commission income	0.97%	1.02%	0.96%	0.98%	1.01%	1.00%
Net trading income	−0.16%	0.10%	0.13%	0.05%	0.12%	0.10%
Other banking income	−0.09%	0.05%	0.03%	0.07%	0.06%	0.04%
Net insurance income	−0.02%	−0.03%	0.02%	−0.01%	0.00%	0.01%
Other operating income	0.26%	0.31%	0.17%	0.16%	0.15%	0.14%
Subtotal non-interest income	0.96%	1.45%	1.33%	1.24%	1.35%	1.29%
Net operating income	5.11%	5.63%	4.66%	4.73%	4.90%	4.95%
Administrative expenses	−1.81%	−1.91%	−1.76%	−1.77%	−1.79%	−1.81%
Depreciation & amortisation	−0.19%	−0.20%	−0.18%	−0.19%	−0.17%	−0.18%
Other operating expenses	−0.04%	−0.17%	−0.08%	−0.02%	−0.02%	−0.05%
Operating expenses	−2.05%	−2.29%	−2.02%	−1.97%	−1.98%	−2.03%
Trading surplus	3.06%	3.34%	2.64%	2.75%	2.92%	2.92%
Impairment charges	−0.55%	−1.15%	−0.31%	−0.23%	−0.30%	−0.28%
Operating profit (pre-goodwill)	2.51%	2.19%	2.32%	2.52%	2.62%	2.64%
Goodwill impairment	0.00%	0.00%	0.00%	0.00%	0.00%	0.00%
Operating profit	2.51%	2.19%	2.32%	2.52%	2.62%	2.64%
Fair value gains/ (losses) on own debt	0.00%	0.00%	0.00%	0.00%	0.00%	0.00%
Changes in fair value of financial assets	−0.08%	0.03%	−0.01%	0.02%	0.00%	0.02%
Income from associates and JVs	0.03%	0.02%	0.02%	0.02%	0.01%	0.01%
Exceptional items	0.00%	0.00%	0.00%	0.00%	0.00%	0.00%
Profit before tax	2.47%	2.24%	2.33%	2.55%	2.63%	2.67%
Income tax	−0.78%	−0.55%	−0.54%	−0.58%	−0.59%	−0.60%
Net profit	1.69%	1.69%	1.79%	1.97%	2.04%	2.07%
Minority interests (non-equity)	0.00%	0.00%	0.00%	0.00%	0.00%	0.00%
Minority interests (equity)	0.00%	0.00%	0.00%	0.00%	0.00%	0.00%
Preference dividends	0.00%	0.00%	0.00%	0.00%	0.00%	0.00%
Net profit attributable to equity shareholders	1.53%	1.65%	1.69%	1.88%	1.94%	1.99%

Source: Bank of China interim and annual reports, author's analysis.

Table 3.4 Bank of China: value levers

Value Levers	2007	2008	2009	2010	2011	2012
RWA growth	**8.2%**	**5.7%**	**30.2%**	**14.0%**	**13.1%**	**9.0%**
Net interest income/Average RWA	4.15%	4.18%	3.33%	3.48%	3.56%	3.66%
Non-interest income/Average RWA	0.96%	1.45%	1.33%	1.24%	1.35%	1.29%
Net fee & commission income/Average RWA	0.97%	1.02%	0.96%	0.98%	1.01%	1.00%
Net trading income/Average RWA	−0.16%	0.10%	0.13%	0.05%	0.12%	0.10%
Other banking income/Average RWA	−0.09%	0.05%	0.03%	0.07%	0.06%	0.04%
Net insurance income growth in period	−397.3%	83.9%	−194.8%	−135.4%	−124.3%	305.0%
Other operating income growth in period	76.2%	25.7%	−31.0%	4.9%	11.5%	4.2%
Administrative expenses/Average RWA	−1.81%	−1.91%	−1.76%	−1.77%	−1.79%	−1.81%
Depreciation expenses/Average RWA	−0.19%	−0.20%	−0.18%	−0.19%	−0.17%	−0.18%
Other operating expenses/Average RWA	−0.04%	−0.17%	−0.08%	−0.02%	−0.02%	−0.05%
Operating expenses/Average RWA	−2.05%	−2.29%	−2.02%	−1.97%	−1.98%	−2.03%
Cost:income ratio	**40.1%**	**40.6%**	**43.4%**	**41.7%**	**40.4%**	**41.0%**
Impairment charges/Average RWA	−0.55%	−1.15%	−0.31%	−0.23%	−0.30%	−0.28%
Interest coupon on subordinated debt	5.00%	5.00%	4.74%	4.77%	4.67%	4.79%
Income tax/Profit before tax	−31.6%	−24.4%	−23.2%	−22.8%	−22.6%	−22.3%
Statutory income tax rate	−33.0%	−25.0%	−25.0%	−25.0%	−25.0%	−25.0%

Source: Bank of China interim and annual reports, author's analysis.

Table 3.5 Bank of China: asset quality

Asset quality	2007	2008	2009	2010	2011	2012
Impaired (non-performing) loans	90,317	90,879	76,006	63,876	63,306	65,455
Gross customer loans	2,850,561	3,296,146	4,910,358	5,660,621	6,342,814	6,864,696
Impairment provisions	96,068	106,494	112,950	122,856	139,676	154,656
Non-performing loans as % Gross customer loans	3.17%	2.76%	1.55%	1.13%	1.00%	0.95%
NPLs as % of RWAs	2.41%	2.29%	1.47%	1.09%	0.95%	0.90%
Provisioning coverage						
Impairment provisions/NPLs	106.4%	117.2%	148.6%	192.3%	220.6%	236.3%
Impairment provisions/RWA	2.56%	2.68%	2.19%	2.09%	2.10%	2.13%
Impairment charges/Average RWA	−0.55%	−1.15%	−0.31%	−0.23%	−0.30%	−0.28%

Source: Bank of China interim and annual reports, author's analysis.

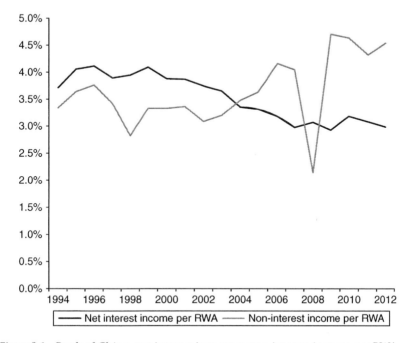

Figure 3.1 Bank of China: net interest income v. non-interest income per RWA
Source: Bank of China interim and annual reports, author's analysis.

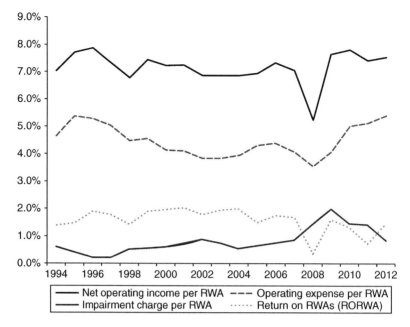

Figure 3.2   Bank of China: key value levers, 2005–2012

Source: Bank of China interim and annual reports, author's analysis.

And looking at the graph of selected value levers, it is clear how the relatively low (and consistent) operating expenses per RWA and low impairment charges per RWA have helped to support the relatively high RORWAs throughout the period.

Forecasts and Valuation

Our forecasts and valuations for Bank of China come with the usual caveats: these are only indicative forecasts that are intended to show how the analyses link with forecasts, and the valuations that flow from these indicative forecasts are only intended to show what can drive a fundamental valuation.

In our forecasts for Bank of China, we have assumed that RWA growth slows as the pace of Chinese GDP growth slows. We have assumed that operating expenses per RWA stay roughly flat, as rising wage expenses are broadly counterbalanced by rising productivity (e.g. with higher usage of more efficient Internet banking and mobile banking platforms). As growth in China slows, and the new Chinese leadership sets out its policies, we expect that bad loans will rise, but we also expect that the vast majority of these bad loans will have been made by Chinese regional banks and shadow banks.

Table 3.6 Bank of China: standard forecast and valuation ratios

Traditional valuation ratios	2010	2011	2012	2013E	2014E	2015E
Share price (CNY) 251						
Profit before tax pre-exceptionals and FV	141,242	168,556	186,261	187,051	198,292	207,612
% growth year-on-year	26.7%	19.3%	10.5%	0.4%	6.0%	4.7%
Net profit pre-exceptionals and FV	103,741	124,210	138,593	134,748	142,955	149,712
% growth year-on-year	27.9%	19.7%	11.6%	–2.8%	6.1%	4.7%
Adjusted EPS, fully-diluted	39.2	42.8	47.7	48.3	51.2	53.6
% growth year-on-year	27.0%	9.1%	11.4%	1.2%	6.1%	4.7%
Adjusted P/E	**6.4**	**5.9**	**5.3**	**5.2**	**4.9**	**4.7**
Dividends per share	15.0	16.0	18.0	18.9	19.8	20.8
% growth year-on-year	15.4%	6.7%	12.5%	5.0%	5.0%	5.0%
Dividend yield	6.0%	6.4%	7.2%	7.5%	7.9%	8.3%
Dividend payout ratio	34.0%	32.8%	31.0%	39.2%	38.8%	38.9%
ROE	18.0%	18.2%	18.0%	15.4%	14.7%	14.1%
Tangible book value per share	230	259	295	332	364	398
Price/Tangible BVPS multiple (x)	**1.09**	**0.97**	**0.85**	**0.76**	**0.69**	**0.63**

Source: Bank of China interim and annual reports, author's analysis.

The end result is that we expect profits in 2013 will only edge up slightly in 2013 versus 2012, and then we expect that profit growth will broadly track the GDP growth rates in the economies of Greater China. This should still enable Bank of China to achieve mid-teens ROEs.

From a fundamental ROIC valuation perspective, what is interesting is that the market appears to be assuming a substantial decline in Bank of China's value-added margins (ROIC–WACC) over time. For example, on the end-2012 valuation, the market appeared to be assuming that Bank of China's value-added margin would fall from 4.6% in 2012 to –0.2% over the next ten years and then staying at –0.2% in perpetuity. This seems counter-intuitive, in our opinion – given Bank of China's competitive strengths in commercial banking and Greater China's macro growth trends, we would expect that ROICs will continue to exceed WACCs for several more decades to come. Indeed, in 2010, the terminal value-added margin appeared substantially higher, at 2.4%.

That said, given the expected near-term turbulence in the Chinese macro outlook, we think it would probably be more reasonable to expect that market expectations for profitability at Bank of China won't be raised overnight; we have therefore used an assumption of a 0% terminal value-

Table 3.7   Bank of China: fundamental ROIC valuation

Fundamental valuation	2010	2011	2012	2013E	2014E	2015E
Value-Added Margin in period	5.25%	4.62%	4.55%	2.19%	1.85%	1.44%
Through-the-cycle Value-Added Margin	3.64%	3.31%	3.13%	1.27%	0.95%	0.69%
Invested Capital growth pa (next 10 years)	4.0%	4.0%	4.0%	4.0%	4.0%	4.0%
Terminal Value-Added Margin assumption	2.38%	0.37%	−0.22%	0.00%	0.00%	0.00%
Assumed continuing growth of Value Added	4.0%	4.0%	4.0%	4.0%	4.0%	4.0%
Invested Capital (beginning of period)	741,165	897,174	1,027,383	1,168,187	1,283,080	1,392,543
PV of Value Created/ (Destroyed) in forecast period	190,508	134,276	118,791	57,467	46,867	37,001
PV of Continuing Value	243,547	36,941	(25,727)	–	–	–
Total firm value	1,175,220	1,068,391	1,120,447	1,225,654	1,329,947	1,429,544
Less: Debt Capital	(90,607)	(123,451)	(146,433)	(150,826)	(160,011)	(169,756)
Less: Equity Adjustments	(162,402)	(180,018)	(197,077)	(204,299)	(214,380)	(225,071)
Target Equity Value	**922,211**	**764,922**	**776,937**	**870,530**	**955,556**	**1,034,717**
Market Capitalisation (end of period)	922,211	764,922	776,937	701,231	701,231	701,231
Target Equity Value per share	3.49	6.16	2.78	3.12	3.42	3.71

Source: Bank of China interim and annual reports, author's analysis.

added margin (i.e. ROIC-WACC = 0%) in our target valuation. This gives a target share price of CNY3.12 at the end of 2013.

2. Barclays

Background

Barclays is a global universal bank; it is engaged in retail banking, wealth management, credit cards, commercial and corporate banking, and investment banking. Barclays has operations in Europe, the Americas, Africa, and Asia; it has its headquarters in London. Barclays was founded over 300 years ago, operates in over 50 countries, and employs 140,000 people.

Barclays: ROIC analysis

Looking at Barclays' standardised income statement and balance sheet items for the past six years (see table below), one of the items that catches the eye is the jump in net operating income in 2009, from £19.5bn in 2008 to £31.2bn in 2009. This was driven by both the acquisition of Lehman Brothers' U.S. business in late 2008 and major trading gains as a result of the first round of quantitative easing in the U.S. and UK; although operating expenses also jumped, these boosts in income still helped Barclays to achieve a trading surplus of £14.5bn in 2009, more than double the $6.3bn achieved in 2008. This jump in trading surplus helped to absorb the increased impairment charges of £8.1bn in 2009 (which were roughly 50% higher than the £5.4bn charge in 2008).

After 2009, net operating income ebbed gently from £31.2bn in 2009 to £29.3bn in 2011 and £29.4bn in 2012. Although administrative expenses went down as well (from a peak of £18.5bn in 2010 to £17.1bn in 2012), other operating expenses (associated with regulatory fines and customer mis-selling redress programmes) appeared in 2011 (£1.3bn) and 2012 (£2.8bn), and total operating expenses rose, from £16.7bn in 2009 to £21.0bn in 2012. The combination of ebbing net operating income and rising operating expenses led to a significant decline in trading surplus, from £14.5bn in 2009 to £8.3bn in 2012.

The 2009–12 drop in trading surplus was partly mitigated by lower impairment charges, which fell from a peak of £8.1bn in 2009 to £3.3bn in 2012. Operating profit before goodwill impairment charges was £6.4bn in 2009 and £5.0bn in 2012.

On a comparative note, Barclays' RWA intensity (its RWA/Total Assets ratio), which was 26.0% at the end of 2012, was significantly lower than at many other banks – for example, HSBC's RWA/Total Assets ratio was

Table 3.8 Barclays: standardised financials

Year-end Dec	2007	2008	2009	2010	2011	2012
Net interest income	9,610	11,469	11,918	12,523	12,201	11,654
Net fee & commission income	7,708	6,491	8,418	8,871	8,622	8,536
Net trading income	3,759	(324)	8,821	7,687	4,952	7,926
Other banking income	923	647	264	1,203	2,018	844
Net insurance income	519	853	341	373	335	296
Other operating income	188	367	1,389	118	1,169	105
Subtotal non-interest income	13,097	8,034	19,233	18,252	17,096	17,707
Net operating income	22,707	19,503	31,151	30,775	29,297	29,361
Administrative expenses	(12,797)	(12,515)	(15,476)	(18,501)	(17,763)	(17,113)
Depreciation & amortisation	(653)	(882)	(1,206)	(1,227)	(1,092)	(1,104)
Other operating expenses	267	148	29	–	(1,325)	(2,795)
Operating expenses	(13,183)	(13,249)	(16,653)	(19,728)	(20,180)	(21,012)
Trading surplus	9,524	6,254	14,498	11,047	9,117	8,349
Impairment charges	(2,795)	(5,419)	(8,071)	(5,672)	(5,602)	(3,340)
Operating profit (pre-goodwill)	6,729	835	6,427	5,375	3,515	5,009
Goodwill impairment	(16)	(142)	(62)	(243)	(597)	–
Operating profit	6,713	693	6,365	5,132	2,918	5,009
Fair value gains/ (losses) on own debt	–	1,663	(1,820)	391	2,708	(4,579)
Changes in fair value of financial assets	293	33	(208)	274	287	–
Income from associates/JVs	42	14	34	58	60	140
Exceptional items	28	3,337	6,991	210	(94)	227
Profit before tax	7,076	5,740	11,362	6,065	5,879	797
Income tax	(1,981)	(453)	(1,074)	(1,516)	(1,928)	(616)
Net profit	5,095	5,287	10,288	4,549	3,951	181
Minority interests (non-equity)	–	–	–	–	–	–

Continued

Table 3.8 Continued

Year-end Dec	2007	2008	2009	2010	2011	2012
Minority interests (equity)	(678)	(905)	(895)	(985)	(944)	(805)
Preference dividends	0	0	0	0	0	0
Net profit attributable to equity shareholders	4,417	4,382	9,393	3,564	3,007	(624)
Dividends	(2,253)	(906)	(113)	(531)	(661)	(793)
Retained earnings	2,164	3,476	9,280	3,033	2,346	(1,417)
Risk-weighted assets (RWA), end of period	353,878	433,302	382,653	398,031	390,999	386,858
RWA growth in period	18.8%	22.4%	–11.7%	0.0%	0.0%	0.0%
Period average RWAs	321,949	373,165	407,016	392,684	394,833	389,576
Total assets	1,227,361	2,052,980	1,378,929	1,489,645	1,563,527	1,488,335
RWA/Assets	28.8%	21.1%	27.8%	26.7%	25.0%	26.0%

Source: Barclays annual and interim reports; author's analysis.

42% at the end of 2012. Another way of putting this would be that if Barclays were to run at the same RWA intensity as HSBC, its RWAs would be 62% higher than reported – and its capital requirements would be correspondingly higher. This is obviously a broad comparison, but in our opinion, it would indicate that Barclays would be at higher risk of having to increase its RWAs (if, for example, the Basel 3 rules were to lead to more standardisation of risk weights across banks in RWA calculations).

Our ROIC drivers table shows how changes in operating performance and capital leverage have affected Barclays' ROIC:

Barclays' capital leverage (average RWAs divided by average invested capital) has dropped markedly, from 6.4x in 2007 to 3.9x in 2010. Capital leverage has been roughly stable at 4x since 2010. This decline in capital leverage has limited the recovery in Barclays' ROIC, and combined with a 10% decline in Barclays' RORWAs from 2009 to 2012 (from 1.62% to 1.46%), these factors drove a 23% fall in ROIC in that period (from 7.5% to 5.8%).

In our ROIC decomposition table, we also show the Core Equity Tier 1 ratio and Debt Capital/Invested Capital ratio; we use these to cross-check the capital leverage ratio (and vice versa). For example, Barclays' Core Equity Tier 1 ratio jumped from 5.6% in 2008 to 10.0% in 2009; in the same period, its RWA/Invested Capital also indicated capital

Table 3.9 Barclays: ROIC decomposition

ROIC drivers	2007	2008	2009	2010	2011	2012
Return on risk-weighted assets (RORWA)	1.68%	0.36%	1.62%	1.31%	0.74%	1.46%
× Avg RWA/Avg Invested Capital	6.4	5.7	4.6	3.9	3.9	4.0
= Return on Invested Capital (ROIC)	10.8%	2.0%	7.5%	5.2%	2.9%	5.8%
NB: Core Equity Tier 1 ratio		5.6%	10.0%	10.8%	11.0%	10.9%
NB: Debt Capital/ Invested Capital	32%	35%	27%	27%	24%	25%
– WACC	7.6%	7.0%	11.5%	11.4%	11.5%	11.0%
= Value-Added Margin	3.2%	–5.0%	–4.0%	–6.2%	–8.6%	–5.2%
Through-the-cycle ROIC	9.8%	2.4%	7.7%	6.2%	4.9%	4.4%
– WACC	7.6%	7.0%	11.5%	11.4%	11.5%	11.0%
= Through-the-cycle Value-Added Margin	2.2%	–4.6%	–3.8%	–5.2%	–6.6%	–6.6%
ROIC/WACC	1.4	0.3	0.7	0.5	0.2	0.5
Enterprise Value/ Invested Capital	0.9	0.5	0.6	0.6	0.5	0.6

Source: Barclays annual and interim reports, author's analysis.

strengthening by falling from 5.7× to 4.6×. Amidst all the changes in Basel capital ratio calculations, the capital leverage ratio is relatively reliable as a ready reckoner.

Looking at Barclays using RORWA analysis gives some deeper insights into what was driving that financial performance over the past several years.

Firstly, looking at the RWA growth (in the table above), there are two interesting points: (1) the 22.4% jump in RWAs from 2008 to 2009 combined with the drop in RWA/Assets (28.8% to 21.1%) in the same period, and (2) the flat RWAs and total assets in 2010 through 2012.

The 2009 jump in assets and RWAs was a result of the Lehman acquisition, but what is interesting is the one-year dip in the RWA/Assets ratio (also called the RWA Intensity ratio) in 2009, from 28.8% to 21.1% and then back up to 27.8% in 2010. This analysis of changes in RWA intensity would encourage an analyst to look at Barclays' disclosure, in order to see if there were any changes in how RWAs were calculated during this period.

Looking at risk-adjusted operating performance by line item in the income statement, we can see that net interest income per RWA was actually quite stable over the entire period 2007–2012, at 3.0–3.2%. Many other line items were also quite stable, including net fee and commission income per RWA, which ranged from a low of 1.7% (in 2008) to a high of 2.4% (in 2007). But net trading income per RWA was much more volatile during that period, ranging from a low of -0.1% in 2008 to a high of 2.2% only a year later. Thus, when making forecasts, we could be reasonably confident when inputting assumptions for net interest income per RWA, whereas we would have less confidence in our forecasts on net trading income per RWA for Barclays, given the relatively volatile performance of that line item.

With operating expenses, it appears that there has been a steady improvement in administrative expense performance since 2010, with administrative expenses per RWA dropping by 21bp (from 4.71% to 4.50%) in 2011 and then by another 11bp (to 4.39%) in 2012. However, this improvement was more than offset by the increase in Other operating expenses per RWA, of 34bp in 2011 and 72bp in 2012.

Most of the key elements in the RORWA performance table are distilled in the Value Levers table. For Barclays, the relative stability of the net interest income per RWA line item can be more easily compared with the more volatile non-interest income per RWA line item (and within that the net trading income line per RWA item).

We also have the cost-income ratio in the Value Levers table; it shows that Barclays' cost-income ratio increased from 53.5% in 2009 to 71.6% in 2012. Note that having done the RORWA and Value Levers analysis beforehand enables us to understand what has driven this deterioration in operating performance.

In order to understand the changes in impairment charges per RWA on the Value Levers table, we also look at some key credit quality indicators for each bank.

Impaired loans (or in earlier years, non-performing loans) are down substantially from their peak of 7.2% of gross customer loans in 2010. Provisioning coverage (impairment provisions/NPLs) has improved, from a low of 39.0% at the end of 2010 to 52.1% by the end of 2012. In other words, things are looking better on the Barclays customer loan book; impaired (or non-performing) loans are down from their peaks, and provisioning coverage has improved, thus supporting a view that impairment charges per RWA are likely to fall further in the near term.

Table 3.10   Barclays: RORWA analysis

Per average risk-weighted asset	2007	2008	2009	2010	2011	2012
Net interest income	2.98%	3.07%	2.93%	3.19%	3.09%	2.99%
Net fee & commission income	2.39%	1.74%	2.07%	2.26%	2.18%	2.19%
Net trading income	1.17%	−0.09%	2.17%	1.96%	1.25%	2.03%
Other banking income	0.29%	0.17%	0.06%	0.31%	0.51%	0.22%
Net insurance income	0.16%	0.23%	0.08%	0.09%	0.08%	0.08%
Other operating income	0.06%	0.10%	0.34%	0.03%	0.30%	0.03%
Subtotal non-interest income	4.07%	2.15%	4.73%	4.65%	4.33%	4.55%
Net operating income	7.05%	5.23%	7.65%	7.84%	7.42%	7.54%
Administrative expenses	−3.97%	−3.35%	−3.80%	−4.71%	−4.50%	−4.39%
Depreciation & amortisation	−0.20%	−0.24%	−0.30%	−0.31%	−0.28%	−0.28%
Other operating expenses	0.08%	0.04%	0.01%	0.00%	−0.34%	−0.72%
Operating expenses	−4.09%	−3.55%	−4.09%	−5.02%	−5.11%	−5.39%
Trading surplus	2.96%	1.68%	3.56%	2.81%	2.31%	2.14%
Impairment charges	−0.87%	−1.45%	−1.98%	−1.44%	−1.42%	−0.86%
Operating profit (pre-goodwill)	2.09%	0.22%	1.58%	1.37%	0.89%	1.29%
Goodwill impairment	0.00%	−0.04%	−0.02%	−0.06%	−0.15%	0.00%
Operating profit	2.09%	0.19%	1.56%	1.31%	0.74%	1.29%
Fair value gains/(losses) on own debt	0.00%	0.45%	−0.45%	0.10%	0.69%	−1.18%
Changes in fair value of financial assets	0.09%	0.01%	−0.05%	0.07%	0.07%	0.00%
Income from associates and JVs	0.01%	0.00%	0.01%	0.01%	0.02%	0.04%
Exceptional items	0.01%	0.89%	1.72%	0.05%	−0.02%	0.06%
Profit before tax	2.20%	1.54%	2.79%	1.54%	1.49%	0.20%
Income tax	−0.62%	−0.12%	−0.26%	−0.39%	−0.49%	−0.16%
Net profit	1.58%	1.42%	2.53%	1.16%	1.00%	0.05%
Minority interests (non-equity)	0.00%	0.00%	0.00%	0.00%	0.00%	0.00%
Minority interests (equity)	0.00%	0.00%	0.00%	0.00%	0.00%	0.00%
Preference dividends	0.00%	0.00%	0.00%	0.00%	0.00%	0.00%
Net profit attributable to equity shareholders	1.37%	1.17%	2.31%	0.91%	0.76%	−0.16%

Table 3.11 Barclays: value levers analysis

Value Levers	2007	2008	2009	2010	2011	2012
RWA growth	18.8%	22.4%	−11.7%	4.0%	−1.8%	−1.1%
Net interest income/Average RWA	2.98%	3.07%	2.93%	3.19%	3.09%	2.99%
Non-interest income/Average RWA	4.07%	2.15%	4.73%	4.65%	4.33%	4.55%
Net fee & commission income/Average RWA	2.39%	1.74%	2.07%	2.26%	2.18%	2.19%
Net trading income/Average RWA	1.17%	−0.09%	2.17%	1.96%	1.25%	2.03%
Other banking income/Average RWA	0.29%	0.17%	0.06%	0.31%	0.51%	0.22%
Net insurance income growth in period	7.0%	64.4%	−60.0%	9.4%	−10.2%	−11.6%
Other operating income growth in period	−12.1%	95.2%	278.5%	−91.5%	890.7%	−91.0%
Administrative expenses/ Average RWA	−3.97%	−3.35%	−3.80%	−4.71%	−4.50%	−4.39%
Depreciation expenses/ Average RWA	−0.20%	−0.24%	−0.30%	−0.31%	−0.28%	−0.28%
Other operating expenses/ Average RWA	0.08%	0.04%	0.01%	0.00%	−0.34%	−0.72%
Operating expenses/ Average RWA	−4.09%	−3.55%	−4.09%	−5.02%	−5.11%	−5.39%
Cost:income ratio	58.1%	67.9%	53.5%	64.1%	68.9%	71.6%
Impairment charges/Average RWA	−0.87%	−1.45%	−1.98%	−1.44%	−1.42%	−0.86%
Interest coupon on subordinated debt	5.29%	5.25%	6.73%	6.53%	7.02%	7.08%
Income tax/Profit before tax	−28.0%	−7.9%	−9.5%	−25.0%	−32.8%	−77.3%
Statutory income tax rate	−30.0%	−28.5%	−28.0%	−28.0%	−26.5%	−24.5%

Table 3.12   Barclays: asset quality

Asset Quality	2007	2008	2009	2010	2011	2012
Impaired (non-performing) loans	9,641	15,700	22,388	31,882	21,342	18,565
Gross customer loans	349,167	468,389	431,020	440,374	442,531	433,582
Impairment provisions	3,772	6,574	10,796	12,432	10,597	9,676
Non-performing loans as % Gross customer loans	2.76%	3.35%	5.19%	7.24%	4.82%	4.28%
NPLs as % of RWAs	2.72%	3.62%	5.85%	8.01%	5.46%	4.80%
Provisioning coverage						
Impairment provisions/NPLs	39.1%	41.9%	48.2%	39.0%	49.7%	52.1%
Impairment provisions/RWA	1.07%	1.52%	2.82%	3.12%	2.71%	2.50%
Impairment charges/Average RWA	−0.87%	−1.45%	−1.98%	−1.44%	−1.42%	−0.86%

Source: Barclays annual and interim reports, author's analysis.

Longer-term trends

Although we have shown the years 2007 through 2012 on the tables above, it has been our practice to go as far back as we can when collecting data. For Barclays, we have collected data on going back to 1989, when Basel I was first implemented, and our Invested Capital and ROIC calculations can go back 1994, which was when enough data became available to make our calculations. For time series that are this long, we find it is easier to discern patterns when we graph a few key line items.

Thus, for an income breakdown, we have chosen to look at Barclays' net interest income per RWA versus its non-interest income per RWA.

From a long-term perspective, the shift in Barclays' business model is clear; net interest income per RWA has declined quite steadily since 1999, and non-interest income per RWA rose markedly from 1998 through 2006 and 2007. In 2008, non-interest income dropped sharply but recovered even more sharply in 2009. Comparing the net interest income and non-interest income per RWA lines, the non-interest income per RWA line is much more volatile.

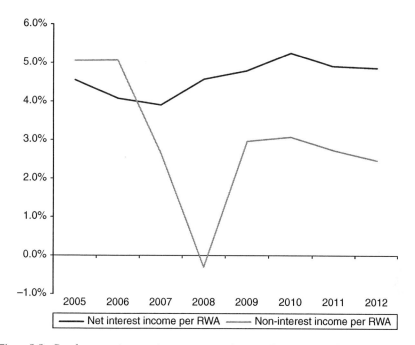

Figure 3.3 Barclays: net interest income v. non-interest income per RWA, 1994–2012
Source: Barclays annual and interim reports, author's analysis.

Graphing some long-term data from the Value Levers table, we can get more perspective on operating performance. (See chart below.)

We know from the net interest income versus non-interest income comparison that the dip in net operating income per RWA in 2009 was caused by the dip in non-interest income; looking at the long data series, it appears that for quite long period (1994–2010) changes in operating expenses per RWA could largely absorb the changes in net operating income per RWA. It is only relatively recently, in 2010 through 2012, that this hasn't been the case. Because of our prior analyses (identifying the increase in Other operating expenses per RWA), we can understand why this relationship appears to have weakened – and we can then take a more informed view in our forecasts as to whether the regulatory fines and other operating expenses will continue.

Looking at the impairment charges per RWA line, it appears that impairment charges and operating expenses are roughly negatively correlated at Barclays; in other words, if impairment charges per RWA are higher in a period, it is likely that operating expenses will be lower. This, too, can inform our forecast assumptions.

Our invested capital calculation for Barclays is in the table below.

From 2007 through 2012, Barclays more than doubled its shareholders' equity, from £23.3bn to £50.6bn; invested capital nearly doubled during this period, from £50.1bn in 2007 to £97.7bn in 2012. The bulk of the increase in invested capital wasn't achieved by debt capital issuance; subordinated debt grew from £18.2bn to £24.0bn during this period. The main driver was the increase in shareholders' equity, along with a major increase in loss provisions (from £3.8bn to £9.7bn).

Our ROIC calculation for Barclays is in the table below:

Barclays' RORWA hit a low of 0.4% in 2008, and then – boosted by net trading income as identified earlier – it recovered to 1.6% in 2009. After dropping to 0.7% in 2011, RORWA recovered to 1.5% in 2012. These swings in RORWA largely translated into swings in ROIC, with a low of 2.0% in 2008 followed by a recovery to 7.5% in 2009. For 2012, we calculate that Barclays generated a ROIC of 5.8%.

A methodological note: In the table above, we show RORWA and ROIC on both period-annualised and 12-month bases. This is because in our models, for reporting periods shorter than one year (e.g. interim results) we calculate RORWA and ROIC by both annualising the results in that

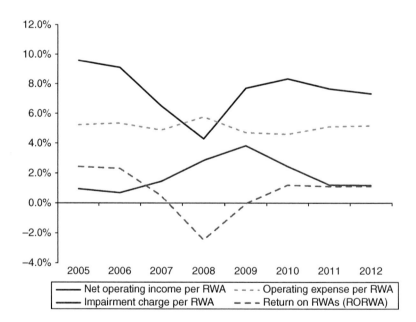

Figure 3.4 Barclays: key value levers, 1994–2012

Source: Barclays annual and interim reports, author's analysis.

Table 3.13 Barclays: Invested Capital

Invested Capital	2007	2008	2009	2010	2011	2012
Adjusted equity						
Shareholders' equity	23,291	36,618	47,277	50,858	55,589	50,615
+ Goodwill written off directly to reserves (pre-98)	215	215	215	215	215	215
+ Cumulative intangibles amortised	904	1,046	1,108	1,351	1,948	1,948
− Cumulative unrealised FV adjustments	(1,129)	(1,162)	(954)	(1,228)	(1,515)	(1,515)
+ Loss provisions (Balance Sheet)	3,772	6,574	10,796	12,432	10,597	9,676
+ Pension liabilities (post IFRS only)	1,537	1,357	769	365	321	1,282
+ Minority Interests (equity)	9,185	10,793	11,201	11,404	9,607	9,371
− Revaluation gains	(26)	(26)	(26)	(29)	(25)	(39)
Adjusted equity	37,749	55,415	70,386	75,368	76,737	71,553
Average adjusted equity in period	34,628	42,889	61,080	73,366	75,150	74,449
Debt capital						
Subordinated debt (ex-IFRS fair value adjustments)	18,150	29,842	25,816	28,499	24,870	24,018
+ Minority interests (non-equity)	–	–	–	–	–	–
+ Preference shares	–	–	–	–	–	–
Debt capital	18,150	29,842	25,816	28,499	24,870	24,018
Average debt capital in period	15,518	22,790	26,549	26,543	26,735	23,267
Invested capital	55,899	85,257	96,202	103,867	101,607	95,571
Invested capital growth in period	20%	53%	13%	8%	−2%	−6%
Average invested capital in period	50,145	65,679	87,629	99,909	101,885	97,716

Source: Barclays annual and interim reports; author's analysis.

Table 3.14   Barclays: ROIC

Return on Invested Capital (ROIC)	2007	2008	2009	2010	2011	2012
Net profit attributable to equity shareholders	4,417	4,382	9,393	3,564	3,007	(624)
+ Goodwill/ intangibles amortisation	16	142	62	243	597	–
+ Exceptional items	(28)	(3,337)	(6,991)	(210)	94	(227)
– Unrealised fair value (gains)/losses	(293)	(1,696)	2,028	(665)	(2,995)	4,579
+ Preference share dividends	–	–	–	–	–	–
+ Interest paid on subordinated debt	878	1,349	1,718	1,778	1,813	1,632
+ Minority Interests charge (non-equity)	–	–	–	–	–	–
+ Minority Interests charge (equity)	678	905	895	985	944	805
+ Provisioning charge (P&L as reported)	2,795	5,419	8,071	5,672	5,602	3,340
+ Tax charge (P&L as reported)	1,981	453	1,074	1,516	1,928	616
Pre-provisioning Operating Profit	10,444	7,617	16,250	12,883	10,990	10,121
– Provisioning charge (P&L as reported)	(2,795)	(5,419)	(8,071)	(5,672)	(5,602)	(3,340)
Adjusted Operating Profit	7,649	2,198	8,179	7,211	5,388	6,781
Operating ROIC (period annualised)	15.25%	3.35%	9.33%	7.22%	5.29%	6.94%
Operating ROIC (12-month)	15.25%	3.35%	9.33%	7.22%	5.29%	6.94%
– Tax charge (P&L as reported)	(1,981)	(453)	(1,074)	(1,516)	(1,928)	(616)
– Implied tax charge on debt capital interest	(263)	(405)	(515)	(533)	(544)	(490)
Adjusted Net Profit	5,405	1,340	6,590	5,162	2,916	5,675
–	–	–	–	–	–	–
Return on risk-weighted assets (period annualised)	1.68%	0.36%	1.62%	1.31%	0.74%	1.46%
RORWA (12-month)	1.68%	0.36%	1.62%	1.31%	0.74%	1.46%
Net ROIC (period annualised)	10.78%	2.04%	7.52%	5.17%	2.86%	5.81%
Net ROIC (12-month)	10.78%	2.04%	7.52%	5.17%	2.86%	5.81%

Source: Barclays annual and interim reports, author's analysis.

period (e.g. doubling the number for a half-yearly interim report) and using the 12-month historical performance as the basis for calculation. We do this because both methods of calculation are useful; the annualised performance in order to highlight a short-term shift, and the 12-month historical to track longer-term trends.

Forecasts and ROIC valuation

Keeping our analyses in mind, we can now make forecasts for Barclays and derive a fundamental ROIC valuation from those forecasts. One key caveat: Because of the inevitable timespan to publication, the forecasts in this text are, by their nature, obsolete. What we want to show, however, is how we can use our ROIC historical analyses to inform our forecasts, and then how we can integrate those forecasts into a robust fundamentally-based valuation methodology.

So, to recap some of our analyses and apply them to a forecast for Barclays:

Looking back over the past two decades and comparing net interest income per RWA with non-interest income, it appears that in circa 2004, Barclays shifted from generating roughly equal amounts of income from net interest income and non-interest income, to a trajectory that strongly favoured non-interest income, and in particular investment banking income. Despite the recent changes in Barclays' management, this preference appears to have remained. We thus expect Barclays' relative emphasis on investment banking-derived non-interest income to continue through 2015. Keeping in mind the historical volatility in Barclays' non-interest income per RWA, we would accordingly expect greater volatility in Barclays' net operating income. In other words, we would have relatively less confidence in our income forecasts for Barclays because of the higher volatility of the investment banking income stream.

Looking at the steady reduction in administrative expenses per RWA over the past few years, and taking into consideration the deep cost-cutting programmes that have been announced by the new management team, we would be inclined to assume further reductions in administrative expenses per RWA in our forecasts. But remembering that the other operating expenses associated with regulatory fines and mis-selling redress programmes had more than offset any administrative cost reductions, and noting that there were several investigations and lawsuits still in process, we would assume that the benefits from administrative cost reductions would be cancelled by continuing other operating expenses. This, in turn, would keep Barclays' cost-income ratio stubbornly high.

From a capital leverage perspective, we can recall that the trends in Barclays' ROICs corresponded reasonably well with changes in capital leverage. Going back several years, RWA/Invested Capital leverage peaked in from 1997 through 1999, when ROICs were also high (although 1998 reflected the RORWA impact of the emerging markets crises). From the late 1990s, as leverage trended downwards, ROICs did, too. In our forecasts, we could expect that Basel III and other regulations will raise capital requirements for investment banking; this would lead to a lower effective cap on leverage for Barclays as a result of its emphasis on investment banking. The result of this, we expect, will be that Barclays' ROICs will remain at circa 5% through 2015.

Putting these assumptions into our Barclays forecast model, we get the following forecasts for EPS, ROE and other traditional ratios:

We also calculate the following through-the-cycle (TTC) ROICs for Barclays, using the average impairment charge since 1989 as the basis for our through-the-cycle impairment charge:

Table 3.15 Barclays: standard forecast and valuation ratios

Traditional Valuation Ratios	2010	2011	2012	2013E	2014E
Share price (GBp): 306.2					
Profit before tax pre-exceptionals & FV	5,433	3,575	5,149	4,310	5,277
% growth year-on-year	−15.9%	−34.2%	44.0%	−16.3%	22.4%
Net profit pre-exceptionals & FV	3,068	754	3,784	2,490	3,291
% growth year-on-year	−52.0%	−75.4%	401.7%	−34.2%	32.2%
Adjusted EPS, fully-diluted	24.6	6.0	29.7	19.5	25.8
% growth year-on-year	−55.7%	−75.6%	393.4%	−34.2%	32.2%
Adjusted P/E	12.4	50.9	10.3	15.7	11.8
Dividends per share	5.5	6.0	6.5	6.8	7.2
% growth year-on-year	120.0%	9.1%	8.3%	5.0%	5.0%
Dividend yield	1.8%	2.0%	2.1%	2.2%	2.3%
Dividend payout ratio	14.9%	21.9%	−117.5%	33.4%	26.6%
ROE	7.3%	5.6%	−1.2%	4.8%	6.1%
Tangible book value per share (GBp)	346	391	350	364	384
Price/Tangible BVPS multiple (x)	0.88	0.78	0.87	0.84	0.80

Table 3.16 Barclays: through-the-cycle (TTC) ROIC

Through-the-cycle (TTC) ROIC	2007	2008	2009	2010	2011	2012
Pre-provisioning Operating Return	10,444	7,617	16,250	12,883	10,990	10,121
Reported provisioning charge as % avg RWA	−0.87%	−1.45%	−1.98%	−1.44%	−1.42%	−0.86%
Long-term average provisioning charge as % RWA	−0.97%	−0.97%	−0.97%	−0.97%	−0.97%	−0.97%
Through-the-cycle (TTC) provisioning charge	(3,115)	(3,611)	(3,938)	(3,800)	(3,820)	(3,770)
TTC post-provisioning Operating Profit	7,329	4,006	12,312	9,083	7,170	6,351
TTC post-provisioning Operating ROIC (12-month)	14.62%	6.10%	14.05%	9.09%	7.04%	6.50%
Reported income tax/Profit before tax	−28.0%	−7.9%	−9.5%	−25.0%	−32.8%	−77.3%
Normalised tax rate	−29.0%	−28.0%	−26.0%	−26.0%	−24.5%	−23.7%
TTC Profit before tax	7,383	7,215	19,275	9,108	6,539	6,718
– Normalised tax	(2,141)	(2,020)	(5,011)	(2,368)	(1,602)	(1,591)
– Implied tax charge on debt capital interest	(263)	(405)	(515)	(533)	(544)	(490)
Through-the-cycle Net Profit	4,924	1,581	6,785	6,182	5,024	4,271
TTC RORWA (12-month)	1.53%	0.42%	1.67%	1.57%	1.27%	1.10%
TTC Net ROIC (12-month)	9.82%	2.41%	7.74%	6.19%	4.93%	4.37%

This, in turn, feeds into our fundamental ROIC valuation for Barclays: From our ROIC perspective, Barclays has been value-destroying for several years. Running our fundamental ROIC valuation backwards, it appears that the market began to agree with that view a few years ago BARC's terminal value-added margin assumption dropped from an

Table 3.17   Barclays: fundamental ROIC valuation

Fundamental valuation	2010	2011	2012	2013E	2014E
Value-Added Margin in period	−6.22%	−8.64%	−5.17%	−6.61%	−5.81%
Through-the-cycle Value-Added Margin	−5.20%	−6.57%	−6.61%	−7.63%	−6.90%
Invested Capital growth pa (next 10 years)	2.0%	2.0%	2.0%	2.0%	2.0%
Terminal Value-Added Margin assumption	0.94%	−2.25%	−0.44%	0.00%	0.00%
Assumed continuing growth of Value Added	0.0%	0.0%	0.0%	0.0%	0.0%
Invested Capital (beginning of period)	96,202	103,867	101,607	95,571	97,958
PV of Value Created/ (Destroyed) in forecast period	(14,385)	(29,051)	(23,015)	(24,844)	(22,694)
PV of Continuing Value	3,066	(7,322)	(1,510)	–	–
Total firm value	84,883	67,494	77,082	70,727	75,264
Less: Debt Capital	(28,499)	(24,870)	(24,018)	(24,258)	(24,746)
Less: Equity Adjustments	(24,510)	(21,148)	(20,938)	(21,345)	(19,528)
Target Equity Value	31,874	21,476	32,126	25,123	30,990
Market Capitalisation (end of period)	31,874	21,476	32,126	37,347	37,347
Target Equity Value per share	2.72	1.79	2.63	2.06	2.54

Source: Barclays annual and interim reports, author's analysis.

implied 0.9% in 2010 to -2.3% in 2011. By the end of 2012 – after the post-LIBOR management changes at Barclays – it appears that the market had trimmed its expectations of value destruction, with the negative value-added margin improving to -0.4%.

Looking ahead, we have used a terminal value-added assumption of 0%. In other words, we have assumed that Barclays management does deliver on its cost-cutting promises, but that the combination of stricter capital requirements and volatile/weaker investment banking income would mean that Barclays' ROIC would not exceed its WACC. Note that we were forecasting a value-added margin (ROIC minus WACC) of -6.6% for 2013, or in other words, this would still imply that the market would continue to expect a significant improvement in profitability at Barclays.

These assumptions produce a fundamental ROIC valuation of 206p per share for Barclays at the end of 2013, and a fundamental valuation of

254p per share at the end of 2014. Again, please note that these valuations should not be taken as actual target valuations; these only illustrate how the fundamental ROIC valuation methodology is integrated with the analysis.

3. Citigroup

Background

Citi is a global financial institution, with 200 million customer accounts in 160 countries. Citi offers retail and business banking, corporate and investment banking, and a range of other financial services. Along with virtually all other Western banks, Citi was hit hard during the financial crisis and has undergone several restructurings, including replacing the CEO twice.

Analysis

Looking at the standardised income statement for Citi, the consistency of a few 'core banking' line items stands out – net interest income throughout most of 2007 through 2012, net fee and commission income from 2010 through 2012, and other banking income from 2010 through 2012. Other line items were significantly more volatile – particularly (and understandably) net trading income during much of the period.

The various restructuring programmes that have been conducted appear to have cut Citi's operating expense base from above $40bn per annum to mid-$30bn, this and lower impairment charges have helped to support Citi's operating profit in recent years. Note that as with all the banks, we have tried to put fair value gains/losses on own debt and other fair value movements below the operating profit line.

Since 2010, despite challenging markets, Citi has produced a profit and even paid a small dividend (although this is at much-reduced levels compared to pre-crisis years). A note on Citi's RWA intensity (RWA/Total Assets ratio): U.S. banks were still reporting under Basel I regulations in their 2012 results, although Citi also released its estimated RWAs using Basel III rules. Basel III RWAs were $1.21 trillion versus $0.97 trillion under Basel I, thus RWA intensity would have been higher as well.

Looking at Citi's ROIC decomposition, it appears that whilst RORWA has recovered from the crisis period of 2007 through 2009 (with a trough RORWA of -2.5% in 2008) to 1.1% in 2012, capital leverage (RWA/Invested Capital) has decreased by more than one-third – from 6.8x in 2007 to 4.0 in 2012. This capital deleveraging has held back the recovery in Citi's ROICs. Of course, the positive aspect of this capital deleveraging has been

Table 3.18 Citi: standardised financials

(US$ millions)	2007	2008	2009	2010	2011	2012
Net interest income	45,389	53,749	48,914	54,186	48,447	47,603
Net fee & commission income	20,068	10,366	17,116	13,658	12,850	12,926
Net trading income	(11,179)	(24,662)	3,022	8,916	4,992	5,389
Other banking income	8,860	8,222	5,195	4,005	3,995	4,012
Net insurance income	2,127	1,818	1,762	1,719	1,675	1,589
Other operating income	11,100	703	3,018	3,551	3,437	95
Subtotal non–interest income	30,976	(3,553)	30,113	31,849	26,949	24,011
Net operating income	76,365	50,196	79,027	86,035	75,396	71,614
Administrative expenses	(43,470)	(42,128)	(32,461)	(31,666)	(33,621)	(34,117)
Depreciation & amortisation	(2,421)	(2,466)	(2,853)	(2,664)	(2,872)	(2,507)
Other operating expenses	(11,318)	(23,096)	(12,621)	(13,045)	(14,440)	(13,894)
Operating expenses	(57,209)	(67,690)	(47,935)	(47,375)	(50,933)	(50,518)
Trading surplus	19,156	(17,494)	31,092	38,660	24,463	21,096
Impairment charges	(16,982)	(33,311)	(39,004)	(25,077)	(11,824)	(10,832)
Operating profit (pre–goodwill)	2,174	(50,805)	(7,912)	13,583	12,639	10,264
Goodwill impairment	–	–	–	–	–	–
Operating profit	2,174	(50,805)	(7,912)	13,583	12,639	10,264
Fair value gains/(losses) on own debt	–	–	–	(399)	1,985	(2,328)
Changes in fair value of financial assets	–	–	–	–	–	–
Income from associates and JVs	–	–	–	–	–	–
Exceptional items	708	4,002	(445)	(68)	112	(149)
Profit before tax	2,882	(46,803)	(8,357)	13,116	14,736	7,787
Income tax	2,546	20,326	6,733	(2,233)	(3,521)	(27)
Net profit	5,428	(26,477)	(1,624)	10,883	11,215	7,760
Minority interests (non-equity)	–	–	–	–	–	–
Minority interests (equity)	(283)	343	(95)	(281)	(148)	(219)
Preference dividends	–36	–1732	–2988	–9	–26	–26
Net profit attributable to equity shareholders	5,109	(27,866)	(4,707)	10,593	11,041	7,515
Dividends	(10,778)	(7,526)	(3,237)	(9)	(107)	(143)
Retained earnings	(5,669)	(35,392)	(7,944)	10,584	10,934	7,372
Risk-weighted assets (RWA), end of period	1,253,321	996,247	1,088,526	977,629	973,369	971,253
RWA growth in period	18.5%	–20.5%	9.3%	0.0%	0.0%	0.0%
Period average RWAs	1,161,988	1,174,049	1,018,900	1,029,003	984,033	975,371
Total assets	2,187,480	1,938,470	1,856,646	1,913,902	1,873,878	1,864,660
RWA/Assets	57.3%	51.4%	58.6%	51.1%	51.9%	52.1%

Source: Citi annual and interim reports, author's analysis.

a strengthening of regulatory capital ratios – Core Equity Tier 1 improved from 9.6% in 2009 to 12.7% in 2012. From an Invested Capital perspective, the drop in debt capital as a percentage of invested capital (from 50% in 2008 to 13% by 2010) would also be regarded as a strengthening of Citi's capital structure.

Citi's RORWA analysis adds a bit more colour – we can see that net interest income per RWA actually increased, from 3.9% in 2007 to 5.3% in 2010, before ebbing slightly to 4.9% in 2011 and 2012. Net interest income per RWA comprised the vast majority of Net operating income per RWA from 2007 through 2012; it was by far the most consistent income line item in the RORWA analysis.

The main cause of the volatility in Non-interest income per RWA was Net trading income per RWA, which ranged from -2.1% (in 2008) to +0.9% (in 2010). These swings are understandable, given the effects of the extraordinary monetary and fiscal programmes that were being implemented in that period (e.g. TARP, QE).

Table 3.19   Citi: ROIC decomposition

ROIC drivers	2007	2008	2009	2010	2011	2012
Return on risk-weighted assets (RORWA)	0.52%	−2.52%	−0.09%	1.21%	1.03%	1.14%
× **Avg RWA/Avg Invested Capital**	6.8	6.0	4.7	4.4	4.1	4.0
= **Return on Invested Capital (ROIC)**	3.5%	−15.2%	−0.4%	5.4%	4.2%	4.6%
NB: Core Equity Tier 1 ratio		2.3%	9.6%	10.8%	11.8%	12.7%
NB: Debt Capital/ Invested Capital	23%	50%	14%	13%	13%	13%
– WACC	7.9%	6.6%	11.6%	11.4%	10.2%	7.4%
= **Value-Added Margin**	−4.4%	−21.8%	−12.0%	−6.0%	−5.9%	−2.8%
Through-the-cycle ROIC	−0.5%	−13.6%	3.7%	5.8%	2.0%	1.1%
– WACC	7.9%	6.6%	11.6%	11.4%	10.2%	7.4%
= **Through-the-cycle Value-Added Margin**	−8.4%	−20.2%	−8.0%	−5.6%	−8.2%	−6.3%
ROIC/WACC	0.4	(2.3)	(0.0)	0.5	0.4	0.6
Enterprise Value/ Invested Capital	**1.1**	**0.7**	**0.6**	**0.7**	**0.4**	**0.6**

Source: Citi annual and interim reports, author's analysis.

Table 3.20   Citi: RORWA analysis

Performance per risk-weighted asset	2007	2008	2009	2010	2011	2012
Net interest income	3.91%	4.58%	4.80%	5.27%	4.92%	4.88%
Net fee & commission income	1.73%	0.88%	1.68%	1.33%	1.31%	1.33%
Net trading income	−0.96%	−2.10%	0.30%	0.87%	0.51%	0.55%
Other banking income	0.76%	0.70%	0.51%	0.39%	0.41%	0.41%
Net insurance income	0.18%	0.15%	0.17%	0.17%	0.17%	0.16%
Other operating income	0.96%	0.06%	0.30%	0.35%	0.35%	0.01%
Subtotal non-interest income	2.67%	−0.30%	2.96%	3.10%	2.74%	2.46%
Net operating income	6.57%	4.28%	7.76%	8.36%	7.66%	7.34%
Administrative expenses	−3.74%	−3.59%	−3.19%	−3.08%	−3.42%	−3.50%
Depreciation & amortisation	−0.21%	−0.21%	−0.28%	−0.26%	−0.29%	−0.26%
Other operating expenses	−0.97%	−1.97%	−1.24%	−1.27%	−1.47%	−1.42%
Operating expenses	−4.92%	−5.77%	−4.70%	−4.60%	−5.18%	−5.18%
Trading surplus	1.65%	−1.49%	3.05%	3.76%	2.49%	2.16%
Impairment charges	−1.46%	−2.84%	−3.83%	−2.44%	−1.20%	−1.11%
Operating profit (pre-goodwill)	0.19%	−4.33%	−0.78%	1.32%	1.28%	1.05%
Goodwill impairment	0.00%	0.00%	0.00%	0.00%	0.00%	0.00%
Operating profit	0.19%	−4.33%	−0.78%	1.32%	1.28%	1.05%
Fair value gains/ (losses) on own debt	0.00%	0.00%	0.00%	−0.04%	0.20%	−0.24%
Changes in fair value of financial assets	0.00%	0.00%	0.00%	0.00%	0.00%	0.00%
Income from associates and JVs	0.00%	0.00%	0.00%	0.00%	0.00%	0.00%
Exceptional items	0.06%	0.34%	−0.04%	−0.01%	0.01%	−0.02%
Profit before tax	0.25%	−3.99%	−0.82%	1.27%	1.50%	0.80%
Income tax	0.22%	1.73%	0.66%	−0.22%	−0.36%	0.00%
Net profit	0.47%	−2.26%	−0.16%	1.06%	1.14%	0.80%
Minority interests (non-equity)	0.00%	0.00%	0.00%	0.00%	0.00%	0.00%
Minority interests (equity)	0.00%	0.00%	0.00%	0.00%	0.00%	0.00%
Preference dividends	0.00%	−0.15%	−0.29%	0.00%	0.00%	0.00%
Net profit attributable to equity shareholders	0.44%	−2.37%	−0.46%	1.03%	1.12%	0.77%

Source: Citi annual and interim reports, author's analysis.

The Value Levers analysis for Citi distils the RORWA analysis. It helps to highlight the operating cost challenges that Citi faces: despite the relatively high levels of Net interest income per RWA, Citi's cost–income ratio has climbed back up from 55.1% in 2010 to 70.5% by 2012, as both Administrative expenses per RWA and Other operating expenses per RWA have climbed back up.

Although Impairment charges per RWA have dropped substantially from their peak in 2009 (at 3.8%) to 1.1% in 2012, on a six-year timeframe, and with several different (and slowing) country macroeconomic forecasts in mind, we might begin to think of Citi's impairment performance in 2012 as a trough – with the possible expectation that impairment charges may begin to increase again as countries recover (haltingly).

Table 3.21   Citi: value levers

Value levers	2007	2008	2009	2010	2011	2012
RWA growth	**18.5%**	**–20.5%**	**9.3%**	**–10.2%**	**–0.4%**	**–0.2%**
Net interest income/ Average RWA	3.91%	4.58%	4.80%	5.27%	4.92%	4.88%
Non-interest income/ Average RWA	2.67%	–0.30%	2.96%	3.10%	2.74%	2.46%
Net fee & commission income/Average RWA	1.73%	0.88%	1.68%	1.33%	1.31%	1.33%
Net trading income/ Average RWA	–0.96%	–2.10%	0.30%	0.87%	0.51%	0.55%
Other banking income/ Average RWA	0.76%	0.70%	0.51%	0.39%	0.41%	0.41%
Net insurance income growth in period	–4.8%	–14.5%	–3.1%	–2.4%	–2.6%	–5.1%
Other operating income growth in period	1.3%	–93.7%	329.3%	17.7%	–3.2%	–97.2%
Administrative expenses/ Average RWA	–3.74%	–3.59%	–3.19%	–3.08%	–3.42%	–3.50%
Depreciation expenses/ Average RWA	–0.21%	–0.21%	–0.28%	–0.26%	–0.29%	–0.26%
Other operating expenses/Average RWA	–0.97%	–1.97%	–1.24%	–1.27%	–1.47%	–1.42%
Operating expenses/ Average RWA	–4.92%	–5.77%	–4.70%	–4.60%	–5.18%	–5.18%
Cost:income ratio	**74.9%**	**134.9%**	**60.7%**	**55.1%**	**67.6%**	**70.5%**
Impairment charges/ Average RWA	–1.46%	–2.84%	–3.83%	–2.44%	–1.20%	–1.11%
Interest coupon on subordinated debt	5.16%	5.60%	5.33%	5.02%	4.81%	4.47%
Income tax/Profit before tax	88.3%	–43.4%	–80.6%	–17.0%	–23.9%	–0.3%
Statutory income tax rate	–35.0%	–35.0%	–35.0%	–35.0%	–35.0%	–35.0%

Source: Citi annual and interim reports, author's analysis.

Table 3.22   Citi: credit quality

Asset quality	2007	2008	2009	2010	2011	2012
Impaired (non–performing) loans	10,295	23,808	33,313	21,138	11,635	11,970
Gross customer loans	777,993	694,216	591,504	648,794	647,242	655,464
Impairment provisions	16,117	29,616	36,033	40,655	30,115	25,455
Non-performing loans as % Gross customer loans	1.32%	3.43%	5.63%	3.26%	1.80%	1.83%
NPLs as % of RWAs	0.82%	2.39%	3.06%	2.16%	1.20%	1.23%
Provisioning coverage						
Impairment provisions/NPLs	157%	124%	108%	192%	259%	213%
Impairment provisions/RWA	1.29%	2.97%	3.31%	4.16%	3.09%	2.62%
Impairment charges/Average RWA	–1.46%	–2.84%	–3.83%	–2.44%	–1.20%	–1.11%

Source: Citi annual and interim reports, author's analysis.

Looking at Citi's credit quality metrics, what is interesting is that whilst the pattern in non-performing (or impaired) loans roughly matches those of many other banks (i.e. with a peak in the 2008–10 period), Citi's provisioning coverage, measured as either impairment provisions/NPLs or impairment provisions/RWAs, is much higher than at many other banks. We think this was due to the proactive approach taken by the U.S. government relatively early in the financial crisis, when it forced U.S. banks to recognise severe impairment charges whilst also providing the funding to recapitalise the banks. This short, sharp shock seemed to do the trick – both non-performing loans and impairment charges fell whilst provisioning coverage ratios remained high.

Looking at Citi's Net interest income per RWA and Non-interest income per RWA on a slightly longer timeframe, what is again quite remarkable

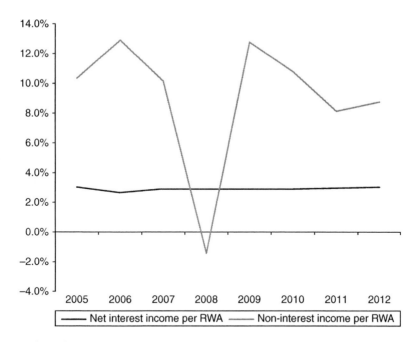

Figure 3.5   Citi: net interest income v. non-interest income per RWA, 2005–2012
Source: Citi annual and interim reports, author's analysis.

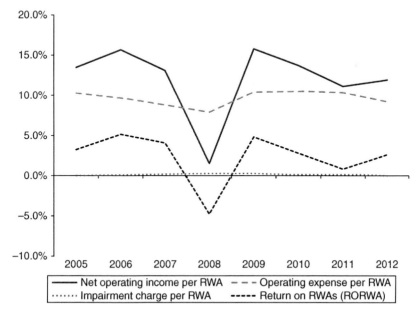

Figure 3.6   Citi: key value levers, 2005–2012
Source: Citi annual and interim reports, author's analysis.

is the relative consistency of Net interest income per RWA versus Non-interest income per RWA.

And looking at Citi's Selected Value Levers analysis on the following page, it appears that Net operating income per RWA has the greatest influence on actual returns on RWAs. It is interesting to note that the dip in Net operating income per RWA that Citi experienced in 2008 effectively dropped through to the bottom line RORWAs. What is also interesting is how much those Value Levers appear to have settled down over the years.

Forecasts and valuation

As with all the banks in this text, these forecasts are merely intended to show how the ROIC for Banks methodology integrates analysis with

Table 3.23   Citi: standard forecast and valuation ratios

Traditional Valuation Ratios	2010	2011	2012	2013E	2014E	2015E
Share price (US cents):						
5160						
Profit before tax pre-exceptionals & FV	13,583	12,639	10,264	19,807	22,311	24,540
% growth year-on-year	−271.7%	−6.9%	−18.8%	93.0%	12.6%	10.0%
Net profit pre-exceptionals & FV	11,036	8,983	9,940	12,719	14,342	15,787
% growth year-on-year	−349.8%	−18.6%	10.6%	28.0%	12.8%	10.1%
Adjusted EPS, fully-diluted	371.9	299.6	329.6	419.9	473.5	521.2
% growth year-on-year	−1118.5%	−19.4%	10.0%	27.4%	12.8%	10.1%
Adjusted P/E	**13.9**	**17.2**	**15.7**	**12.3**	**10.9**	**9.9**
Dividends per share	0.3	3.7	4.7	5.0	5.2	5.5
% growth year-on-year	−99.7%	1081.6%	29.0%	5.0%	5.0%	5.0%
Dividend yield	0.0%	0.1%	0.1%	0.1%	0.1%	0.1%
Dividend payout ratio	0.1%	1.0%	1.9%	1.2%	1.1%	1.0%
ROE	6.7%	6.5%	4.1%	6.6%	7.0%	7.1%
Tangible book value per share (GBp)	4,457	4,976	5,121	5,536	6,005	6,521
Price/Tangible BVPS multiple (x)	**1.16**	**1.04**	**1.01**	**0.93**	**0.86**	**0.79**

Source: Citi annual and interim reports, author's analysis.

valuation. In our indicative forecast for Citi, we have assumed that net operating income per RWA remains strong, and RWA will begin to grow again, driven by both the gradual transition from Basel I to III, and a gradual macro-recovery in the U.S. We assume that cost-cutting initiatives are reasonably successful in reducing operating expenses per RWA – although conduct risk charges remain a chunk of operating expenses in Citi and other large global banks. This combination would result in an improvement in Citi's cost–income ratio. If the U.S. macro-recovery does endure, then we would expect that impairment charges per RWA could

Table 3.24   Citi: fundamental ROIC valuation

Fundamental valuation	2010	2011	2012	2013E	2014E	2015E
Value-Added Margin in period	−6.04%	−5.94%	−2.81%	−2.76%	−2.38%	−2.18%
Through-the-cycle Value-Added Margin	−5.56%	−8.19%	−6.30%	−5.00%	−4.82%	−4.80%
Invested Capital growth pa (next 10 years)	2.0%	2.0%	2.0%	2.0%	2.0%	2.0%
Terminal Value-Added Margin assumption	−1.06%	−2.40%	−0.43%	0.50%	0.50%	0.50%
Assumed continuing growth of Value Added	2.0%	2.0%	2.0%	2.0%	2.0%	2.0%
Invested Capital (beginning of period)	222,774	235,855	239,920	244,765	256,647	269,274
PV of Value Created/ (Destroyed) in forecast period	(50,207)	(86,584)	(61,284)	(41,218)	(41,504)	(43,779)
PV of Continuing Value	(9,735)	(29,736)	(10,756)	10,310	10,788	11,400
Total firm value	162,832	119,534	167,880	213,857	225,930	236,896
Less: Debt Capital	(29,723)	(30,544)	(30,875)	(31,441)	(32,903)	(34,750)
Less: Equity Adjustments	(42,976)	(31,882)	(27,403)	(26,148)	(23,126)	(24,416)
Target Equity Value	**90,133**	**57,108**	**109,602**	**156,268**	**169,902**	**177,729**
Market Capitalisation (end of period)	137,446	76,927	119,823	156,290	156,290	156,290
Target Equity Value per share	31.32	19.63	37.40	51.59	56.09	58.68

Source: Citi annual and interim reports, author's analysis.

reduce further, although we would remain wary of a pickup in impairment charges – especially if U.S. monetary policies begin to normalise.

Running our fundamental ROIC valuation methodology backwards, we can estimate that the market's implied terminal value-added margin assumption for Citi was -1.1% at the end of 2010 and -2.4% at the end of 2011, recovering to -0.4% at the end of 2012. We have assumed that the market is assuming that Citi's long-term profitability will improve further, and thus we have used the assumption of a terminal value-added margin of 0.5%. The combination of all these assumptions and data gives a share price target of $52 for the end of 2013, and $56 at the end of 2014.

4. Credit Suisse

Background

Credit Suisse is a major financial services group, with 47,000 employees in 50 countries. It is divided into two main businesses – Private Banking & Wealth Management (which includes corporate banking), based mainly in Switzerland, and Investment Banking, which operates globally.

Analysis

As with nearly all the banks, Credit Suisse recorded a major (CHF8.3bn) loss in 2008, driven by CHF14.9bn in net trading losses; this swung into CHF16.2bn of positive net trading income a year later, driving a CHF32bn positive swing in operating profit before fair value items. Operating profit then dipped to CHF1.4bn in 2011 and recovered to CHF5.8bn in 2012, but this was less than half the operating profit that Credit Suisse had produced in 2007.

Throughout this period, net interest income stayed relatively stable; net interest income tended to be half the level of non-interest income, with the non-interest income being much more volatile due mainly to swings in net trading income.

Credit Suisse's RWA intensity, at 21–24% RWA/Total Assets, is quite low in comparison with other banks; we would keep an eye on this, given both the expected increase in risk weightings from Basel II.5 to Basel III, as well as a potentially higher Total Assets figure as the US GAAP reporting standards (which Credit Suisse uses) and IFRS standards are brought closer together.

Looking at the ROIC decomposition table for Credit Suisse, we can see that whilst capital leverage ratios (RWA/Invested Capital) have been relatively stable since 2009 (at 3.6–3.8x), RORWA has swung from -4.8% to +4.8% in the period 2007–12, dragging ROIC along with it. ROIC went from -24.6% in 2008 to 17.9% in 2009 – a swing of more than 40% in a

Table 3.25 Credit Suisse: standardised financials

(U.S.$ millions)	2007	2008	2009	2010	2011	2012
Net interest income	8,442	8,536	6,891	6,541	6,433	7,150
Net fee & commission income	16,519	12,518	11,753	11,930	10,960	11,298
Net trading income	4,942	(14,869)	16,155	8,969	2,939	4,812
Other banking income	5,804	(4,200)	502	1,429	1,820	2,548
Net insurance income	–	–	–	–	–	–
Other operating income	–	–	–	–	–	–
Subtotal non-interest income	27,265	(6,551)	28,410	22,328	15,719	18,658
Net operating income	35,707	1,985	35,301	28,869	22,152	25,808
Administrative expenses	(22,038)	(19,889)	(21,600)	(20,664)	(19,389)	(18,546)
Depreciation & amortisation	(893)	(1,174)	(1,114)	(1,166)	(1,196)	(1,294)
Other operating expenses	–	–	–	–	–	–
Operating expenses	(22,931)	(21,063)	(22,714)	(21,830)	(20,585)	(19,840)
Trading surplus	12,776	(19,078)	12,587	7,039	1,567	5,968
Impairment charges	(240)	(813)	(506)	79	(187)	(170)
Operating profit (pre-goodwill)	12,536	(19,891)	12,081	7,118	1,380	5,798
Goodwill impairment	–	–	–	–	–	–
Operating profit	12,536	(19,891)	12,081	7,118	1,380	5,798
Fair value gains/(losses) on own debt	1,204	4,989	(4,004)	341	1,210	(1,663)
Changes in fair value of financial assets	–	–	–	28	871	(1,954)
Income from associates and JVs	–	–	–	–	–	–
Exceptional items	6	(531)	169	(19)	–	–
Profit before tax	13,746	(15,433)	8,246	7,468	3,461	2,181
Income tax	(1,248)	4,596	(1,835)	(1,548)	(671)	(496)
Net profit	12,498	(10,837)	6,411	5,920	2,790	1,685
Minority interests (non-equity)	–	–	–	–	–	–
Minority interests (equity)	(4,738)	2,619	313	(822)	(837)	(336)
Preference dividends	0	–60	–131	–162	–216	–231
Net profit attributable to equity shareholders	7,760	(8,278)	6,593	4,936	1,737	1,118
Dividends	(2,552)	(116)	(2,338)	(1,526)	(915)	(970)
Retained earnings	5,209	(8,394)	4,255	3,410	822	148
Risk-weighted assets (RWA), end of period	323,640	257,467	221,609	218,702	241,753	224,296
RWA growth in period	27.6%	–20.4%	–13.9%	0.0%	0.0%	0.0%
Period average RWAs	292,537	296,185	237,211	226,560	216,984	233,365
Total assets	1,360,680	1,170,350	1,031,427	1,032,005	1,049,165	924,280
RWA/Assets	23.8%	22.0%	21.5%	21.2%	23.0%	24.3%

Source: Credit Suisse annual and interim reports, author's analysis.

year. ROIC has been volatile even recently, going to 10.6% in 2010 to 3.1% in 2011 and then back to 10.3% in 2012.

We think that this ROIC volatility must be challenging for Credit Suisse management; this level of uncertainty in past profitability would probably translate into uncertainty in resource/capital allocation. It would probably be more difficult to commit resources and capital to a long-term project with returns that might vary from –20% to +20% than going for a short-term project with 0–5% returns. In addition, we think this volatility would probably lead to lower ratings by credit agencies, on the view that returns (and thus ability to service debts) were less certain.

This uncertainty might help explain why Credit Suisse shares have seemed to trade at a discount to their 'rule of thumb' valuation – as a rule of thumb, ROIC/WACC multiples tend to roughly match Enterprise Value/Invested Capital multiples, but in the case of Credit Suisse, the ROIC/WACC multiple has tended to be higher than the Enterprise Value/

Table 3.26   Credit Suisse: ROIC decomposition

ROIC drivers	2007	2008	2009	2010	2011	2012
Return on risk-weighted assets (RORWA)	**4.17%**	**–4.82%**	**4.84%**	**2.98%**	**0.83%**	**2.66%**
× Avg RWA/Avg Invested Capital	**4.6**	**5.1**	**3.7**	**3.6**	**3.7**	**3.8**
= Return on Invested Capital (ROIC)	**19.2%**	**–24.6%**	**17.9%**	**10.6%**	**3.1%**	**10.3%**
NB: Core Equity Tier 1 ratio		8.6%	10.8%	12.2%	10.7%	15.5%
NB: Debt Capital/ Invested Capital	30%	49%	42%	44%	47%	37%
– WACC	7.0%	8.4%	9.1%	8.5%	7.5%	6.0%
= Value-Added Margin	**12.2%**	**–33.0%**	**8.8%**	**2.1%**	**–4.5%**	**4.2%**
Through-the-cycle ROIC	16.4%	–24.6%	16.3%	9.7%	3.1%	8.5%
– WACC	7.0%	8.4%	9.1%	8.5%	7.5%	6.0%
= Through-the-cycle Value-Added Margin	9.4%	–32.9%	7.2%	1.2%	–4.4%	2.4%
ROIC/WACC	2.7	(2.9)	2.0	1.2	0.4	1.7
Enterprise Value/ Invested Capital	**1.5**	**1.1**	**1.4**	**1.2**	**0.9**	**0.9**

Source: Credit Suisse annual and interim reports, author's analysis.

Invested Capital multiple – except, of course, in 'bad' years when the relationship seems to flip to its opposite.

Looking at Credit Suisse from an RORWA perspective, it becomes clearer that net interest income per RWA, at circa 3% throughout the period, contributes a relatively small proportion of net operating income, which with the exception of 2008 ranged between 10% and 15% per RWA. As described earlier, net trading income per RWA, which ranged between -5.0% (in 2008) and 6.8% (in 2009), has been the main contributor to the volatility in net operating income.

Looking at administrative expenses per RWA, the swings roughly match the swings in net operating income; we can interpret this as indicating that Credit Suisse's relatively heavy weighting in investment banking has kept its cost base relatively high.

Looking at impairment charges per RWA, these look quite low in comparison to other banks. In our opinion, this would reflect both the relatively low weighting of retail banking (as evidenced by the low net interest income per RWA) as well as the private banking bias in the retail banking operations. Historically, private banking operations have generated much lower levels of bad debts – but it has generally cost more to operate a private bank than a regular retail bank; this would help to explain both the consistently low impairment charges and the consistently high operating expenses per RWA.

The Value Levers analysis distils the RORWA analysis. Here we can see that Credit Suisse's cost–income ratio seems to settle at 64–77% in 'good' years, but then goes up to 93–106% in 'bad' years. Although roughly half of non-interest income per RWA is quite stable (with net fee and commissions per RWA at circa 5%), the –5% to +7% swing in net trading income (excluding fair value changes in own debt) has led to overall volatility in net operating income, and the relatively high operating cost structure makes it hard to compensate for this volatility.

A look at Credit Suisse's asset quality provides more justification for its relatively low impairment charges per RWA. Non-performing loans (or impaired loans in IFRS) peaked at 1.15% in 2008 – far below the levels of NPLs reported by many other banks. Looking into Credit Suisse's loan book, this was largely a reflection of both a high proportion of Swiss loans and a conservative Swiss approach to lending that the regulators encouraged.

Provisioning coverage was also robust, at 53% in 2011 and 2012. So, in other words, bad debts would not be our main concern for Credit Suisse when making forecasts for the bank.

Table 3.27   Credit Suisse: RORWA analysis

Performance per risk-weighted asset	2007	2008	2009	2010	2011	2012
Net interest income	2.89%	2.88%	2.91%	2.89%	2.96%	3.06%
Net fee and commission income	5.65%	4.23%	4.95%	5.27%	5.05%	4.84%
Net trading income	1.69%	−5.02%	6.81%	3.96%	1.35%	2.06%
Other banking income	1.98%	−1.42%	0.21%	0.63%	0.84%	1.09%
Net insurance income	0.00%	0.00%	0.00%	0.00%	0.00%	0.00%
Other operating income	0.00%	0.00%	0.00%	0.00%	0.00%	0.00%
Subtotal non-interest income	9.32%	−2.21%	11.98%	9.86%	7.24%	8.00%
Net operating income	12.21%	0.67%	14.88%	12.74%	10.21%	11.06%
Administrative expenses	−7.53%	−6.72%	−9.11%	−9.12%	−8.94%	−7.95%
Depreciation and amortisation	−0.31%	−0.40%	−0.47%	−0.51%	−0.55%	−0.55%
Other operating expenses	0.00%	0.00%	0.00%	0.00%	0.00%	0.00%
Operating expenses	−7.84%	−7.11%	−9.58%	−9.64%	−9.49%	−8.50%
Trading surplus	4.37%	−6.44%	5.31%	3.11%	0.72%	2.56%
Impairment charges	−0.08%	−0.27%	−0.21%	0.03%	−0.09%	−0.07%
Operating profit (pre-goodwill)	4.29%	−6.72%	5.09%	3.14%	0.64%	2.48%
Goodwill impairment	0.00%	0.00%	0.00%	0.00%	0.00%	0.00%
Operating profit	4.29%	−6.72%	5.09%	3.14%	0.64%	2.48%
Fair value gains/ (losses) on own debt	0.41%	1.68%	−1.69%	0.15%	0.56%	−0.71%
Changes in fair value of financial assets	0.00%	0.00%	0.00%	0.01%	0.40%	−0.84%
Income from associates and JVs	0.00%	0.00%	0.00%	0.00%	0.00%	0.00%
Exceptional items	0.00%	−0.18%	0.07%	−0.01%	0.00%	0.00%
Profit before tax	4.70%	−5.21%	3.48%	3.30%	1.60%	0.93%
Income tax	−0.43%	1.55%	−0.77%	−0.68%	−0.31%	−0.21%
Net profit	4.27%	−3.66%	2.70%	2.61%	1.29%	0.72%
Minority interests (non-equity)	0.00%	0.00%	0.00%	0.00%	0.00%	0.00%
Minority interests (equity)	0.00%	0.00%	0.00%	0.00%	0.00%	0.00%
Preference dividends	0.00%	−0.02%	−0.06%	−0.07%	−0.10%	−0.10%
Net profit attributable to equity shareholders	2.65%	−2.79%	2.78%	2.18%	0.80%	0.48%

Source: Credit Suisse annual and interim reports, author's analysis.

Table 3.28 Credit Suisse: value levers

Value Levers	2007	2008	2009	2010	2011	2012
RWA growth	27.6%	–20.4%	–13.9%	–1.3%	10.5%	–7.2%
Net interest income/Average RWA	2.89%	2.88%	2.91%	2.89%	2.96%	3.06%
Non-interest income/Average RWA	9.32%	–2.21%	11.98%	9.86%	7.24%	8.00%
Net fee and commission income/Average RWA	5.65%	4.23%	4.95%	5.27%	5.05%	4.84%
Net trading income/Average RWA	1.69%	–5.02%	6.81%	3.96%	1.35%	2.06%
Other banking income/Average RWA	1.98%	–1.42%	0.21%	0.63%	0.84%	1.09%
Net insurance income growth in period	#DIV/0!	#DIV/0!	#DIV/0!	#DIV/0!	#DIV/0!	#DIV/0!
Other operating income growth in period	#DIV/0!	#DIV/0!	#DIV/0!	#DIV/0!	#DIV/0!	#DIV/0!
Administrative expenses/ Average RWA	–7.53%	–6.72%	–9.11%	–9.12%	–8.94%	–7.95%
Depreciation expenses/ Average RWA	–0.31%	–0.40%	–0.47%	–0.51%	–0.55%	–0.55%
Other operating expenses/ Average RWA	0.00%	0.00%	0.00%	0.00%	0.00%	0.00%
Operating expenses/ Average RWA	–7.84%	–7.11%	–9.58%	–9.64%	–9.49%	–8.50%
Cost:income ratio	64.2%	1061.1%	64.3%	75.6%	92.9%	76.9%
Impairment charges/Average RWA	–0.08%	–0.27%	–0.21%	0.03%	–0.09%	–0.07%
Interest coupon on subordinated debt	6.95%	6.45%	7.07%	7.09%	6.93%	7.37%
Income tax/Profit before tax	–9.1%	–29.8%	–22.3%	–20.7%	–19.4%	–22.7%
Statutory income tax rate	–22.0%	–22.0%	–22.0%	–22.0%	–22.0%	–22.0%

Source: Credit Suisse annual and interim reports, author's analysis.

Table 3.29 Credit Suisse: credit quality

Asset quality	2007	2008	2009	2010	2011	2012
Impaired (non-performing) loans	1,946	2,725	2,297	1,863	1,718	1,729
Gross customer loans	241,788	237,463	238,600	219,891	234,357	243,204
Impairment provisions	1,234	1,639	1,395	1,017	910	922
Non-performing loans as % Gross customer loans	0.80%	1.15%	0.96%	0.85%	0.73%	0.71%
NPLs as % of RWAs	0.60%	1.06%	1.04%	0.85%	0.71%	0.77%
Provisioning coverage						
Impairment provisions/NPLs	63.4%	60.1%	60.7%	54.6%	53.0%	53.3%
Impairment provisions/RWA	0.38%	0.64%	0.63%	0.47%	0.38%	0.41%
Impairment charges/ Average RWA	−0.08%	−0.27%	−0.21%	0.03%	−0.09%	−0.07%

Source: Credit Suisse annual and interim reports, author's analysis.

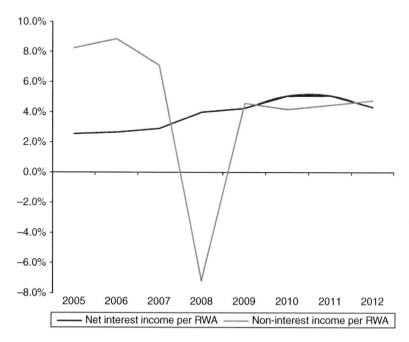

Figure 3.7 Credit Suisse: net interest income v. non-interest income per RWA

Source: Credit Suisse annual and interim reports, author's analysis.

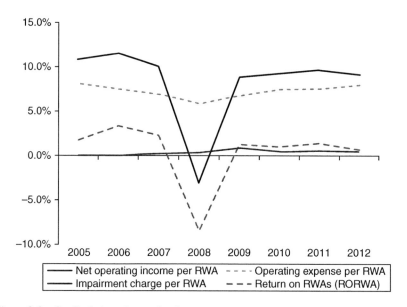

Figure 3.8 Credit Suisse: key value levers

Source: Credit Suisse annual and interim reports, author's analysis.

Looking at a graph of net interest income versus non-interest income per RWA, Credit Suisse's reliance on non-interest income is clear, as is the stable, yet relatively low, contribution of net interest income.

Looking at key value levers over a slightly longer timeframe, we can also see that Credit Suisse's operating expenses per RWA haven't been able to compensate for swings in net operating income, despite impairment charges per RWA that are extremely low in comparison to net operating income (impairments are the dotted line that skims above the 0% line on the graph). Thus, swings in net operating income per RWA tend to fall directly to the bottom line. This was especially the case with the dip in 2008, but looking at the period of 2005 through 2012, we can see that net return on RWAs roughly paralleled net operating income throughout the period.

Forecasts and Valuation

In our forecasts for Credit Suisse, we have assumed that the distinguishing features of the Credit Suisse RORWA, Value Levers and ROIC profiles have remained in place, namely a relatively high reliance on non-interest income (and especially a volatile net trading income line item), a low impairment charge, and a high operating cost base.

These assumptions have led to estimates that Credit Suisse's profit before tax, fair value changes and extraordinary items will dip slightly in 2013, followed by 9% growth in 2014 and 5% growth in 2015.

Whilst our forecast of circa 11% ROE from 2013 through 2015 may imply stability, we expect that Credit Suisse's actual performance will remain volatile, driven by continued swings in net trading income. Management, we expect, may try to compensate for this earnings volatility by decreeing relatively steady growth in dividends.

Table 3.30 Credit Suisse: standard forecast and valuation ratios

Traditional valuation ratios	2010	2011	2012	2013E	2014E	2015E
Share price (CHF centimes): 2875						
Profit before tax pre-exceptionals and FV	7,118	1,380	5,798	5,775	6,279	6,594
% growth year-on-year	−41.1%	−80.6%	320.1%	−0.4%	8.7%	5.0%
Net profit pre-exceptionals and FV	4,588	(152)	4,305	3,990	4,373	4,606
% growth year-on-year	−56.2%	−103.3%	−2925.3%	−7.3%	9.6%	5.3%
Adjusted EPS, fully-diluted	382.0	(12.6)	334.7	305.9	329.8	341.9
% growth year-on-year	−55.8%	−103.3%	−2750.4%	−8.6%	7.8%	3.7%
Adjusted P/E	**7.5**	**(227.7)**	**8.6**	**9.4**	**8.7**	**8.4**
Dividends per share	130.0	75.0	75.0	78.8	82.7	86.8
% growth year-on-year	−35.0%	−42.3%	0.0%	5.0%	5.0%	5.0%
Dividend yield	4.5%	2.6%	2.6%	2.7%	2.9%	3.0%
Dividend payout ratio	30.9%	52.7%	86.8%	26.0%	25.3%	25.6%
ROE	13.9%	5.2%	3.2%	10.8%	10.9%	10.6%
Tangible book value per share	2,077	2,032	2,077	2,272	2,486	2,704
Price/Tangible BVPS multiple (x)	**1.38**	**1.41**	**1.38**	**1.27**	**1.16**	**1.06**

Source: Credit Suisse annual and interim reports, author's analysis.

When we ran our fundamental ROIC valuation of Credit Suisse backwards in order to derive the market's implied expectation of terminal value-added margins, it appears that the market shifted from an expectation of circa 0.4% terminal value-added margins in 2010 and 2011, to an expectation of -1.0% in 2012. Note that this implied a significant future deterioration; we calculated that Credit Suisse's value-added margin was 4.2% in 2012 (and 2.4% on a through-the-cycle basis with long-term average provisioning), versus the expectation (implied in the end-2012 share price) that Credit Suisse's value-added margin would drop to -1.0% in ten years' time and remain at that level thereafter.

Table 3.31 Credit Suisse: fundamental ROIC valuation

Fundamental valuation	2010	2011	2012	2013E	2014E	2015E
Value-Added Margin in period	2.11%	−4.46%	4.22%	1.80%	2.00%	1.83%
Through-the-Cycle Value-Added Margin	1.18%	−4.41%	2.42%	1.41%	1.62%	1.54%
Invested Capital growth pa (next 10 years)	2.0%	2.0%	2.0%	2.0%	2.0%	2.0%
Terminal Value-Added Margin assumption	0.38%	0.35%	−1.04%	0.10%	0.10%	0.10%
Assumed continuing growth of Value Added	2.0%	2.0%	2.0%	2.0%	2.0%	2.0%
Invested Capital (beginning of period)	62,920	56,987	56,810	56,027	58,962	62,259
PV of Value Created/ (Destroyed) in forecast period	3,596	(8,880)	3,103	3,241	3,886	3,951
PV of Continuing Value	1,872	2,050	(9,982)	586	611	643
Total firm value	68,388	50,157	49,931	59,854	63,460	66,853
Less: Debt Capital	(25,246)	(26,865)	(20,629)	(20,983)	(21,899)	(23,057)
Less: Equity Adjustments	1,541	3,729	100	539	1,495	1,524
Target Equity Value	**44,683**	**27,021**	**29,402**	**39,409**	**43,056**	**45,320**
Market Capitalisation (end of period)	44,683	27,021	29,402	37,504	37,504	37,504
Target Equity Value per share	37.40	22.55	22.98	30.21	32.47	33.64

Source: Credit Suisse annual and interim reports, author's analysis.

For our valuations, we have assumed a terminal value-added margin of 0.10% for Credit Suisse, implying that the market's expectation of performance for Credit Suisse improves somewhat. This would imply a target share price of CHF30 at end-2013, rising to above CHF32 by end-2014. Note that because we expect the volatility of non-interest income will continue, we also expect that share price targets will be quite volatile.

5. Deutsche Bank

Background

Deutsche Bank, headquartered in Germany, has corporate and investment banking operations around the world, with a leading position in fixed-income investment banking. It also has wealth management and transaction banking businesses.

Analysis

Deutsche Bank, with its relatively heavy emphasis on fixed-income investment banking, was hit particularly hard in the financial crisis. Although the net loss attributable to shareholders was 'only' EUR3.8bn in 2008, this included a EUR28.6bn in gains on the fair value of own debt; excluding this and a EUR4.8bn loss of fair value changes in other financial assets, we calculate that Deutsche Bank had a EUR29.6bn operating loss in 2008. To set this in context, we calculate that Deutsche Bank had tangible shareholders' equity of EUR28.5bn at the end of 2007.

The main cause of the operating loss in 2008 was EUR33.8bn in net trading losses in 2008 (again, this didn't include fair value gains on own debt); EUR5.6bn in trading income by 2009 helped to swing Deutsche Bank back into operating profit (of EUR3.7bn excluding fair value changes) for 2009.

Operating recovered in 2010 and 2011 as net operating income recovered, but a large increase in administrative expenses (from EUR22bn in 2011 to EUR25bn in 2012) led to another dip in operating income (from EUR5.1bn in 2011 to EUR0.7bn in 2012).

Throughout this period, swings in fair value items – both on own debt and with other financial instruments – added to the volatility in Deutsche Bank's earnings.

Looking at Deutsche Bank's ROIC drivers, we can see that RORWAs are now roughly half the level achieved prior to the crisis. Capital leverage (RWA/Invested Capital) ratios are quite high – implying that the strength of Deutsche Bank's capital ratios may be a concern. As we discussed earlier, given that Deutsche Bank's RWA intensity (RWA/Total Assets) ratios are low compared to peers, we would keep a close track on regulatory

Table 3.32 Deutsche Bank: standardised financials

(US$ millions)	2007	2008	2009	2010	2011	2012
Net interest income	8,849	12,453	12,459	15,583	17,445	15,891
Net fee & commission income	12,289	9,741	8,911	10,669	11,544	11,510
Net trading income	7,175	(33,829)	5,634	3,658	2,749	5,562
Other banking income	1,146	712	(344)	(1,803)	(141)	460
Net insurance income	(193)	252	(542)	(485)	(207)	(414)
Other operating income	1,286	699	(183)	764	1,322	281
Subtotal non-interest income	21,703	(22,425)	13,476	12,803	15,267	17,399
Net operating income	30,552	(9,972)	25,935	28,386	32,712	33,290
Administrative expenses	(19,345)	(14,898)	(17,930)	(18,549)	(22,095)	(25,307)
Depreciation & amortisation	(1,731)	(3,047)	(1,782)	(4,255)	(3,697)	(3,235)
Other operating expenses	13	–	–	–	–	(394)
Operating expenses	(21,063)	(17,945)	(19,712)	(22,804)	(25,792)	(28,936)
Trading surplus	9,489	(27,917)	6,223	5,582	6,920	4,354
Impairment charges	(612)	(1,076)	(2,630)	(1,274)	(1,839)	(1,721)
Operating profit (pre-goodwill)	8,877	(28,993)	3,593	4,308	5,081	2,633
Goodwill impairment	(128)	(585)	134	(29)	–	(1,886)
Operating profit	8,749	(29,578)	3,727	4,279	5,081	747
Fair value gains/(losses) on own debt	–	28,630	(2,550)	83	1,772	(698)
Changes in fair value of financial assets	–	(4,793)	4,025	(387)	(1,463)	735
Income from associates and JVs	–	–	–	–	–	–
Exceptional items	–	–	–	–	–	–
Profit before tax	8,749	(5,741)	5,202	3,975	5,390	784
Income tax	(2,239)	1,845	(244)	(1,645)	(1,064)	(493)
Net profit	6,510	(3,896)	4,958	2,330	4,326	291
Minority interests (non-equity)	–	–	–	–	–	–
Minority interests (equity)	(36)	61	15	(20)	(194)	(54)
Preference dividends	0	0	0	0	0	0
Net profit attributable to equity shareholders	6,474	(3,835)	4,973	2,310	4,132	237
Dividends	(2,005)	(2,274)	(309)	(465)	(691)	(689)
Retained earnings	4,469	(6,109)	4,664	1,845	3,441	(452)
Risk-weighted assets (RWA), end of period	328,818	307,732	273,476	346,204	381,246	333,605
RWA growth in period	0.0%	0.0%	0.0%	0.0%	0.0%	0.0%
Period average RWAs	304,958	311,599	292,850	306,650	341,697	365,030
Total assets	1,925,003	2,202,423	1,500,664	1,905,630	2,164,103	2,012,329
RWA/Assets	17.1%	14.0%	18.2%	18.2%	17.6%	16.6%

Source: Deutsche Bank interim and annual reports, author's analysis.

Table 3.33   Deutsche Bank: ROIC decomposition

ROIC drivers	2007	2008	2009	2010	2011	2012
Return on risk-weighted assets (RORWA)	2.33%	–8.58%	1.27%	1.02%	1.35%	0.73%
× Avg RWA/Avg Invested Capital	6.2	9.0	9.3	7.3	6.4	6.4
= Return on Invested Capital (ROIC)	14.3%	–77.3%	11.8%	7.4%	8.6%	4.7%
NB: Core Equity Tier 1 ratio		7.0%	8.7%	8.7%	9.5%	11.4%
NB: Debt Capital/ Invested Capital	16%	39%	29%	28%	25%	19%
– WACC	7.8%	7.4%	9.7%	9.5%	9.2%	8.8%
= Value-Added Margin	**6.6%**	**–84.7%**	**2.1%**	**–2.0%**	**–0.6%**	**–4.1%**
Through-the-Cycle ROIC	10.8%	–58.2%	11.9%	8.0%	8.0%	5.1%
– WACC	7.8%	7.4%	9.7%	9.5%	9.2%	8.8%
= Through-the-cycle Value-Added Margin	3.1%	–65.6%	2.2%	–1.5%	–1.2%	–3.6%
ROIC/WACC	1.8	(10.5)	1.2	0.8	0.9	0.5
Enterprise Value/ Invested Capital	**1.0**	**1.2**	**1.5**	**1.1**	**0.8**	**0.8**

Source: Deutsche Bank interim and annual reports, author's analysis

trends that might indicate stricter risk weight calculations and/or higher capital requirements.

Although Deutsche Bank's ROIC, at 4.7% in 2012, was not that bad compared to the other banks we have analysed, our ROIC decomposition highlights (1) the relatively weak RORWAs, and (2) the relatively high capital leverage ratios. We would interpret the combination of relatively weaker operating profitability and relatively higher capital leverage ratios as an indication of a relatively higher risk profile.

Also, in terms of valuation, we would note that whereas in 2007 Deutsche Bank's ROIC/WACC multiple of 1.8x was higher than its EV/IC (Enterprise Value/Invested Capital) multiple of 1.0x, since 2008 the ROIC/WACC multiple has been lower than the EV/IC multiple, with the minor exception of 2011.

Looking at Deutsche Bank's performance from an RORWA perspective, we can see that net interest income per RWA at Deutsche Bank is actually quite robust, at 4–5% from 2008 through 2012. Non-interest income per RWA has also been quite strong (with the exception of 2008 and its trading losses) at 4–5%. Net operating income per RWA, at 8–10% from 2009 through 2013, is thus quite strong relative to the other banks we have analysed.

Relatively high operating expenses per RWA, at 7–8% throughout most of this period, use up most of this top-line income strength, however. Although impairment charges per RWA are quite low, at 20–50p, the relatively high cost structure leads to weaker operating profit margins: in 2012, operating profit per RWA dipped to 0.2%, versus 2.9% in 2007.

Table 3.34   Deutsche Bank: RORWA analysis

Performance per risk-weighted asset	2007	2008	2009	2010	2011	2012
Net interest income	2.90%	4.00%	4.25%	5.08%	5.11%	4.35%
Net fee & commission income	4.03%	3.13%	3.04%	3.48%	3.38%	3.15%
Net trading income	2.35%	–10.86%	1.92%	1.19%	0.80%	1.52%
Other banking income	0.38%	0.23%	–0.12%	–0.59%	–0.04%	0.13%
Net insurance income	–0.06%	0.08%	–0.19%	–0.16%	–0.06%	–0.11%
Other operating income	0.42%	0.22%	–0.06%	0.25%	0.39%	0.08%
Subtotal non-interest income	7.12%	–7.20%	4.60%	4.18%	4.47%	4.77%
Net operating income	10.02%	–3.20%	8.86%	9.26%	9.57%	9.12%
Administrative expenses	–6.34%	–4.78%	–6.12%	–6.05%	–6.47%	–6.93%
Depreciation & amortisation	–0.57%	–0.98%	–0.61%	–1.39%	–1.08%	–0.89%
Other operating expenses	0.00%	0.00%	0.00%	0.00%	0.00%	–0.11%
Operating expenses	–6.91%	–5.76%	–6.73%	–7.44%	–7.55%	–7.93%
Trading surplus	3.11%	–8.96%	2.12%	1.82%	2.03%	1.19%
Impairment charges	–0.20%	–0.35%	–0.90%	–0.42%	–0.54%	–0.47%
Operating profit (pre-goodwill)	2.91%	–9.30%	1.23%	1.40%	1.49%	0.72%
Goodwill impairment	–0.04%	–0.19%	0.05%	–0.01%	0.00%	–0.52%
Operating profit	2.87%	–9.49%	1.27%	1.40%	1.49%	0.20%
Fair value gains/(losses) on own debt	0.00%	9.19%	–0.87%	0.03%	0.52%	–0.19%
Changes in fair value of financial assets	0.00%	–1.54%	1.37%	–0.13%	–0.43%	0.20%
Income from associates and JVs	0.00%	0.00%	0.00%	0.00%	0.00%	0.00%
Exceptional items	0.00%	0.00%	0.00%	0.00%	0.00%	0.00%
Profit before tax	2.87%	–1.84%	1.78%	1.30%	1.58%	0.21%
Income tax	–0.73%	0.59%	–0.08%	–0.54%	–0.31%	–0.14%
Net profit	2.13%	–1.25%	1.69%	0.76%	1.27%	0.08%
Minority interests (non-equity)	0.00%	0.00%	0.00%	0.00%	0.00%	0.00%
Minority interests (equity)	0.00%	0.00%	0.00%	0.00%	0.00%	0.00%
Preference dividends	0.00%	0.00%	0.00%	0.00%	0.00%	0.00%
Net profit attributable to equity shareholders	2.12%	–1.23%	1.70%	0.75%	1.21%	0.06%

Source: Deutsche Bank interim and annual reports, author's analysis.

Table 3.35 Deutsche Bank: value levers

Value levers	2007	2008	2009	2010	2011	2012
RWA growth	**19.4%**	**-6.4%**	**-11.1%**	**26.6%**	**10.1%**	**-12.5%**
Net interest income/ Average RWA	2.90%	4.00%	4.25%	5.08%	5.11%	4.35%
Non-interest income/ Average RWA	7.12%	–7.20%	4.60%	4.18%	4.47%	4.77%
Net fee & commission income/Average RWA	4.03%	3.13%	3.04%	3.48%	3.38%	3.15%
Net trading income/ Average RWA	2.35%	–10.86%	1.92%	1.19%	0.80%	1.52%
Other banking income/Average RWA	0.38%	0.23%	–0.12%	–0.59%	–0.04%	0.13%
Net insurance income growth in period	188.1%	–230.6%	–315.1%	–10.5%	–57.3%	100.0%
Other operating income growth in period	230.6%	–45.6%	–126.2%	–517.5%	73.0%	–78.7%
Administrative expenses/Average RWA	–6.34%	–4.78%	–6.12%	–6.05%	–6.47%	–6.93%
Depreciation expenses/Average RWA	–0.57%	–0.98%	–0.61%	–1.39%	–1.08%	–0.89%
Other operating expenses/Average RWA	0.00%	0.00%	0.00%	0.00%	0.00%	–0.11%
Operating expenses/ Average RWA	–6.91%	–5.76%	–6.73%	–7.44%	–7.55%	–7.93%
Cost:income ratio	**68.9%**	**–180.0%**	**76.0%**	**80.3%**	**78.8%**	**86.9%**
Impairment charges/ Average RWA	–0.20%	–0.35%	–0.90%	–0.42%	–0.54%	–0.47%
Interest coupon on subordinated debt	7.56%	6.99%	7.14%	6.21%	7.08%	7.30%
Income tax/Profit before tax	–25.6%	–32.1%	–4.7%	–41.4%	–19.7%	–62.9%
Statutory income tax rate	–38.4%	–29.6%	–29.6%	–29.6%	–29.6%	–29.6%

Source: Deutsche Bank interim and annual reports, author's analysis.

Table 3.36 Deutsche Bank: credit quality

Credit quality	2007	2008	2009	2010	2011	2012
Impaired (non-performing) loans	2,645	3,682	7,201	6,313	10,070	10,335
Gross customer loans	200,597	271,219	261,448	411,025	416,676	401,985
Impairment provisions	1,705	1,938	3,343	3,296	4,162	4,696
Non-performing loans as % Gross customer loans	1.32%	1.36%	2.75%	1.54%	2.42%	2.57%
NPLs as % of RWAs	0.80%	1.20%	2.63%	1.82%	2.64%	3.10%
Provisioning coverage						
Impairment provisions/NPLs	64.5%	52.6%	46.4%	52.2%	41.3%	45.4%
Impairment provisions/RWA	0.52%	0.63%	1.22%	0.95%	1.09%	1.41%
Impairment charges/ Average RWA	–0.20%	–0.35%	–0.90%	–0.42%	–0.54%	–0.47%

Source: Deutsche Bank interim and annual reports, author's analysis.

The relatively large swings in fair value items – both in own long-term debt as well as in fair value movements with other financials – added to the volatility of reported earnings.

A note about Deutsche Bank's RWA intensity (RWA/Total Assets): at 14–18% from 2007 through 2012, this is amongst the lowest of the banks that we have analysed. Some of the other banks have RWA intensity 3x that reported by Deutsche Bank.

As regulators work to amalgamate global standards, e.g. by reviewing risk weighting methodologies amongst banks, we think that Deutsche Bank could face a higher risk of having to increase its RWAs; this would lead to both a shift downward in per RWA ratios, but also potentially higher capital requirements.

The Value Levers analysis offers a more distilled version of the RORWA analysis. It highlights how the relatively high operating expenses per RWA have used up most of the relatively strong net operating income per RWA. Deutsche Bank's cost–income ratio, at 87% in 2012, reflects this.

Looking at asset quality, Deutsche Bank's relatively low impairment charge per RWA (at 20–90bp per RWA and 47bp in 2012) is largely justified by the relatively low levels of non-performing loans (at 1.3–2.8%). NPLs did pick up in 2012, however (from 2.4% at the end of 2011 to 2.6%

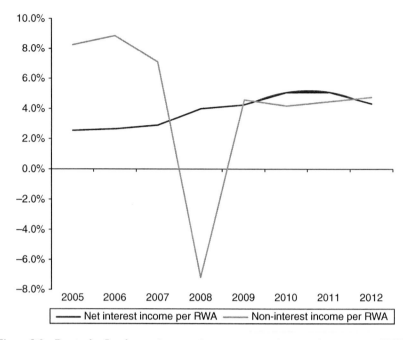

Figure 3.9   Deutsche Bank: net interest income v. non-interest income per RWA
Source: Deutsche Bank interim and annual reports, author's analysis.

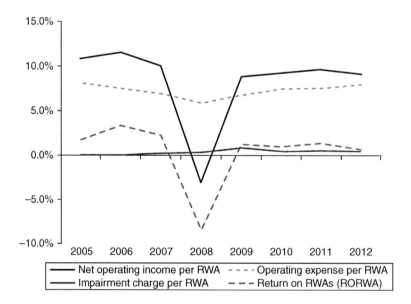

Figure 3.10   Deutsche Bank: key value levers
Source: Deutsche Bank interim and annual reports, author's analysis.

at the end of 2012), so impairment charges might tick up in the future, albeit from relatively low levels.

Looking at Deutsche Bank's performance over a slightly longer time-frame, we can see that non-interest income had contributed a much greater proportion of income prior to 2008. We think this reflects Deutsche Bank's relatively heavy emphasis on investment banking, and particularly fixed-income investment banking, as a source of income. In 2008, this bias meant that Deutsche Bank's income was particularly badly affected. Although there was a partial recovery in non-interest income per RWA in 2009, it did not regain the levels achieved prior to the financial crisis.

Looking at selected value levers over a longer timeframe, it becomes clear that Deutsche Bank was not able to cut operating expenses per RWA to compensate adequately for the dip in net operating income per RWA in 2008. Although net operating income did recover in 2009, it has not

Table 3.37 Deutsche Bank : standard forecast and valuation ratios

Traditional Valuation Ratios	2010	2011	2012	2013E	2014E	2015E
Share price (EUR cents)						
3634						
Profit before tax pre-exceptionals & FV	4,308	5,081	2,633	3,362	4,244	4,441
% growth year-on-year	19.9%	17.9%	−48.2%	27.7%	26.2%	4.6%
Net profit pre-exceptionals & FV	2,529	3,391	2,303	3,432	4,052	4,189
% growth year-on-year	−44.5%	34.1%	−32.1%	49.0%	18.1%	3.4%
Adjusted EPS, fully-diluted	319.7	354.3	239.9	364.8	420.3	424.3
% growth year-on-year	−49.7%	10.8%	−32.3%	52.1%	15.2%	0.9%
Adjusted P/E	**11.4**	**10.3**	**15.1**	**10.0**	**8.6**	**8.6**
Dividends per share	75.0	–	–	–	–	–
% growth year-on-year	50.0%	−100.0%	#DIV/0!	5.0%	5.0%	5.0%
Dividend yield	2.1%	0.0%	0.0%	0.0%	0.0%	0.0%
Dividend payout ratio	20.1%	16.7%	290.7%	0.0%	0.0%	0.0%
ROE	5.4%	8.1%	0.4%	−0.6%	0.6%	0.8%
Tangible book value per share	3,615	4,155	4,282	4,144	4,076	4,025
Price/Tangible BVPS multiple (x)	**1.01**	**0.87**	**0.85**	**0.88**	**0.89**	**0.90**

Source: Deutsche Bank interim and annual reports, author's analysis

regained the levels achieved from 2005 through 2007, and that combined with slightly higher impairment charges per RWA have kept operating profitability (Net RORWA) weaker than before the crisis.

Forecasts and valuation

In our forecasts for Deutsche Bank, we have assumed that the cost-cutting and restructuring programme announced in 2012 gradually shows results over the next few years, mainly in the form of a lower cost–income ratio and lower operating expenses per RWA. Given the RORWA performance over the past several years, we would regard this as a significant accomplishment for Deutsche Bank.

Table 3.38 Deutsche Bank: fundamental ROIC valuation

Fundamental valuation	2010	2011	2012	2013E	2014E	2015E
Value-Added Margin in period	−2.04%	−0.58%	−4.08%	−1.02%	−0.29%	−0.67%
Through-the-cycle Value-Added Margin	−1.47%	−1.21%	−3.63%	−0.56%	0.17%	−0.08%
Invested Capital growth pa (next 10 years)	2.0%	2.0%	2.0%	2.0%	2.0%	2.0%
Terminal Value-Added Margin assumption	1.70%	−3.80%	−2.76%	−2.00%	−1.00%	0.00%
Assumed continuing growth of Value Added	2.0%	2.0%	2.0%	2.0%	2.0%	2.0%
Invested Capital (beginning of period)	26,103	43,541	47,812	46,955	50,010	53,266
PV of Value Created/ (Destroyed) in forecast period	256	(9,347)	(12,994)	(4,363)	(1,496)	(166)
PV of Continuing Value	4,298	(13,145)	(11,249)	(6,475)	(3,433)	–
Total firm value	30,657	21,049	23,569	36,118	45,081	53,100
Less: Debt Capital	(12,353)	(11,775)	(8,785)	(8,961)	(9,414)	(9,987)
Less: Equity Adjustments	17,631	17,353	15,833	12,634	10,131	6,202
Target Equity Value	**35,935**	**26,627**	**30,617**	**39,791**	**45,798**	**49,315**
Market Capitalisation (end of period)	35,935	26,627	30,617	34,188	34,188	34,188
Target Equity Value per share	47.72	28.69	32.78	42.30	47.51	49.96

Source: Deutsche Bank interim and annual reports, author's analysis.

We also assume that regulatory pressures to both increase risk weightings and carry higher levels of core capital will force Deutsche Bank to bring down its capital leverage ratio by raising more capital.

Please note our usual caveats regarding these forecasts; they are not intended as 'true' analyst forecasts, they are included in order to show how the ROIC analysis and valuation models interact.

In terms of our fundamental ROIC valuation, when we run our model backwards, it appears that since 2011, the market has assumed that Deutsche Bank will be destroying value in perpetuity, with an implied terminal value-added margin of -2.8% at the end of 2012 and -3.8% at the end of 2011.

For our end-2013 valuation, we have assumed a terminal value-added margin of 2.0% – this implies that we think that whilst the market will tend to give Deutsche Bank the benefit of the doubt in the first few years of its announced restructuring programme, given the concerns about RWA intensity and capital leverage, it will continue to assume that Deutsche Bank will remain value-destroying. This gives an end-2013 share price target of EUR42.

Looking further ahead, we think that if by 2015, the market has been convinced that Deutsche Bank can eventually earn its cost of capital (i.e. ROIC equals WACC, or the terminal value-added margin is zero), then the end-2015 target share price would EUR50.

6. JP Morgan Chase

Background

JP Morgan Chase & Co is a large global financial services firm, with 260,000 employees and 50 million customers worldwide. It offers investment banking, retail and business banking, commercial and corporate banking, transactions processing, asset management and private equity services. It has one of the largest U.S. banking operations.

Analysis

Looking at the standardised financial statement for JP Morgan, the large operating loss in 2008 sticks out; this was driven by -$18bn of net trading income, due to both trading losses and the acquisition of Bear Stearns in that year. Net trading income recovered strongly in 2009 (to $17bn) and then ebbed to $7bn by 2012. Note that this standardised net trading income line item differs significantly from the reported income statement line item, because we have taken out fair value changes and shown them

Table 3.39   JP Morgan Chase: standardised financials

(U.S.$ millions)	2007	2008	2009	2010	2011	2012
Net interest income	26,406	38,779	51,152	51,001	47,689	44,910
Net fee and commission income	27,563	27,187	27,383	25,458	24,101	26,801
Net trading income	7,861	(17,693)	16,675	10,764	5,936	6,780
Other banking income	6,911	7,419	7,110	5,891	6,158	5,658
Net insurance income	–	–	–	–	–	–
Other operating income	1,829	2,829	1,647	2,307	2,624	4,597
Subtotal non-interest income	44,164	19,742	52,815	44,420	38,819	43,836
Net operating income	70,570	58,521	103,967	95,421	86,508	88,746
Administrative expenses	(33,859)	(34,800)	(39,919)	(41,673)	(44,247)	(45,550)
Depreciation and amortisation	(3,821)	(4,528)	(4,358)	(4,965)	(5,105)	(5,147)
Other operating expenses	(4,023)	(4,172)	(8,075)	(14,558)	(13,559)	(14,032)
Operating expenses	(41,703)	(43,500)	(52,352)	(61,196)	(62,911)	(64,729)
Trading surplus	28,867	15,021	51,615	34,225	23,597	24,017
Impairment charges	(6,864)	(20,979)	(32,015)	(16,639)	(7,574)	(3,385)
Operating profit (pre-goodwill)	22,003	(5,958)	19,600	17,586	16,023	20,632
Goodwill impairment	–	–	–	–	–	–
Operating profit	22,003	(5,958)	19,600	17,586	16,023	20,632
Fair value gains/(losses) on own debt	(468)	17,376	(4,097)	1,697	1,249	(1,860)
Changes in fair value of financial assets	1,270	(8,645)	564	5,584	9,472	10,145
Income from associates and JVs	–	–	–	–	–	–
Exceptional items	–	1,906	76	–	–	–
Profit before tax	22,805	4,679	16,143	24,867	26,744	28,917
Income tax	(7,440)	926	(4,415)	(7,489)	(7,773)	(7,633)
Net profit	15,365	5,605	11,728	17,378	18,971	21,284
Minority interests (non-equity)	–	–	–	–	–	–
Minority interests (equity)	–	(189)	(515)	(964)	(779)	(754)
Preference dividends	0	−674	−2439	−642	−629	−653
Net profit attributable to equity shareholders	15,365	4,742	8,774	15,772	17,563	19,877
Dividends	(4,984)	(5,674)	(788)	(782)	(3,773)	(4,565)
Retained earnings	10,381	(932)	7,986	14,990	13,790	15,312
Risk-weighted assets (RWA), end of period	1,244,659	1,244,659	1,198,006	1,174,978	1,221,198	1,270,378
RWA growth in period	33.0%	0.0%	-3.7%	0.0%	0.0%	0.0%
Period average RWAs	1,053,158	1,163,933	1,240,785	1,158,691	1,198,400	1,282,261
Total assets	1,562,147	2,175,052	2,031,989	2,117,605	2,265,792	2,358,141
RWA/Assets	79.7%	57.2%	59.0%	55.5%	53.9%	53.9%

Source: JP Morgan Chase, author's analysis.

separately; these fair value items (gains/losses on own debt and other changes in fair value items) have been major contributors to earnings volatility since the U.S. GAAP fair value accounting rules were introduced in 2007.

The other line items in JP Morgan's standardised income statement are markedly less volatile; broadly speaking, net operating income in 2012 roughly matched the level of 2007, whilst operating expenses climbed, leading to a drop in trading surplus (i.e. pre-provisioning). Impairment charges are down markedly from their peak in 2009, but despite the improvement, operating profit (pre-fair value items) in 2012 was still lower than 2007. RWA intensity (RWA/Total Assets) declined substantially, from 80% in 2007 to 54% in 2012. Note that these are still Basel I RWAs

Table 3.40 JP Morgan: ROIC decomposition

ROIC drivers	2007	2008	2009	2010	2011	2012
Return on risk-weighted assets (RORWA)	1.55%	–0.28%	1.36%	1.09%	0.89%	1.17%
× **Avg RWA/ Avg Invested Capital**	6.4	6.1	5.3	4.5	4.7	5.0
= **Return on Invested Capital (ROIC)**	10.0%	–1.7%	7.1%	4.9%	4.1%	5.9%
NB: Core Equity Tier 1 ratio		7.0%	8.8%	9.8%	10.1%	11.0%
NB: Debt Capital/ Invested Capital	23%	33%	26%	25%	25%	21%
– WACC	8.1%	9.0%	10.7%	10.4%	9.4%	7.1%
= **Value-Added Margin**	1.9%	–10.7%	–3.5%	–5.5%	–5.2%	–1.3%
Through-the-cycle ROIC	7.7%	1.1%	10.9%	6.1%	3.3%	3.1%
– WACC	8.1%	9.0%	10.7%	10.4%	9.4%	7.1%
= **Through-the-cycle Value-Added Margin**	–0.3%	–7.9%	0.3%	–4.3%	–6.1%	–4.0%
ROIC/WACC	1.2	(0.2)	0.7	0.5	0.4	0.8
Enterprise Value/Invested Capital	1.1	0.9	0.9	0.9	0.8	0.9

Source: JP Morgan Chase annual and interim reports, author's analysis.

as for all U.S.-based banks, although Basel III disclosures are becoming available.

Looking at ROIC drivers, JP Morgan's RORWAs of circa 1% since 2010 are relatively low compared to, for example, many of the UK and international banks. With the shift from Basel I to III, we expect that RWAs will increase by 20–30% whilst net returns will remain relatively stable, and thus RORWAs for JP Morgan could shift downwards.

In terms of capital leverage (RWA/Invested Capital), although JP Morgan's capital leverage has come down since 2007 (or in other words, core capital ratios have strengthened), under Basel III and its potentially higher RWAs we would expect capital leverage to rise (and core capital ratios to fall). The resulting ROIC – of 5.9% in 2012 – whilst an improvement on the 4.9% in 2010 and 4.1% in 2011 – still remains below our estimated WACC for JP Morgan, and thus the Value-Added Margin has remained negative since 2008.

Using RORWA analysis, it appears that whilst net operating income per RWA has gone from 7% in 2007 up to 8% in 2009 and 2010 and then back to 7% in 2012, operating expenses per RWA have shifted up from 4% in 2007 to 5% in 2012. This has driven a drop in JP Morgan's trading surplus, from 2.7% in 2007 to 1.9% in 2012, via a peak of 4.1% in 2009 driven largely by 1.3% in net trading income per RWA (versus a roughly normal level of 0.5% in the period).

The line-by-line RORWA table does highlight just how much the fair value items contribute to the volatility of JP Morgan's income and earnings; for example, fair value on own debt (FVOOD) items swung from −0.04% in 2007 to +1.5% in 2008 and then back to −0.3% in 2009 and changes in the fair value of other financial assets per RWA ranged from −0.7% to +0.7% in the period. Given that operating profit per RWA (pre-fair value items) ranged from −0.5% to +2.0% during this period, swings of +/− 1.5% had a major impact on reported earnings.

It is important to note that we are not making value judgements about whether or not the influence of fair value items is a good or bad thing; however, noting the relative size and volatility of the fair value items, we think that extracting them from the operating line items does help in analysing JP Morgan's performance.

The Value Levers analysis distils the RORWA analysis; here it is clearer that JP Morgan has returned to a pace of (Basel I) RWA growth that roughly paces the U.S. macro recovery – reflecting JP Morgan's large presence in the U.S.

JP Morgan's weighting towards non-interest income versus net interest income is also evident; looking at individual components, net fee and commissions (which include investment banking fees) are the main

Table 3.41 JP Morgan Chase: RORWA analysis

Performance per risk-weighted asset	2007	2008	2009	2010	2011	2012
Net interest income	2.51%	3.33%	4.12%	4.40%	3.98%	3.50%
Net fee & commission income	2.62%	2.34%	2.21%	2.20%	2.01%	2.09%
Net trading income	0.75%	−1.52%	1.34%	0.93%	0.50%	0.53%
Other banking income	0.66%	0.64%	0.57%	0.51%	0.51%	0.44%
Net insurance income	0.00%	0.00%	0.00%	0.00%	0.00%	0.00%
Other operating income	0.17%	0.24%	0.13%	0.20%	0.22%	0.36%
Subtotal non-interest income	4.19%	1.70%	4.26%	3.83%	3.24%	3.42%
Net operating income	6.70%	5.03%	8.38%	8.24%	7.22%	6.92%
Administrative expenses	−3.21%	−2.99%	−3.22%	−3.60%	−3.69%	−3.55%
Depreciation & amortisation	−0.36%	−0.39%	−0.35%	−0.43%	−0.43%	−0.40%
Other operating expenses	−0.38%	−0.36%	−0.65%	−1.26%	−1.13%	−1.09%
Operating expenses	−3.96%	−3.74%	−4.22%	−5.28%	−5.25%	−5.05%
Trading surplus	2.74%	1.29%	4.16%	2.95%	1.97%	1.87%
Impairment charges	−0.65%	−1.80%	−2.58%	−1.44%	−0.63%	−0.26%
Operating profit (pre-goodwill)	2.09%	−0.51%	1.58%	1.52%	1.34%	1.61%
Goodwill impairment	0.00%	0.00%	0.00%	0.00%	0.00%	0.00%
Operating profit	2.09%	−0.51%	1.58%	1.52%	1.34%	1.61%
Fair value gains/ (losses) on own debt	−0.04%	1.49%	−0.33%	0.15%	0.10%	−0.15%
Changes in fair value of financial assets	0.12%	−0.74%	0.05%	0.48%	0.79%	0.79%
Income from associates and JVs	0.00%	0.00%	0.00%	0.00%	0.00%	0.00%
Exceptional items	0.00%	0.16%	0.01%	0.00%	0.00%	0.00%
Profit before tax	2.17%	0.40%	1.30%	2.15%	2.23%	2.26%
Income tax	−0.71%	0.08%	−0.36%	−0.65%	−0.65%	−0.60%
Net profit	1.46%	0.48%	0.95%	1.50%	1.58%	1.66%
Minority interests (non-equity)	0.00%	0.00%	0.00%	0.00%	0.00%	0.00%
Minority interests (equity)	0.00%	0.00%	0.00%	0.00%	0.00%	0.00%
Preference dividends	0.00%	−0.06%	−0.20%	−0.06%	−0.05%	−0.05%
Net profit attributable to equity shareholders	1.46%	0.41%	0.71%	1.36%	1.47%	1.55%

Source: JP Morgan Chase, author's analysis.

contributors, as well as net trading income in most years. The net trading income line item, however, is quite volatile.

Looking ahead towards Basel III and other regulatory changes, we expect that the bulk of increased risk weightings, and thus RWAs, will fall in areas covered by investment banking, for example, in trading. This could affect JP Morgan disproportionately given its relative emphasis on investment banking.

Table 3.42 JP Morgan Chase: value levers

Value Levers	2007	2008	2009	2010	2011	2012
RWA growth	**33.0%**	**0.0%**	**–3.7%**	**–1.9%**	**3.9%**	**4.0%**
Net interest income/ Average RWA	2.51%	3.33%	4.12%	4.40%	3.98%	3.50%
Non-interest income/ Average RWA	4.19%	1.70%	4.26%	3.83%	3.24%	3.42%
Net fee & commission income/Average RWA	2.62%	2.34%	2.21%	2.20%	2.01%	2.09%
Net trading income/ Average RWA	0.75%	–1.52%	1.34%	0.93%	0.50%	0.53%
Other banking income/ Average RWA	0.66%	0.64%	0.57%	0.51%	0.51%	0.44%
Net insurance income growth in period						
Other operating income growth in period	–15.9%	54.7%	–41.8%	40.1%	13.7%	75.2%
Administrative expenses/Average RWA	–3.21%	–2.99%	–3.22%	–3.60%	–3.69%	–3.55%
Depreciation expenses/ Average RWA	–0.36%	–0.39%	–0.35%	–0.43%	–0.43%	–0.40%
Other operating expenses/Average RWA	–0.38%	–0.36%	–0.65%	–1.26%	–1.13%	–1.09%
Operating expenses/ Average RWA	–3.96%	–3.74%	–4.22%	–5.28%	–5.25%	–5.05%
Cost:income ratio	**59.1%**	**74.3%**	**50.4%**	**64.1%**	**72.7%**	**72.9%**
Impairment charges/ Average RWA	–0.65%	–1.80%	–2.58%	–1.44%	–0.63%	–0.26%
Interest coupon on subordinated debt	6.69%	6.97%	6.48%	7.06%	7.07%	7.26%
Income tax/Profit before tax	–32.6%	19.8%	–27.3%	–30.1%	–29.1%	–26.4%
Statutory income tax rate	–35.0%	–35.0%	–35.0%	–35.0%	–35.0%	–35.0%

Source: JP Morgan Chase, author's analysis.

Looking at operating expense breakdowns, administrative expenses and other operating expenses per RWA have both increased in the past few years. With relatively flat income per RWA and rising operating costs, JP Morgan's cost–income ratio has risen accordingly, from 59% in 2007 to 73% in 2012. This is probably a reflection of the relative emphasis on investment banking; note that the fair value items have been excluded from this cost–income ratio calculation.

Impairment charges have dropped substantially, from a peak of 2.6% in 2009 to one-tenth of that in 2012. One question for forecasting would be whether or not impairment charges could remain at such low levels.

In our ROIC models, we also track loan quality and provisioning. For JP Morgan, non-performing loans have reduced from 2.8% of loans at end-2009 to 1.4% at end-2011; NPLs began to edge up again, to 1.5% by end-2012. As a percentage of RWAs, NPLs at 0.8% at end-2012 were higher than the levels in 2007 and 2008 but well off of the peak of 1.5% at end-2009.

Impairment provisions have remained much higher than NPLs – probably a feature of the U.S. GAAP provisioning methodology – with impairment provisions/NPLs falling from 281% in 2007 and 256% in 2008 back to 205% in 2012. Beyond the methodological differences between U.S. GAAP and

Table 3.43   JP Morgan Chase: credit quality

Credit Quality	2007	2008	2009	2010	2011	2012
Impaired (non-performing) loans	3,282	8,953	17,564	14,841	9,993	10,720
Gross customer loans	519,374	744,898	633,458	692,927	723,720	733,796
Impairment provisions	9,234	23,164	31,602	32,266	27,609	21,936
Non-performing loans as % Gross customer loans	0.63%	1.20%	2.77%	2.14%	1.38%	1.46%
NPLs as % of RWAs	0.26%	0.72%	1.47%	1.26%	0.82%	0.84%
Provisioning coverage						
Impairment provisions/NPLs	281.4%	258.7%	179.9%	217.4%	276.3%	204.6%
Impairment provisions/RWA	0.74%	1.86%	2.64%	2.75%	2.26%	1.73%
Impairment charges/Average RWA	−0.65%	−1.80%	−2.58%	−1.44%	−0.63%	−0.26%

Source: JP Morgan Chase, author's analysis.

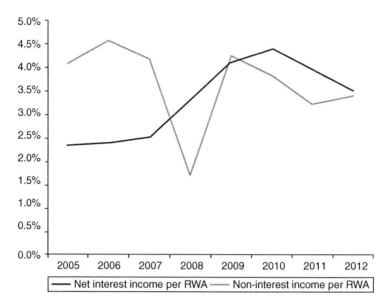

Figure 3.11 JP Morgan Chase: net interest income v. non-interest income per RWA

Source: JP Morgan Chase annual and interim reports, author's analysis.

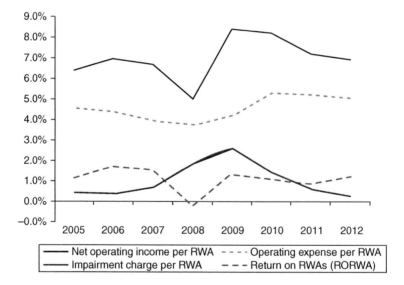

Figure 3.12 JP Morgan Chase: key value levers

Source: JP Morgan Chase annual and interim reports, author's analysis.

IFRS/IAS accounting, we still have the sense that JP Morgan's provisioning seemed quite conservative, especially versus many non-American peers.

Looking ahead, we are also sceptical that JP Morgan's extremely low levels of impairment charges per RWA can be maintained, especially if NPLs are beginning to tick upwards again. At 26bp in 2012 – one-tenth the level in 2009 – we would assume rising impairment charges per RWA in our forecasts.

On a slightly longer timeframe (2005–12); the following charts shows how non-interest income went from comprising the majority of net operating income at JP Morgan (from 2005 through 2007) to roughly level-pegging in 2012. Net interest income per RWA is also markedly less volatile than non-interest income per RWA.

Table 3.44 JP Morgan Chase: standard forecast and valuation ratios

Traditional valuation ratios	2010	2011	2012	2013E	2014E	2015E
Share price (U.S. cents): 5160						
Profit before tax pre-exceptionals & FV	17,586	16,023	20,632	19,881	21,908	22,586
% growth year-on-year	–10.3%	–8.9%	28.8%	–3.6%	10.2%	3.1%
Net profit pre-exceptionals & FV	10,445	10,157	15,143	11,382	12,667	13,074
% growth year-on-year	–16.1%	–2.8%	49.1%	–24.8%	11.3%	3.2%
Adjusted EPS, fully diluted	262.7	259.1	396.2	298.7	331.1	340.5
% growth year-on-year	–18.2%	–1.4%	52.9%	–24.6%	10.9%	2.8%
Adjusted P/E	**19.6**	**19.9**	**13.0**	**17.3**	**15.6**	**15.2**
Dividends per share	20.0	100.0	120.0	126.0	132.3	138.9
% growth year-on-year	0.0%	400.0%	20.0%	5.0%	5.0%	5.0%
Dividend yield	0.4%	1.9%	2.3%	2.4%	2.6%	2.7%
Dividend payout ratio	5.0%	21.5%	23.0%	42.3%	40.0%	40.9%
ROE	9.7%	10.2%	10.7%	5.7%	6.2%	6.1%
Tangible book value per share (GBp)	2,602	3,105	3,627	3,789	3,976	4,166
Price/Tangible BVPS multiple (x)	**1.98**	**1.66**	**1.42**	**1.36**	**1.30**	**1.24**

Source: JP Morgan Chase annual and interim reports, author's analysis.

Looking at the longer-term chart for selected value levers, we can see how the uptick in net operating income per RWA in 2009 and 2010 was not sustained, whereas operating expenses per RWA shifted higher from 2010 through 2012; despite the significant fall in impairment charges per RWA, this deterioration in the cost–income ratio kept net RORWAs roughly flat.

Table 3.45 JP Morgan Chase: fundamental ROIC valuation

Fundamental valuation	2010	2011	2012	2013E	2014E	2015E
Value-Added Margin in period	−5.45%	−5.11%	−1.00%	−1.71%	−1.25%	−1.26%
Through-the-Cycle Value-Added Margin	−4.21%	−5.97%	−3.86%	−4.48%	−4.10%	−4.06%
Invested Capital growth pa (next 10 years)	2.0%	2.0%	2.0%	2.0%	2.0%	2.0%
Terminal Value-Added Margin assumption	1.81%	−0.21%	0.15%	0.50%	0.50%	0.50%
Assumed continuing growth of Value Added	2.0%	2.0%	2.0%	2.0%	2.0%	2.0%
Invested Capital (beginning of period)	247,076	249,173	239,072	233,848	239,362	244,614
PV of Value Created/ (Destroyed) in forecast period	(21,604)	(54,432)	(34,166)	(34,780)	(32,088)	(32,838)
PV of Continuing Value	22,127	(3,311)	3,939	10,672	10,936	11,302
Total firm value	247,599	191,430	208,845	209,740	218,210	223,079
Less: Debt Capital	(61,882)	(59,692)	(49,188)	(49,991)	(52,062)	(54,681)
Less: Equity Adjustments	(18,985)	(3,607)	10,351	12,334	16,879	15,940
Target Equity Value	**166,732**	**128,131**	**170,008**	**172,084**	**183,027**	**184,338**
Market Capitalisation (end of period)	165,875	125,442	167,260	196,658	196,658	196,658
Target Equity Value per share	42.14	32.85	44.63	45.15	47.84	48.00

Source: JP Morgan Chase annual and interim reports, author's analysis.

Forecasts and valuations

In our forecasts for JP Morgan, we have assumed that net operating income per RWA remains relatively flat, whilst cost-cutting measures enable operating expenses per RWA to edge lower. Impairment charges do edge up but remain quite a bit lower than the average impairment charge of 2005 through 2012. The result is that JP Morgan's profit before tax (excluding fair value adjustments) edges down 4% in 2013 before growing in 2014 and 2015. ROEs remain around 6% in our forecasts for 2013 through 2015.

For our fundamental ROIC valuation, we first look at the implied market terminal value-added margins for JP Morgan, which were 0.15% in 2012 and -0.21% in 2011. For our target valuations, we have assumed a terminal value-added margin of 0.50%. This gives an end-2013 share price target of $45 for end-2013 and $48 for end-2014.

7. Lloyds Banking Group

Background and analysis

Lloyds Banking Group's main businesses are retail, commercial and corporate banking, life insurance and general insurance, pensions, and investment funds. In 2009, Lloyds acquired HBOS, another major UK bank; this made Lloyds Banking Group the UK's largest retail bank.

The acquisition of HBOS in 2009 presented challenges for Lloyds, both operationally and in terms of accounting. Because of the size of the acquisition, its price (a substantial discount to book value) and the extreme volatility and uncertainty of asset values at the time of the acquisition, there was a significant degree of judgement that was required in terms of how to account for the acquisition.

After the HBOS acquisition, Lloyds management chose a core/non-core approach for the bulk of its financial reporting, and there was also a substantial 'fair value unwind' that affected many of the line items in the statutory income statement. As a result of these significant 'fair value unwind' distortions, it became difficult to analyse several of the line items in the statutory income statement. Lloyds thus developed a 'management accounts' perspective on its financial performance, which was widely adopted by analysts.

In other words, there have been far less 'usable' financial data for Lloyds since the HBOS acquisition. As we mentioned earlier, we tend to ignore core/non-core distinctions in our ROIC analysis, on the fundamental view that a bank should be analysed and valued on a 'whole entity' basis.

This relative lack of data is reflected in the standardised income statement for Lloyds; for example, much of the detail in non-interest income

Table 3.46   Lloyds: standardised financials

(In £ millions)	2007	2008	2009	2010	2011	2012
Net interest income	13,403	14,903	12,726	14,143	12,233	9,075
Net fee & commission income	3,884	–	–	–	–	3,293
Net trading income	178	–	–	–	–	13,346
Other banking income	–	–	–	–	–	–
Net insurance income	3,559	–	–	–	–	(10,112)
Other operating income	3,756	6,452	8,738	9,394	8,964	4,700
Subtotal non-interest income	11,377	6,452	8,738	9,394	8,964	11,227
Net operating income	24,780	21,355	21,464	23,537	21,197	20,302
Administrative expenses	(9,916)	(12,236)	(11,609)	(10,882)	(10,253)	(9,630)
Depreciation & amortisation	(1,839)	–	–	–	–	(2,126)
Other operating expenses	–	–	(1,096)	(1,439)	(5,195)	(4,175)
Operating expenses	(11,755)	(12,236)	(12,705)	(12,321)	(15,448)	(15,931)
Trading surplus	13,025	9,119	8,759	11,216	5,749	4,371
Impairment charges	(3,868)	(14,880)	(23,988)	(13,181)	(9,787)	(5,149)
Operating profit (pre-goodwill)	9,157	(5,761)	(15,229)	(1,965)	(4,038)	(778)
Goodwill impairment	(198)	–	(993)	(629)	(562)	–
Operating profit	8,959	(5,761)	(16,222)	(2,594)	(4,600)	(778)
Fair value gains/(losses) on own debt	–	–	–	–	–	(270)
Changes in fair value of financial assets	(467)	–	17,751	3,331	1,031	478
Income from associates and JVs	234	(952)	(767)	(91)	27	–
Exceptional items	752	–	280	(365)	–	–
Profit before tax	9,478	(6,713)	1,042	281	(3,542)	(570)
Income tax	(2,044)	38	1,911	(539)	828	(773)
Net profit	7,434	(6,675)	2,953	(258)	(2,714)	(1,343)
Minority interests (non-equity)	(32)	(26)	(126)	(62)	(73)	(84)
Minority interests (equity)	(68)	–	–	–	–	–
Preference dividends	–	–	–	–	–	–
Net profit attributable to equity shareholders	7,334	(6,701)	2,827	(320)	(2,787)	(1,427)
Dividends declared (not IFRS format)	(3,851)	(648)	–	–	–	–
Retained earnings	3,483	(7,349)	2,827	(320)	(2,787)	(1,427)
Risk-weighted assets (RWA), end of period	502,838	498,500	493,307	406,372	352,341	310,299
RWA growth in period	16.4%	–0.9%	–1.0%	–17.6%	–13.3%	–11.9%
Period average RWAs	456,806	493,062	489,179	456,518	381,312	331,904
Total assets		1,127,725	1,027,255	991,574	970,546	924,552
RWA/Assets		44%	48%	41%	36%	34%

Source: Lloyds Banking Group annual and interim reports, author's analysis.

line items either has not been available or has been badly distorted by the fair value unwind. For 2013, management have stated that the remaining pool of fair value unwind items is much smaller, and, thus, we have begun to shift back to the statutory accounts as the basis for our ROIC analysis.

That said, looking at Lloyds' operating profit before fair value and other items, it seems clear that Lloyds was loss-making from 2008 through 2012. However, by 2012, this loss was beginning to taper off, particularly driven by lower impairment charges. Lloyds' operating loss prior to fair value and other items shrank from a £4.6bn loss in 2011 to a £0.8bn loss in 2012, as impairment charges fell from £9.8bn to £5.1bn. Net operating income appeared to ebb from £23.5bn in 2010 to £20.3bn in 2012;

Table 3.47 Lloyds: ROIC decomposition

ROIC drivers	2007	2008	2009	2010	2011	2012
Return on risk-weighted assets (RORWA)	1.79%	−1.00%	−2.50%	−0.27%	−0.44%	−0.01%
× **Avg RWA/Avg Invested Capital**	5.4	5.3	5.1	4.5	3.9	3.7
= **Return on Invested Capital (ROIC)**	9.70%	−5.37%	−12.77%	−1.23%	−1.75%	−0.02%
NB: Core Equity Tier 1 ratio		1.9%	8.1%	10.2%	10.8%	12.0%
NB: Debt Capital/ Invested Capital	48%	39%	35%	36%	37%	40%
− WACC	6.72%	7.22%	10.61%	10.05%	9.77%	9.39%
= **Value-Added Margin**	2.98%	−12.59%	−23.38%	−11.28%	−11.52%	−9.41%
Through-the-cycle ROIC	3.05%	−0.57%	0.24%	5.14%	2.05%	1.41%
− WACC	6.72%	7.22%	10.61%	10.05%	9.77%	9.39%
= Through-the-cycle Value-Added Margin	−3.67%	−7.79%	−10.38%	−4.91%	−7.72%	−7.98%
ROIC/WACC	1.44	(0.74)	(1.20)	(0.12)	(0.18)	(0.00)
Enterprise Value/ Invested Capital	1.10	0.46	0.68	0.80	0.56	0.80
EBITDA	12,626	(4,255)	(13,374)	(114)	(1,885)	3,655
EBITDA growth in period	−6%	−134%	214%	−99%	1554%	−294%
EV/EBITDA, period average	7.6	(11.8)	(5.0)	(710.1)	(28.1)	18.5

Source: Lloyds Banking Group annual and interim reports, author's analysis.

total assets shrank from £992bn to £925bn during this period, and RWAs dropped substantially, from £406bn to £310bn.

In 2011, Lloyds appointed a new CEO who initiated a major restructuring programme; many non-core assets were sold at a loss for 'capital accretion', meaning that the negative effect on capital ratios from a loss on disposal was outweighed by the positive effect on capital ratios from the risk-weighted assets that were taken off the Lloyds balance sheet. Many of the senior executives in the core businesses were replaced. One of the indications that the restructuring programme was having an effect was a drop in administrative expenses, from £10.8bn in 2010 to £10.3bn in 2011 and £9.6bn in 2012. (Note, however, there were significant 'fair value unwind' effects during this period.) Also, in 2011 and 2012, Lloyds recognised significant Other operating expense items, mainly related to customer rebates for the mis-selling of payment protection insurance.

The ROIC decomposition table for Lloyds sums it up:

RORWA has been negative since 2008, although in 2012 it was only -0.01%. In recent years, however, there has been a major reduction in capital leverage, with Lloyds' RWA/Invested Capital ratio falling from 5.1x in 2009 to 3.7x in 2012. This has helped to improve ROIC, from -13% in 2009 to -0.02% in 2012.

Interestingly, on a through-the-cycle basis (using the long-term average impairment charge to calculate ROIC instead of the charge in that period), Lloyds' ROIC would have been positive for most of the period, e.g. at 1.4% in 2012. This would indicate that as impairments 'normalise', we could expect Lloyds to return to profitability from a ROIC perspective.

Looking at the value levers for Lloyds, the drop in RWAs from 2010 onwards is significant; RWAs fell by 18% in 2010, 13% in 2011, and 12% in 2012. There also appeared to be a substantial shift in income; net interest income per RWA dropped from 3.1% in 2010 to 2.7% in 2012, whilst non-interest income per RWA increased from 2.1% to 3.4% in the same period.

Although administrative expenses fell in absolute terms from 2010 to 2012, on a per RWA basis there was actually an increase, from 2.4% in 2010 to 2.9% in 2012 as the decline in RWAs outpaced the drop in administrative expenses. Viewed on a per RWA basis, the mis-selling provisions in Other operating expenses were substantial, at 1.4% in 2011 and 1.3% in 2012. This was a key factor behind a jump in the cost–income ratio, from 52% in 2010 to 79% in 2012.

Looking at Lloyds' credit quality table, it is obvious by the jump in gross customer loans from £213bn at the end of 2007 to £705bn at the end of 2008 that the HBOS acquisition had a major impact on Lloyds'

Table 3.48 Lloyds: value levers

Value levers	2007	2008	2009	2010	2011	2012
RWA growth	**16.4%**	**–0.9%**	**–1.0%**	**–17.6%**	**–13.3%**	**–11.9%**
Net interest income/Average RWA	2.93%	3.02%	2.60%	3.10%	3.21%	2.73%
Non-interest income/Average RWA	2.49%	1.31%	1.79%	2.06%	2.35%	3.38%
Net fee & commission income/Average RWA	0.85%					0.99%
Net trading income/Average RWA	0.04%					4.02%
Other banking income/Average RWA						
Net insurance income growth in period						
Other operating income growth in period	98.4%	71.8%	35.4%	7.5%	–4.6%	–47.6%
Administrative expenses/Average RWA	–2.17%	–2.48%	–2.37%	–2.38%	–2.69%	–2.90%
Depreciation expenses/Average RWA						
Other operating expenses/Average RWA	0.00%	0.00%	–0.22%	–0.32%	–1.36%	–1.26%
Operating expenses/Average RWA	–2.57%	–2.48%	–2.60%	–2.70%	–4.05%	–4.80%
Cost:income ratio	**47.4%**	**57.3%**	**59.2%**	**52.3%**	**72.9%**	**78.5%**
Impairment charges/Average RWA	–0.85%	–3.02%	–4.90%	–2.89%	–2.57%	–1.55%
Interest coupon on subordinated debt	5.49%	5.97%	7.98%	5.43%	6.02%	7.49%
Income tax/Profit before tax	–21.6%	–0.6%	183.4%	–191.8%	–23.4%	135.6%
Statutory income tax rate	–30.0%	–28.5%	–28.0%	–28.0%	–26.5%	–24.5%

Source: Lloyds Banking Group annual and interim reports, author's analysis.

Table 3.49   Lloyds: credit quality

Asset quality	2007	2008	2009	2010	2011	2012
Impaired (non-performing) loans	8,899	31,304	58,833	64,606	60,269	46,293
Gross customer loans	212,652	704,910	660,004	626,378	595,443	540,071
Impairment provisions	5,781	14,152	25,988	29,635	27,718	21,772
Non-performing loans as % Gross customer loans	4.18%	4.44%	8.91%	10.31%	10.12%	8.57%
NPLs as % of RWAs	1.77%	6.28%	11.93%	15.90%	17.11%	14.92%
Provisioning coverage						
Impairment provisions/ NPLs	65.0%	45.2%	44.2%	45.9%	46.0%	47.0%
Impairment provisions/ RWA	1.15%	5.55%	6.70%	8.31%	8.46%	7.36%
Impairment charges/ Average RWA	−0.85%	−3.02%	−4.90%	−2.89%	−2.57%	−1.55%

Source: Lloyds Banking Group annual and interim reports, author's analysis.

balance sheet, operations, and – as the financial crisis deepened in 2009 – credit quality. Interestingly, in 2008 non-performing (or impaired) loans as a percentage of customer loans increased by far less as a percentage of customer loans (4.2% to 4.4%) than as a percentage of RWAs (from 1.8% to 6.3%); this implied that Lloyds and HBOS had quite different approaches to calculating their RWAs. By 2009, however, this discrepancy had reduced considerably.

As credit quality improved, Lloyds' impairment charges per RWA declined accordingly. For example, NPLs fell from 10.1% of gross customer loans at the end of 2011 to 8.6% by the end of 2012, and impairment charges per RWA correspondingly fell from 2.6% to 1.6% during that period. Looking ahead, one of the key questions when analysing Lloyds would be how long this improving trend would last – especially if interest rates in the UK were to begin to rise again. A large proportion of Lloyds' mortgage book is either interest-only mortgages or on tracker

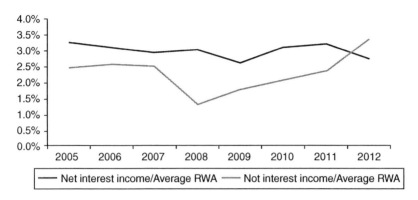

Figure 3.13   Lloyds: net interest income v. non-interest income per RWA, 2005–2012
Source: Lloyds Banking Group annual and interim reports, author's analysis.

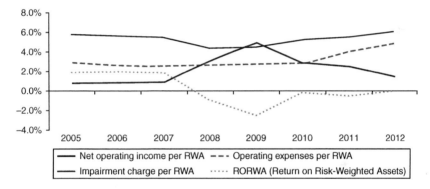

Figure 3.14   Lloyds: key value levers, 2005–2012
Source: Lloyds Banking Group annual and interim reports, author's analysis.

rates; both of these would be affected by higher rates, potentially lead-ing to another increase in, arrears and a reversal of, these impairment trends. On the other hand, if the rate environment were to remain at these extreme lows for another several years, non-performing loans could carry on trending downwards. Looking at the sheer quantum of non-performing (or impaired) loans, however – still at 8.6% of gross customer loans and £46bn at the end of 2012 – these improved impairment trends would have to carry on for several more years before Lloyds' non-perform-ing loans could be classified as 'performing' again.

With a slightly longer timeframe (using pro forma income statements and balance sheets that combined Lloyds and HBOS before the acquisi-tion), it appears that net interest income per RWA has been more sta-ble as an income contributor than non-interest income. The 2012 uptick in non-interest income per RWA appears to be the anomaly from this perspective.

Looking at key value levers in a longer timeframe, the jump in impairment charges per RWA in 2008–11 (with a super-peak in 2009) could be an anomaly, especially considering the sub-1% level of impairments per RWA prior to the financial crises.

Also, from our earlier analysis we know that the mis-selling provisions in Other operating expenses was a major factor behind the rise in operating expenses per RWA in 2011 and 2012. In our forecasts, we would take a view on whether these provisions are likely to continue at those levels. However, even if we were to take the view that other operating expenses per RWA are likely to drop, we would still need to take a view as to whether the recent increase in administrative expenses per RWA constituted a lasting trend.

In broad terms, the improvement in net operating income per RWA and falling impairment charges per RWA over the past few years appear to have been cancelled by rising operating expenses per RWA, leaving Lloyds with a slightly negative RORWA over the past few years. In terms of forecasts and valuations, the question is whether or not the trends in those value levers will continue.

Lloyds: forecasts and valuation

The usual caveat applies: In this text, our forecasts are merely indicative; we are showing how various assumptions and expectations translate into traditional earnings forecasts as well as our ROIC-based fundamental valuation.

For Lloyds, we think that the key value levers that would influence future profitability, and thus valuations are (1) operating expenses per RWA, including both administrative expenses and other operating expenses, and (2) impairment charges per RWA.

For operating expenses per RWA, we expect that although various regulatory charges will continue, it is likely that they will diminish from the substantial levels that were recorded in 2011 and 2012. It is the increasing trend in administrative expenses per RWA that is of greater concern; this trend could reverse itself if there is a significant time-lag element related to disposals and headcount reductions (in other words, some employee-related expenses could carry on for a while after the disposal of a unit), but if the trend was related to the recent shift to non-interest income versus net interest income per RWA and more costly non-interest income operating structures (for example, in investment banking), then we would assume that administrative expenses

Table 3.50 Lloyds: standard forecast and valuation ratios

Traditional valuation ratios	2010	2011	2012	2013E	2014E
Share price (GBp): 54					
Profit before tax, pre-exceptionals & FV	(2,056)	(4,011)	(778)	4,346	1,388
% growth year-on-year	−87.1%	95.1%	−80.6%	−658.6%	−68.1%
Net profit pre-exceptionals & FV	(1,827)	(2,983)	(1,518)	3,224	993
% growth year-on-year	−80.1%	63.3%	−49.1%	−312.4%	−69.2%
Adjusted EPS, fully-diluted	(2.7)	(4.4)	(2.2)	4.7	1.4
% growth year-on-year	−88.7%	60.1%	−49.3%	−312.4%	−69.2%
Adjusted P/E	**(19.8)**	**(12.4)**	**(24.5)**	**11.5**	**37.4**
Dividends per share	–	–	–	–	–
% growth year-on-year	0.0%	0.0%	0.0%	0.0%	0.0%
Dividend yield	0.0%	0.0%	0.0%	0.0%	0.0%
Dividend payout ratio	0.0%	0.0%	0.0%	0.0%	0.0%
ROE	−0.7%	−6.1%	−3.2%	7.5%	1.8%
P/BVPS multiple	**0.80**	**0.81**	**0.84**	**0.83**	**0.81**
Book value per share	68	67	64	65	66
% growth in period	−0.3%	−1.3%	−4.2%	1.9%	1.9%
Balance sheet goodwill	5,512	5,212	5,212	5,212	5,212
Tangible shareholders' equity	40,549	40,708	38,787	39,622	40,458
Tangible book value per share (GBp)	60	59	56	58	59
Price/Tangible BVPS multiple (x)	**0.91**	**0.91**	**0.96**	**0.94**	**0.92**

Source: Lloyds Banking Group annual and interim reports, author's analysis.

per RWA would continue to rise. In our forecasts, we have assumed a bit of both; thus, administrative expenses per RWA are expected to remain roughly flat.

For impairment expenses per RWA, we have assumed that they continue to trend downwards. Although we do not expect a strong recovery in the UK macroeconomic environment, nor do we expect another collapse; implicit in our forecasts is the assumption that house prices remain relatively stable for the next few years.

Table 3.51   Lloyds: fundamental ROIC valuation

Fundamental valuation	2010	2011	2012	2013E	2014E
Value-Added Margin in period	–11.28%	–11.52%	–9.41%	–3.37%	–5.83%
Through-the-cycle Value-Added Margin	–4.91%	–7.72%	–7.98%	–4.57%	–7.05%
Invested Capital growth pa (next 10 years)	0.0%	0.0%	0.0%	0.0%	0.0%
Terminal Value-Added Margin assumption	5.74%	–3.57%	1.18%	0.00%	0.00%
Assumed continuing growth of Value Added	0.0%	0.0%	0.0%	0.0%	0.0%
Invested Capital (beginning of period)	98,597	100,584	94,646	84,221	81,452
PV of Value Created/ (Destroyed) in forecast period	740	(34,584)	(20,591)	(12,196)	(18,101)
PV of Continuing Value	(89)	530	(128)	–	–
Total firm value	99,248	66,530	73,927	72,025	63,350
Less: Debt Capital	(36,232)	(35,089)	(34,092)	(34,777)	(34,085)
Less: Equity Adjustments	(18,291)	(13,637)	(6,130)	(1,841)	1,630
Target Equity Value	**44,725**	**17,804**	**33,705**	**35,406**	**30,896**
Market Capitalisation (end of period)	44,725	17,804	33,705	37,113	37,113
Target Equity Value per share	0.67	0.26	0.49	0.52	0.45

Source: Lloyds Banking Group annual and interim reports, author's analysis.

The bottom line is that we expect Lloyds will return to profitability in 2013, on both a statutory basis and on a ROIC basis. We also expect that with this return to relative normalcy (and the declining balance of fair value items) the statutory financial statements will become more usable.

Our indicative forecast for Lloyds is below:

Our indicative valuation for Lloyds, based on the assumptions outlined above, is below:

Note that although we forecast a return to a positive ROIC, we continue to expect that Lloyds' ROIC will remain below its WACC – leading to expected negative Value-Added Margins of -3% for 2013 and -6% for 2014.

If we look at the implied market expectations of terminal (10 years onwards) value-added margins for Lloyds, we estimate that the market expected that Lloyds' profitability would improve substantially over the next decade, from -9% in 2012 to +1%, based on Lloyds' equity valuation at the end of 2012. Looking back, these implied market expectations of long-term profitability swung around in a wide range, from a terminal value-added margin of +5.7% at the end of 2010 to -3.6% at the end of 2011.

We decided to use a terminal value-added of 0% in our fundamental valuation for Lloyds. Our main assumptions behind this were that although impairment charges should fall back to the long term through-the-cycle average as the macroeconomic environment normalised, it would be difficult to cut operating expenses much further, especially if Lloyds were to continue to shift towards sources of non-interest income that had higher operating cost structures.

Putting these forecasts and assumptions into our fundamental ROIC valuation model produced a share price target of 52p for the end of 2013 and a target of 45p for the end of 2014.

8. RBS

Background

RBS has over 30 million customers worldwide, with operations in the UK, the U.S., Europe and Asia. The Group offers retail and business banking, corporate banking and some investment banking and insurance services.

In 2007 and 2008, RBS acquired much of the U.S. and UK operations of ABN AMRO; in 2008 and 2009, the enlarged group began a major restructuring, where virtually the entire management team and board were replaced, and many businesses were either sold or closed. The new

Table 3.52   RBS: standardised financials

(In £ millions)	2007	2008	2009	2010	2011	2012
Net interest income	12,382	18,675	13,388	14,209	12,679	11,402
Net fee and commission income	7,024	7,445	5,948	5,982	4,924	4,875
Net trading income	3,540	(8,477)	3,761	4,517	2,701	1,675
Other banking income	2,300	2,148	1,563	1,959	2,251	2,081
Net insurance income	1,641	1,844	1,065	435	1,275	1
Other operating income	430	(370)	(410)	(197)	254	172
Subtotal non-interest income	14,935	2,590	11,927	12,696	11,405	8,804
Net operating income	27,317	21,265	25,315	26,905	24,084	20,206
Administrative expenses	(11,154)	(13,003)	(11,757)	(12,073)	(11,129)	(10,308)
Depreciation and amortisation	(1,697)	(3,154)	(1,873)	(2,150)	(1,875)	(1,802)
Other operating expenses	(3,767)	(5,464)	(3,979)	(3,995)	(4,931)	(5,593)
Operating expenses	(16,618)	(21,621)	(17,609)	(18,218)	(17,935)	(17,703)
Trading surplus	10,699	(356)	7,706	8,687	6,149	2,503
Impairment charges	(2,104)	(8,072)	(13,899)	(9,256)	(8,709)	(5,279)
Operating profit (pre-goodwill)	8,595	(8,428)	(6,193)	(569)	(2,560)	(2,776)
Goodwill impairment	–	(32,581)	–	(10)	(91)	(124)
Operating profit	8,595	(41,009)	(6,193)	(579)	(2,651)	(2,900)
Fair value gains/(losses) on own debt	–	977	51	249	1,621	(2,836)
Changes in fair value of financial assets	318	(1,816)	(75)	(585)	11	(7)
Income from associates and JVs	66	69	(268)	70	26	29
Exceptional items	309	4,914	3,574	418	274	377
Profit before tax	9,288	(36,865)	(2,911)	(427)	(719)	(5,337)
Income tax	(1,709)	2,323	339	(663)	(1,250)	(469)
Net profit	7,579	(34,542)	(2,572)	(1,090)	(1,969)	(5,806)
Minority interests (non-equity)	(184)	10,832	(648)	(61)	(28)	123
Minority interests (equity)	–	–	–	–	–	–
Preference dividends	(246)	(596)	(935)	(124)	–	(288)
Net profit attributable to equity shareholders	7,149	(24,306)	(4,155)	(1,275)	(1,997)	(5,971)
Dividends declared (not IFRS format)	(3,873)	–	–	–	–	–
Retained earnings	3,276	(24,306)	(4,155)	(1,275)	(1,997)	(5,971)
Risk-weighted assets (RWA), end of period	486,100	577,800	438,200	462,600	439,000	459,600
RWA growth in period	8.4%	18.9%	−24.2%	5.6%	−5.1%	4.7%
Period average RWAs	470,260	511,825	527,650	462,150	442,150	442,000
Total assets	1,595,066	2,218,693	1,522,481	1,452,634	1,506,867	1,312,295
RWA/Assets	30%	26%	29%	32%	29%	35%

Source: RBS annual and interim reports, author's analysis.

Table 3.53 RBS: ROIC decomposition

ROIC-based ratios	2007	2008	2009	2010	2011	2012
Return on risk-weighted assets (RORWA)	1.69%	−0.73%	−1.03%	−0.14%	−0.37%	−1.26%
x Avg RWA/Avg Invested Capital	4.6	4.2	3.3	2.8	2.7	2.7
= Return on Invested Capital(ROIC)	7.8%	−3.1%	−3.4%	−0.4%	−1.0%	−3.4%
NB: Core Equity Tier 1 ratio	0.0%	0.0%	11.0%	10.7%	10.6%	10.3%
NB: Debt Capital/ Invested Capital	43%	43%	26%	21%	19%	21%
- WACC	6.3%	6.0%	10.5%	10.8%	10.7%	9.8%
= Value-Added Margin	1.5%	−9.1%	−13.9%	−11.2%	−11.7%	−13.2%
Through-the-cycle ROIC	4.9%	4.6%	0.9%	2.1%	1.9%	−1.9%
- WACC	6.3%	6.0%	10.5%	10.8%	10.7%	9.8%
= Through-the-cycle Value-Added Margin	−1.4%	−1.4%	−9.6%	−8.7%	−8.7%	−11.6%
ROIC/WACC	1.2	(0.5)	(0.3)	(0.0)	(0.1)	(0.4)
Enterprise Value/ Invested Capital	0.9	0.5	0.4	0.5	0.3	0.4
EBITDA	11,876	(2,084)	(3,245)	2,317	1,702	(2,966)
EBITDA growth in period	−4%	−118%	56%	−171%	−27%	−274%
EV/EBITDA, period average	7.3	(44.0)	(23.5)	33.1	31.8	(23.5)

management team expects to have largely completed the restructuring by 2015.

Analysis

In the standardised financials for RBS have used pro forma financial statements reflecting the ABN AMRO acquisition. Even on a pro forma basis, the change from 2007 to 2008 was stark: RBS went from a £7bn net profit in 2007 to a £24bn loss in 2008, RWAs jumped from £486bn to £578bn during that same period (largely because the risk weightings on many assets had jumped), and net operating income fell from £27bn to £21bn as net trading income swung from +£3.5bn to -£8.5bn. After the new management team and board were appointed in 2009, an aggressive programme of disposals cut total assets from £1.5 trillion at the end of 2009 to £1.2 trillion at the end of 2012 – but increasing risk weights meant that RWAs actually increased in that same period, from £438bn to £460bn. From 2009 through 2012, net operating income declined from £25bn to £20bn, whilst operating expenses stayed relatively flat, at circa £18bn. Operating profits were thus highly exposed to impairment charges, which reduced from £14bn in 2009 to £5bn in 2012.

ROIC decomposition

Looking at RBS' ROIC decomposition table, the swing from a positive RORWA of 1.7% in 2007 to -1.3% in 2012 catches the eye. The major reduction in capital leverage does as well, with RBS' RWA/Invested Capital ratio falling from 4.6x in 2007 and 4.2x in 2008, to 2.8x by 2010 and edging further down to 2.7x in 2011 and 2012.

In other words, although the negative RORWAs must have been painful, RBS' capital ratios actually looked reasonably robust. A cross-check with the Core Equity Tier 1 ratio (at 10–11%) confirms this. The comparatively low Debt Capital/Invested Capital ratio of 21% by 2012 gives further reassurance that RBS' capital structure is actually reasonably robust.

Remembering that RBS' RWA/Assets ratio is relatively low, at 35% at the end of 2012, we would look out for potential weakening of capital ratios (and increasing of capital leverage ratios) as Basel 3 and other rules on RWA calculations are finalised, but it is obvious that the main driver behind the weak ROICs over the past few years has been the weak RORWAs. Accordingly, we would focus our analysis on judging whether or not a recovery in RORWAs were possible.

RORWA and value levers analyses

Combining the declining top-line income with rising RWAs meant that on an RORWA basis, there was significant margin compression. Although net interest income per RWA remained reasonably robust at 2.5–3.1% during the period, non-interest income per RWA fell from 2.3% in 2009 to 2.0% in 2012. And although administrative expenses per RWA were controlled relatively well, running from 2.2% in 2009 up to 2.6% in 2010 but then falling back to 2.3% in 2012, Other operating expenses per RWA rose from 0.8% in 2009 to 1.3% in 2012, driving total operating expenses per RWA up from 3.3% in 2009 to 4.0% in 2012. As a result of the above, trading surplus (pre-impairment) per RWA fell from 1.5% in 2009 to 0.6% in 2012. And although impairment charges per RWA dropped from 2.6% in 2009 to 1.2% in 2012, this still kept RBS loss-making, with an operating loss per RWA of -1.2% in 2009 shrinking to a -0.7% in 2012.

Table 3.54 RBS: RORWA analysis

Performance per risk-weighted asset	2007	2008	2009	2010	2011	2012
Net interest income	2.63%	3.65%	2.54%	3.07%	2.87%	2.58%
Net fee and commission income	1.49%	1.45%	1.13%	1.29%	1.11%	1.10%
Net trading income	0.75%	−1.66%	0.71%	0.98%	0.61%	0.38%
Other banking income	0.49%	0.42%	0.30%	0.42%	0.51%	0.47%
Net insurance income	0.35%	0.36%	0.20%	0.09%	0.29%	0.00%
Other operating income	0.09%	−0.07%	−0.08%	−0.04%	0.06%	0.04%
Subtotal non-interest income	3.18%	0.51%	2.26%	2.75%	2.58%	1.99%
Net operating income	5.81%	4.15%	4.80%	5.82%	5.45%	4.57%
–	0.00%	0.00%	0.00%	0.00%	0.00%	0.00%
Administrative expenses	−2.37%	−2.54%	−2.23%	−2.61%	−2.52%	−2.33%
Depreciation and amortisation	−0.36%	−0.62%	−0.35%	−0.47%	−0.42%	−0.41%
Other operating expenses	−0.80%	−1.07%	−0.75%	−0.86%	−1.12%	−1.27%
Operating expenses	−3.53%	−4.22%	−3.34%	−3.94%	−4.06%	−4.01%
Trading surplus	2.28%	−0.07%	1.46%	1.88%	1.39%	0.57%
Impairment charges	−0.45%	−1.58%	−2.63%	−2.00%	−1.97%	−1.19%
Operating profit (pre-goodwill)	1.83%	−1.65%	−1.17%	−0.12%	−0.58%	−0.63%
Goodwill impairment	0.00%	−6.37%	0.00%	0.00%	−0.02%	−0.03%
Operating profit	1.83%	−8.01%	−1.17%	−0.13%	−0.60%	−0.66%
Fair value gains/ (losses) on own debt	0.00%	0.00%	0.00%	0.00%	0.00%	0.00%
Changes in fair value of financial assets	0.07%	−0.35%	−0.01%	−0.13%	0.00%	0.00%
Income from associates and JVs	0.01%	0.01%	−0.05%	0.02%	0.01%	0.01%
Exceptional items	0.07%	0.96%	0.68%	0.09%	0.06%	0.09%
Profit before tax	1.98%	−7.20%	−0.55%	−0.09%	−0.16%	−1.21%
Income tax	−0.36%	0.45%	0.06%	−0.14%	−0.28%	−0.11%
Net profit	1.61%	−6.75%	−0.49%	−0.24%	−0.45%	−1.31%
Minority interests (non-equity)	−0.04%	2.12%	−0.12%	−0.01%	−0.01%	0.03%
Minority interests (equity)	0.00%	0.00%	0.00%	0.00%	0.00%	0.00%
Preference dividends	−0.05%	−0.12%	−0.18%	−0.03%	0.00%	−0.07%
Net profit attributable to equity shareholders	1.52%	−4.75%	−0.79%	−0.28%	−0.45%	−1.35%

Source: RBS annual and interim reports, author's analysis.

Table 3.55 RBS: value levers analysis

Value Levers	2007	2008	2009	2010	2011	2012
RWA growth	**8.4%**	**18.9%**	**−24.2%**	**5.6%**	**−5.1%**	**4.7%**
Net interest income/ Average RWA	2.63%	3.65%	2.54%	3.07%	2.87%	2.58%
Non-interest income/ Average RWA	3.18%	0.51%	2.26%	2.75%	2.58%	1.99%
Net fee and commission income/Average RWA	1.49%	1.45%	1.13%	1.29%	1.11%	1.10%
Net trading income/ Average RWA	0.75%	−1.66%	0.71%	0.98%	0.61%	0.38%
Other banking income/Average RWA	0.49%	0.42%	0.30%	0.42%	0.51%	0.47%
Net insurance income growth in period	8.3%	12.4%	−42.2%	−59.2%	193.1%	−99.9%
Other operating income growth in period	−87.2%	−186.0%	10.8%	−52.0%	−228.9%	−32.3%
Administrative expenses/Average RWA	−2.37%	−2.54%	−2.23%	−2.61%	−2.52%	−2.33%
Depreciation expenses/Average RWA	−0.36%	−0.62%	−0.35%	−0.47%	−0.42%	−0.41%
Other operating expenses/Average RWA	−0.80%	−1.07%	−0.75%	−0.86%	−1.12%	−1.27%
Operating expenses/ Average RWA	−3.53%	−4.22%	−3.34%	−3.94%	−4.06%	−4.01%
Cost:income ratio	**60.8%**	**101.7%**	**69.6%**	**67.7%**	**74.5%**	**87.6%**
Impairment charges/ Average RWA	−0.45%	−1.58%	−2.63%	−2.00%	−1.97%	−1.19%

Source: RBS annual and interim reports, author's analysis.

RBS' Value Levers table distils the RORWA analysis into fewer line items. It also shows that despite major achievements in its restructuring, RBS' cost–income ratio remains stubbornly high (at 88% for 2012, for example), because of both a weaker top-line income per RWA and stubbornly high operating expenses per RWA.

Going into more detail on RBS' credit quality, we can see that impaired loans (or NPLs) rose by more than 6x from the end of 2007 (when NPLs/ Gross customer loans stood at 1.47%) to the end of 2012 (when it was

Table 3.56 RBS: credit quality

Asset quality	2007	2008	2009	2010	2011	2012
Impaired (non-performing) loans	8,251	18,791	34,989	38,598	40,845	41,140
Gross customer loans	563,028	701,200	569,670	520,803	473,872	453,099
Impairment provisions	4,953	9,324	15,173	18,055	19,883	21,148
Non-performing loans as % Gross customer loans	1.47%	2.68%	6.14%	7.41%	8.62%	9.08%
NPLs as % of RWAs	1.70%	3.25%	7.98%	8.34%	9.30%	8.95%
Provisioning coverage						
Impairment provisions/NPLs	60.0%	49.6%	43.4%	46.8%	48.7%	51.4%
Impairment provisions/RWA	**1.02%**	**1.61%**	**3.46%**	**3.90%**	4.53%	4.60%
Impairment charges/Average RWA	–0.45%	–1.58%	–2.63%	–2.00%	–1.97%	–1.19%

Source: RBS annual and interim reports, author's analysis.

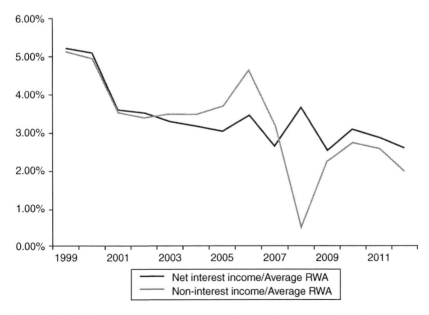

Figure 3.15 RBS: net interest income v. non-interest income per RWA, 1999–2012
Source: RBS annual and interim reports, author's analysis.

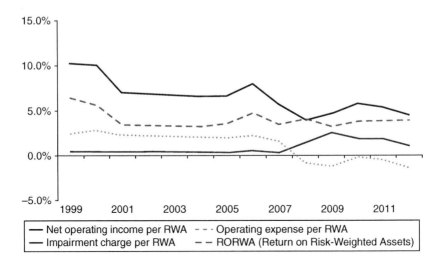

Figure 3.16   RBS: key value levers
Source: RBS annual and interim reports, author's analysis.

9.08%). Note that there was less of an increase in NPLs as a percentage of RWAs (from 1.70% to 8.95%) – this was because as loans became non-performing, their risk weights increased significantly.

What is interesting is that impairment charges per RWA have come down even whilst the percentage of NPLs continued to rise – and even whilst provisioning coverage ratios (impairment provisions/NPLs) have improved. If provisioning coverage had decreased, we would be concerned by this seeming discrepancy, but because provisioning coverage levels have actually risen, we are willing to accept that the trends in impairment charges are really improving at RBS.

Looking at selected value levers for RBS over a longer timeframe, the decline in net operating income per RWA becomes quite clear. Most of the decline appears to be driven by a weakening in non-interest income per RWA, though; RBS' net interest income per RWA appears to have held up relatively well, even though there was some volatility in the rocky 2007–09 period.

Looking at selected value levers on a longer timeframe, it appears that net operating income per RWA has trended downwards for over a decade, whilst operating expenses per RWA have remained relatively flat. This has meant that trading surplus per RWA was under constant pressure, and was in particular exposed to the spike in impairment charges per RWA in 2009 (and its relatively slow recovery since then). The bottom line is that RORWA remained negative from 2008 through 2012.

From a forecast perspective, however, knowing that RBS intends to divest itself of several more key businesses over the next few years

Table 3.57 RBS: standard forecast and valuation ratios

Traditional valuation ratios	2010	2011	2012	2013E	2014E
Share price (GBp): 290.00					
Profit before tax pre-exceptionals & FV	(499)	(2,534)	(2,747)	1,038	3,949
% growth year-on-year	−92.3%	407.8%	8.4%	−137.8%	280.6%
Net profit pre-exceptionals and FV	(1,394)	(3,736)	(3,290)	651	2,959
% growth year-on-year	−79.3%	168.1%	−11.9%	−119.8%	354.4%
Adjusted EPS, fully-diluted	(13.0)	(34.5)	(30.2)	5.9	26.8
% growth year-on-year	−89.8%	165.7%	−12.7%	−119.6%	354.4%
Adjusted P/E	**(22.3)**	**(8.4)**	**(9.6)**	**49.1**	**10.8**
Dividends per share	–	–	–	–	–
% growth year-on-year	0.0%	0.0%	0.0%	0.0%	0.0%
Dividend yield	0.0%	0.0%	0.0%	0.0%	0.0%
Dividend payout ratio	0.0%	0.0%	0.0%	0.0%	0.0%
ROE	−1.8%	−2.8%	−8.9%	1.0%	4.5%
P/BVPS multiple	**0.44**	**0.45**	**0.50**	**0.50**	**0.48**
Book value per share	656	648	581	581	608
% growth in period	−50.3%	−1.3%	−10.3%	0.0%	4.6%
Balance sheet goodwill	14,448	14,592	14,592	14,592	14,592
Tangible shareholders' equity	55,940	55,483	48,794	49,445	52,404
Tangible book value per share (GBp)	5,210	503	443	449	475
Price/Tangible BVPS multiple (x)	**0.06**	**0.58**	**0.66**	**0.65**	**0.61**

Source: RBS annual and interim reports, author's analysis.

(e.g. the remaining Direct Line insurance business, the Williams & Glyn's UK retail/SME branches, Citizens Bank in the US), we could expect significant capital relief as RWAs are sold off, as well as off-loading of some major operating expenses. A reduction in RWAs, coupled with a reduction in operating expenses per RWA and falling impairment charges per RWA, could result in a return to positive RORWAs as early as 2013.

Forecasts and valuation

With the usual caveat that these are only indicative forecasts, we have assumed that RBS does continue with its restructuring/disposal programmes, thereby reducing operating expenses per RWA and getting some capital relief from the sale of RWAs. We also assume that the impairments

Table 3.58   RBS: fundamental ROIC valuation

Fundamental valuation	2010	2011	2012	2013E	2014E
Value-Added Margin in period	–11.18%	–11.66%	–13.20%	–9.08%	–7.70%
Through-the-cycle Value-Added Margin	–8.66%	–8.74%	–11.63%	–9.08%	–8.23%
Invested Capital growth pa (next 10 years)	0.0%	0.0%	0.0%	0.0%	0.0%
Terminal Value-Added Margin assumption	1.03%	–0.25%	2.84%	1.00%	1.00%
Assumed continuing growth of Value Added	1.0%	1.0%	1.0%	1.0%	1.0%
Invested Capital (beginning of period)	171,939	164,344	163,869	161,759	160,209
PV of Value Created/ (Destroyed) in forecast period	(40,900)	(46,934)	(48,079)	(43,038)	(37,904)
PV of Continuing Value	5,682	(1,372)	18,833	6,467	6,285
Total firm value	136,721	116,038	134,623	125,188	128,589
Less: Debt Capital	(33,887)	(31,866)	(33,404)	(34,373)	(33,012)
Less: Equity Adjustments	(60,069)	(61,928)	(64,969)	(61,799)	(58,362)
Target Equity Value	**42,765**	**22,244**	**36,250**	**29,017**	**37,216**
Market Capitalisation (end of period)	42,765	22,244	36,250	31,966	31,966
Target Equity Value per share	3.99	2.06	3.32	2.63	3.38

Source: RBS annual and interim reports, author's analysis.

charges per RWA do continue to improve, albeit at a slow pace given weak macro recoveries.

Putting these together, we get a forecasted return to profit for RBS in 2013. By 2014, our indicative forecasts produce an ROE of 4.5% – still below WACC, but vastly better than showing an operating loss.

Running our fundamental ROIC valuation backwards to derive the implicit market expectation for RBS' terminal value-added margin, we can infer that the market was expecting the RBS would generate a terminal value-added margin of 1.0% in 2010 – in other words, in ten years' time, RBS' ROIC would be 1.0% higher than its WACC. By the end of 2011, based on the closing share price, the market's expectations for a terminal value-added margin had fallen back, to -0.3%, but by the end of 2012, the implied market assumption for terminal value-added margin had increased to 2.8%. All of these implied market expectations for value-added margins were far higher than the actual value-added margins in that period; for example, the value-added margin in 2012 was -13%.

In our indicative ROIC valuation for RBS, we have used a terminal value-added margin assumption of 1.0%. This results in a target equity value per share of 263p for the end of 2013, and an end-2014 target valuation of 338p.

9. Standard Chartered

Background

Standard Chartered offers retail and business banking, trade finance, corporate and investment banking, and wealth management. It has 89,000 employees in 68 markets, with a footprint mainly in the developing markets of Asia, Africa, and the Middle East.

Analysis

Looking at its standardised performance summary for 2007–12, what is apparent in Standard Chartered's results is the steady growth in net operating income – and the growth in net profit – throughout a period when most other banks had wide swings in income and profitability. The operating profit line item – which excludes changes in fair value of own debt and other fair value changes – showed steady growth from 2007 until 2012, when administrative expenses jumped from $9.3bn to $10.2bn, largely because of $0.7bn in regulatory fines associated with past violations of U.S. anti-Iranian banking rules.

Besides those fines, the other line item that was quite volatile was the impairment charge, which more than doubled from $0.8bn in 2007 to $1.8bn in 2008, and then peaked at $2.1bn in 2009, dipped to $1.0bn in 2010 and then climbed back up to $1.4bn in 2012. Given the volatility of the impairment charge line item, the relatively lower volatility of the operating profit line item is quite impressive, indicating an ability to re-price and reposition the loan book quickly in order to adapt to changes in the credit environment.

It is also worth noting that Standard Chartered's RWA intensity (its RWA/Assets ratio) of 43–52% is higher than the 25–40% with many other banks. We think this is a reflection of Standard Chartered's bias towards trade finance, business lending, and other lending areas that carry higher risk weightings.

Looking at Standard Chartered's ROIC decomposition table, it seems clear that the consistency of strong RORWA and capital leverage (RWA/Invested Capital) ratios have delivered a consistently strong ROIC. As

Table 3.59   Standard Chartered: standardised financials

Performance summary	2007	2008	2009	2010	2011	2012
Net interest income	6,265	7,387	7,623	8,470	10,153	11,010
Net fee and commission income	2,661	2,941	3,370	4,238	4,046	4,121
Net trading income	1,254	2,373	2,798	2,390	3,031	2,775
Other banking income	–	–	–	–	–	–
Net insurance income	–	–	–	–	–	–
Other operating income	880	1,235	1,301	777	793	1,192
Subtotal non-interest income	4,795	6,549	7,469	7,405	7,870	8,088
Net operating income	11,060	13,936	15,092	15,875	18,023	19,098
Administrative expenses	(5,870)	(7,186)	(7,432)	(8,464)	(9,296)	(10,228)
Depreciation and amortisation	(345)	(425)	(520)	(559)	(621)	(668)
Other operating expenses	–	–	–	–	–	–
Operating expenses	(6,215)	(7,611)	(7,952)	(9,023)	(9,917)	(10,896)
Trading surplus	4,845	6,325	7,140	6,852	8,106	8,202
Impairment charges	(818)	(1,790)	(2,102)	(959)	(1,019)	(1,415)
Operating profit (pre-goodwill)	4,027	4,535	5,038	5,893	7,087	6,787
Goodwill impairment	–	–	–	–	–	–
Operating profit	4,027	4,535	5,038	5,893	7,087	6,787
Fair value gains/(losses) on own debt	(37)	(118)	70	(14)	(438)	(256)
Changes in fair value of financial assets	44	150	22	201	52	229
Income from associates and JVs	1	1	21	42	74	116
Exceptional items	–	233	–	–	–	–
Profit before tax	4,035	4,801	5,151	6,122	6,775	6,876
Income tax	(1,046)	(1,290)	(1,674)	(1,708)	(1,842)	(1,891)
Net profit	2,989	3,511	3,477	4,414	4,933	4,985
Minority interests (non-equity)	–	–	–	–	–	–
Minority interests (equity)	(148)	(103)	(97)	(82)	(84)	(98)
Preference dividends	–	–	–	–	–	0
Net profit attributable to equity shareholders	2,841	3,408	3,380	4,332	4,849	4,887
Dividends declared (not IFRS format)	(1,117)	(1,165)	(1,329)	(1,570)	(1,802)	(2,016)
Retained earnings	1,724	2,243	2,051	2,762	3,047	2,871
Risk-weighted assets (RWA), end of period	171,833	188,821	213,923	245,077	270,690	301,861
RWA growth in period	12.0%	9.9%	13.3%	14.6%	10.5%	11.5%
Period average RWAs	160,942	195,724	203,194	231,842	260,086	286,297
Total assets	329,871	435,068	436,653	516,560	599,070	636,518
RWA/Assets	52%	43%	49%	47%	45%	47%

Source: Standard Chartered annual and interim reports, author's analysis.

Table 3.60 Standard Chartered: ROIC decomposition

ROIC-based ratios	2007	2008	2009	2010	2011	2012
Return on risk-weighted assets (RORWA)	2.18%	1.97%	2.00%	2.05%	2.10%	1.87%
x Avg RWA/Avg Invested Capital	4.4	4.7	4.6	4.8	4.5	4.6
= Return on Invested Capital (ROIC)	9.7%	9.2%	9.2%	9.8%	9.4%	8.6%
NB: Core Equity Tier 1 ratio	0.0%	7.5%	8.9%	11.8%	11.8%	11.7%
NB: Debt Capital/ Invested Capital	46%	48%	38%	29%	29%	29%
– WACC	6.9%	6.7%	8.0%	8.4%	8.1%	7.4%
= Value-Added Margin	2.8%	2.6%	1.2%	1.4%	1.3%	1.2%
Through-the-cycle ROIC	8.1%	9.1%	10.1%	8.3%	8.0%	7.8%
– WACC	6.9%	6.7%	8.0%	8.4%	8.1%	7.4%
= Through-the-cycle Value-Added Margin	1.2%	2.4%	2.1%	–0.1%	–0.2%	0.4%
ROIC/WACC	1.4	1.4	1.1	1.2	1.2	1.2
Enterprise Value/ Invested Capital	2.2	1.0	1.5	1.4	1.2	1.2
EBITDA	5,147	5,892	6,523	7,253	8,186	8,186
EBITDA growth in period	26%	14%	11%	11%	13%	0%
EV/EBITDA, period average	17.0	7.5	10.5	11.0	8.5	9.9

Source: Standard Chartered annual and interim reports, author's analysis.

described in an earlier section, we think that the markets tend to reward well-capitalised banks that produce consistently strong returns with lower funding costs, both in terms of debt capital and in terms of lower equity betas. This tends to result in significantly lower WACCs. In other words, these may be the dynamics of how valuation premiums are developed.

This is an opportune moment to discuss another valuation metric that ROIC can use – ROIC/WACC versus Enterprise Value/Invested Capital comparisons. In our experience, this tends to be a decent ready reckoner for valuations: a listed company's ROIC/WACC multiple usually roughly matches its Enterprise Value/Invested Capital multiple. The problem for banks has been how debt capital and thus Enterprise Value and Invested Capital can be calculated; the ROIC for Banks methodology addresses those problems.

Table 3.61   Standard Chartered: RORWA analysis

Performance per risk-weighted asset	2007	2008	2009	2010	2011	2012
Net interest income	3.89%	3.77%	3.75%	3.65%	3.90%	3.85%
Net fee and commission income	1.65%	1.50%	1.66%	1.83%	1.56%	1.44%
Net trading income	0.78%	1.21%	1.38%	1.03%	1.17%	0.97%
Other banking income	0.00%	0.00%	0.00%	0.00%	0.00%	0.00%
Net insurance income	0.00%	0.00%	0.00%	0.00%	0.00%	0.00%
Other operating income	0.55%	0.63%	0.64%	0.34%	0.30%	0.42%
Subtotal non-interest income	2.98%	3.35%	3.68%	3.19%	3.03%	2.83%
Net operating income	6.87%	7.12%	7.43%	6.85%	6.93%	6.67%
Administrative expenses	−3.65%	−3.67%	−3.66%	−3.65%	−3.57%	−3.57%
Depreciation and amortisation	−0.21%	−0.22%	−0.26%	−0.24%	−0.24%	−0.23%
Other operating expenses	0.00%	0.00%	0.00%	0.00%	0.00%	0.00%
Operating expenses	−3.86%	−3.89%	−3.91%	−3.89%	−3.81%	−3.81%
Trading surplus	3.01%	3.23%	3.51%	2.96%	3.12%	2.86%
Impairment charges	−0.51%	−0.91%	−1.03%	−0.41%	−0.39%	−0.49%
Operating profit (pre-goodwill)	2.50%	2.32%	2.48%	2.54%	2.72%	2.37%
Goodwill impairment	0.00%	0.00%	0.00%	0.00%	0.00%	0.00%
Operating profit	2.50%	2.32%	2.48%	2.54%	2.72%	2.37%
Fair value gains/ (losses) on own debt	0.00%	0.00%	0.00%	0.00%	0.00%	0.00%
Changes in fair value of financial assets	0.03%	0.08%	0.01%	0.09%	0.02%	0.08%
Income from associates and JVs	0.00%	0.00%	0.01%	0.02%	0.03%	0.04%
Exceptional items	0.00%	0.12%	0.00%	0.00%	0.00%	0.00%
Profit before tax	2.51%	2.45%	2.54%	2.64%	2.60%	2.40%
Income tax	−0.65%	−0.66%	−0.82%	−0.74%	−0.71%	−0.66%
Net profit	1.86%	1.79%	1.71%	1.90%	1.90%	1.74%
Minority interests (non-equity)	0.00%	0.00%	0.00%	0.00%	0.00%	0.00%
Minority interests (equity)	−0.09%	−0.05%	−0.05%	−0.04%	−0.03%	−0.03%
Preference dividends	0.00%	0.00%	0.00%	0.00%	0.00%	0.00%
Net profit attributable to equity shareholders	1.77%	1.74%	1.66%	1.87%	1.86%	1.71%

Source: Standard Chartered annual and interim reports, author's analysis.

EV/EBITDA multiples can be created for the banks as well; this tends to be a comparative valuation tool rather than a fundamental valuation model that gives a set of bottom-up price targets, however.

Looking at our RORWA table for Standard Chartered, however, and seeing that net profit per RWA has been consistently strong (at 1.7–1.9%), we would not view the higher RWA intensity as a concern; rather, we would regard this as an indicator that Standard Chartered's business model does differ from those of many other banks.

The Value Levers table helps to distil the RORWA analysis. Standard Chartered RWA's growth is much higher than that of its UK-listed peers – but the more valid comparison is probably with other emerging markets

Table 3.62 Standard Chartered: value levers

Value Levers	2007	2008	2009	2010	2011	2012
RWA growth	**12.0%**	**9.9%**	**13.3%**	**14.6%**	**10.5%**	**11.5%**
Net interest income/ Average RWA	3.89%	3.77%	3.75%	3.65%	3.90%	3.85%
Non-interest income/ Average RWA	2.98%	3.35%	3.68%	3.19%	3.03%	2.83%
Net fee & commission income/Average RWA	1.65%	1.50%	1.66%	1.83%	1.56%	1.44%
Net trading income/ Average RWA	0.78%	1.21%	1.38%	1.03%	1.17%	0.97%
Other banking income/Average RWA	0.00%	0.00%	0.00%	0.00%	0.00%	0.00%
Net insurance income growth in period						
Other operating income growth in period	79.2%	40.3%	5.3%	−40.3%	2.1%	50.3%
Administrative expenses/Average RWA	−3.65%	−3.67%	−3.66%	−3.65%	−3.57%	−3.57%
Depreciation expenses/ Average RWA	−0.21%	−0.22%	−0.26%	−0.24%	−0.24%	−0.23%
Other operating expenses/Average RWA	0.00%	0.00%	0.00%	0.00%	0.00%	0.00%
Operating expenses/ Average RWA	−3.86%	−3.89%	−3.91%	−3.89%	−3.81%	−3.81%
Cost:income ratio	**56.2%**	**54.6%**	**52.7%**	**56.8%**	**55.0%**	**57.1%**
Impairment charges/ Average RWA	−0.51%	−0.91%	−1.03%	−0.41%	−0.39%	−0.49%

Source: Standard Chartered annual and interim reports, author's analysis.

banks like Bank of China. Standard Chartered's net interest income per RWA is also significantly higher than many of the developed country banks – we would interpret this as indicating that the lending margins available in the emerging markets where Standard Chartered does the vast bulk of its banking are higher than those generally available in the developed markets. This higher net operating income per RWA appears to allow Standard Chartered to spend a bit more on its operating expenses, e.g. by investing in growth areas; its operating expenses per RWA are higher than at, for example, HSBC. But Standard Chartered's cost–income ratio actually doesn't suffer too much (at 57% in 2012), because of the strength in net operating income.

Looking at the components of non-interest income in the Value Levers table, the net trading income per RWA (at 0.8% to 1.4%) is quite a significant component, accounting for nearly half of non-interest income. Although Standard Chartered's net trading income per RWA line item is less volatile than at many other banks (especially those with large investment banking divisions), we would still keep an eye on this line item because of this general potential volatility.

Looking at Standard Chartered's credit quality metrics, it becomes clearer why its impairment charges per RWA have been so low in comparison to

Table 3.63   Standard Chartered: credit quality

	2007	2008	2009	2010	2011	2012
Impaired (non-performing) loans	2,316	3,007	4,012	4,631	4,618	5,600
Gross customer loans	157,517	179,163	202,677	247,164	269,513	289,607
Impairment provisions	1,809	1,981	2,627	2,679	2,972	3,175
Non-performing loans as % Gross customer loans	1.47%	1.68%	1.98%	1.87%	1.71%	1.93%
NPLs as % of RWAs	1.35%	1.59%	1.88%	1.89%	1.71%	1.86%
Provisioning coverage						
Impairment provisions/NPLs	78.1%	65.9%	65.5%	57.8%	64.4%	56.7%
Impairment provisions/RWA	1.05%	1.05%	1.23%	1.09%	1.10%	1.05%
Impairment charges/Average RWA	−0.51%	−0.91%	−1.03%	−0.41%	−0.39%	−0.49%

Source: Standard Chartered annual and interim reports, author's analysis.

the other banks that we have analysed: Standard Chartered's non-performing (or impaired) loans as a percentage of gross customer loans have remained remarkably low throughout the past several years whilst the financial and sovereign debt crises have ravaged many Western developed market economies. NPLs as a percentage of gross customer loans peaked at 1.98% in 2009 – well below the peak NPLs seen at other banks with developed markets exposures. Standard Chartered's provisioning coverage (impairment provisions as a percentage of NPLs) was also relatively high in comparison to Western banks, at 57% in 2012.

The reason for the strong credit metrics is because nearly all of Standard Chartered's loan portfolio is in the developing markets of Asia, Africa and

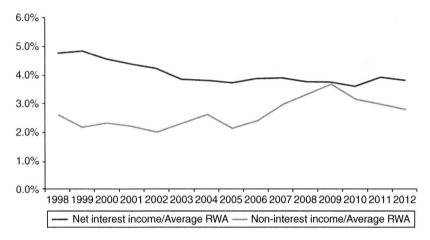

Figure 3.17 Standard Chartered: net interest income v. non-interest income per RWA

Source: Standard Chartered annual and interim reports, author's analysis.

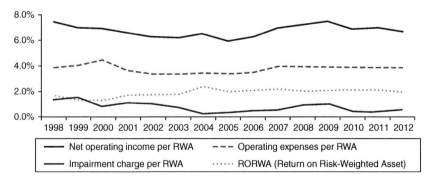

Figure 3.18 Standard Chartered: key value levers

Source: Standard Chartered annual and interim reports, author's analysis.

the Middle East – regions which weathered the recent crises far better than the developed countries. Looking at this historical performance, and taking a view on the relative macroeconomic prospects, these developing markets could be expected to continue to outperform developed markets – and thus Standard Chartered's banking franchise would continue to thrive.

We can also look at Standard Chartered on a longer timeframe, picking out some key value levers (see charts below):

Looking at the net interest income versus non-interest income per RWA, it is quite clear that Standard Chartered still derives the majority of its income from net interest income, and that the level of net interest income per RWA has remained relatively high versus many of its competitors.

Table 3.64 Standard Chartered: standard forecast and valuation ratios

Traditional Valuation Ratios	2010	2011	2012	2013E	2014E
GBP 1,585 **2409** **1.5197**					
Profit before tax pre-exceptionals & FV	5,935	7,161	6,903	7,642	8,964
% growth year-on-year	17.3%	20.7%	−3.6%	10.7%	17.3%
Net profit pre-exceptionals & FV	4,201	5,249	4,970	5,757	6,927
% growth year-on-year	27.5%	24.9%	−5.3%	15.8%	20.3%
Adjusted EPS, fully diluted	191.6	219.1	205.6	237.7	285.6
% growth year-on-year	19.7%	14.3%	−6.2%	15.6%	20.1%
Adjusted P/E	**12.6**	**11.0**	**11.7**	**10.1**	**8.4**
Dividends per share	69.0	76.0	84.0	92.4	101.6
% growth year-on-year	9.5%	10.1%	10.5%	10.0%	10.0%
Dividend yield	2.9%	3.2%	3.5%	3.8%	4.2%
Dividend payout ratio	36.2%	37.2%	41.3%	38.4%	35.2%
ROE	14.1%	12.8%	11.8%	12.6%	13.9%
P/BVPS multiple	**1.41**	**1.45**	**1.31**	**1.21**	**1.11**
Book value per share	1,704	1,659	1,839	1,989	2,180
% growth in period	40.1%	−2.6%	10.8%	8.2%	9.6%
Balance sheet goodwill	6,998	7,061	7,312	7,312	7,312
Tangible shareholders' equity	29,720	32,159	36,555	40,230	44,873
Tangible book value per share (USD cents)	1,266	1,349	1,531	1,682	1,873
Price/Tangible BVPS multiple (x)	**1.90**	**1.79**	**1.57**	**1.43**	**1.29**

Source: Standard Chartered annual and interim reports, author's analysis.

Non-interest income per RWA increased up to a peak in 2009 but has ebbed back since then. As noted above, trading income forming a large portion of non-interest income, we would want to monitor this potentially volatile line item.

Looking at other selected value levers, what is quite impressive in our view is how stable and solid the RORWA line item has been; this seems to have been a function of net operating income, operating expenses and impairment charges all having been managed to roughly offset each other in aggregate. The period-to-period interaction of these line items would be worth exploring in detail.

Forecast and Valuation

Our forecasts for Standard Chartered are only indicative; in our experience, forecasts tend to change every time one looks at them. Behind those

Table 3.65   Standard Chartered: fundamental ROIC valuation

Fundamental valuation	2010	2011	2012	2013E	2014E
Value-Added Margin in period	1.40%	1.28%	1.20%	1.89%	2.67%
Through-the-cycle Value-Added Margin	−0.13%	−0.16%	0.40%	0.77%	1.34%
Invested Capital growth pa (next 10 years)	8.0%	8.0%	8.0%	8.0%	8.0%
Terminal Value-Added Margin assumption	3.02%	1.07%	1.08%	1.30%	1.30%
Assumed continuing growth of Value Added	4.0%	4.0%	4.0%	4.0%	4.0%
Invested Capital (beginning of period)	45,421	56,430	60,168	66,888	72,950
PV of Value Created/ (Destroyed) in forecast period	7,600	2,952	4,990	7,625	10,365
PV of Continuing Value	29,858	13,662	19,532	25,163	27,515
Total firm value	82,879	73,044	84,690	99,677	110,830
Less: Debt Capital	(16,592)	(17,378)	(19,492)	(21,695)	(24,146)
Less: Equity Adjustments	(3,120)	(3,570)	(3,529)	(3,714)	(4,093)
Target Equity Value	**63,167**	**52,096**	**61,669**	**74,268**	**82,591**
Market Capitalisation (end of period)	63,167	52,096	61,669	57,569	57,569
Target Equity Value per share (USD)	29.31	22.03	25.85	31.07	34.50
Target Equity Value per share (GBP)	**18.80**	**14.21**	**15.91**	**20.45**	**22.70**

Source: Standard Chartered annual and interim reports, author's analysis.

forecasts, we make several key assumptions for Standard Chartered, namely (1) RWA growth continues at a relatively strong (high single-digit) pace, and that this reflects more true credit growth rather than an increase in risk weightings, (2) net interest income per RWA remains relatively stable, but non-interest income per RWA ebbs as the boosts to trading income (from QE-supported markets, for example) fade, (3) operating expenses per RWA show some slight improvement but remain higher than at many other banks because of Standard Chartered's continuing investment programmes (e.g. branch openings in China), and (4) although impairment charges continue to edge up, they remain relatively lower than in many developed markets because the bulk of the emerging markets in which Standard Chartered operates continue to show relatively benign credit characteristics – with the exception of Korea and, possibly, mainland China.

In our traditional forecast valuation ratios, these assumptions drive continuing strong growth in earnings and ROEs in the mid-teens. The mid-teens ROEs, in turn, enable a relatively good dividend yield whilst also maintaining strong capital ratios.

Running our fundamental ROIC valuation model backwards, the market's implied terminal value-added margin assumption (based on the year-end share price and historical ROIC performance) was 1.1% at end-2012 and 1.1% at end-2011. In 2010, the implied market expectation of Standard Chartered's terminal value-added margin was 3.0%. Note that in 2011 and 2012, Standard Chartered's ROICs in those periods actually appeared to be higher than the market's implied assumption of terminal value-added margin. In other words, the market appeared to expecting that Standard Chartered's profitability would deteriorate in the long term, whereas for most of the other banks, the market appeared to hold the opposite expectation, that profitability would improve (significantly in most cases).

In our indicative fundamental ROIC valuation for Standard Chartered, we have used a terminal value-added margin of 1.3% – still lower than what we expect in 2013 and 2014. With this relatively conservative assumption, Standard Chartered's target share price would be £20.45 at the end of 2013 and £22.70 at the end of 2014.

Index

Printed and bound in Great Britain by
CPI Group (UK) Ltd, Croydon, CR0 4YY